Lone Pine

Perennials
for
Georgia

Tara Dillard
Don Williamson

Distributed by Lone Pine Publishing
1808 B Street NW, Suite 140
Auburn, WA, USA 98001
Website: www.lonepinepublishing.com

Library and Archives Canada Cataloguing in Publication

Dillard, Tara, 1960-
    Perennials for Georgia / Tara Dillard, Don Williamson.

Includes index.
ISBN-13: 978-976-8200-34-1

    1. Perennials--Georgia. I. Williamson, Don, 1962- II. Title.

SB434.D54 2007   635.9'3209758   C2006-903543-1

Photography: All photos by Tamara Eder, Derek Fell, Tim Matheson, Alison Penko and Laura Peters except: Pam Beck 286, 287; Rob Broekhuis 214, 215a; Callaway Gardens 316a; Karen Carriere 147b, 194a, 194b, 315; Stacey Carr Cyrus 232, 233b; Therese D'Monte 79b, 159a; Joan de Grey 137a; Elliot Engley 46a, 46b, 46c, 47; Erv Evans 215b; Erika Flatt 19, 123a; Anne Gordon 114; Chris Hansen and Terra Nova Nurseries 314; Richard Hawke and CBG 243a; Liz Klose 76b, 83, 300a; Debra Knapke 115b, 159b; Cal Lemke 233a; Janet Loughrey 105a, 189a, 229a, 230; Erica Markham 49a, 49b, 50; Marilynn McAra 153a; Kim O'Leary 44a, 73, 115a, 122a, 271a, 271b, 272a, 272c, 273a, 295a; Photos.com 62, 64, 66b, 241a, 247b; PPA 235b; Robert Ritchie 59b, 67, 69, 94, 95b, 117, 142b, 166, 167, 191b, 246a; Saxon Holt 107b, 108, 195, 229b, 259a, 261, 272b, 288; Peter Thompstone 104a, 164, 173b, 177b, 247b; Mark Turner 106, 107a, 86, 129, 184, 189b, 205a, 312, 313b; Valleybrook Gardens 113a, 158, 193a, 193b; Don Williamson 152, 153b, 239b, 247a; Carol Woo 70.

PC: 13

Contents

4

Acknowledgments

Thank you Barbara Allen, former program chair and president of the Georgia Perennial Plant Association, for bringing the worlds most talented perennial experts to the podiums of our hometown, Atlanta, GA. How do I thank the many volunteers that comprised GPPA when I joined? Without you, there would have been no monthly meetings, yearly symposiums and plant sales, nor plant exchanges to attend. Thank you, volunteers.

In my garden are perennials that were gifts from acquaintances who soon became close friends. The perennials are thriving and the love of the friendships remains, though several of those gardening friends have died. I'm thankful for the legacy of friends that are gone; beauty and life moving forward.
—*Tara Dillard*

I am blessed to work with many wonderful people, including my new and very knowledgeable friend Tara Dillard, and all the great folks at Lone Pine Publishing. I also thank The Creator. —*Don Williamson*

We thank the following people and organizations for their valuable time and beautiful images: Anne Gordon; Cal Lemke; Callaway Gardens in Stone Mountain, GA; Chris Hansen and Terra Nova Nurseries; Debra Knapke; Derek Fell; Erv Evans and NCSU Extension; Horticolor; Janet Loughrey; Joan de Grey; Liz Klose; Marilynn McAra; Mark Turner; Pam Beck; Perennial Plant Association; Peter Thompstone; Richard Hawke and the Chicago Botanic Gardens; Rob Broekhuis and robsplants.com; Saxon Holt; Stacey Carr Cyrus; Therese D'Monte; Valleybrooke Gardens and all those who allowed us to photograph their gardens.

The Flowers at a Glance

Pictorial Guide in Alphabetical Order

Artemisia
p. 74

Aster
p. 78

Astilbe
p. 82

Autumn Fern
p. 86

Beebalm
p. 90

Black-Eyed Susan
p. 94

Barrenwort
p. 88

Blackberry Lily
p. 96

Blanket Flower
p. 98

Blazing Star
p. 100

Bloodroot
p. 106

Blue Lyme Grass
p. 108

Bluestar
p. 110

Bleeding Heart
p. 102

Boltonia
p. 114

Butterfly Weed
p. 116

Candyturf
p. 118

Canna Lily
p. 120

Cardinal Flower
p. 124

Carolina Lupine
p. 128

Christmas Fern
p. 130

Christmas Rose
p. 132

Chrysanthemum
p. 136

Cinnamon Fern
p. 138

Columbine
p. 140

Coral Bells
p. 144

Coreopsis
p. 148

Crocosmia
p. 150

Daffodil
p. 152

Daylily
p. 154

Dwarf Plumbago
p. 158

Eulalia Grass
p. 160

Evening Primrose
p. 164

False Indigo
p. 166

False Sunflower
p. 168

Feather Reed Grass
p. 170

Foamflower
p. 172

Gaura
p. 178

Golden Hakone Grass
p. 180

Goldenrod
p. 182

Foxglove
p. 174

Green and Gold
p. 184

Hardy Ageratum
p. 186

Hardy Begonia
p. 188

Hardy Hibiscus
p. 192

Hosta
p. 196

Iris
p. 202

Hardy Geranium
p. 190

Japanese Anemone
p. 206

Japanese Painted Fern
p. 210

Kalimeris
p. 214

Meadow Rue
p. 220

Northern Maidenhair
p. 226

Lily
p. 216

Mondo Grass
p. 222

Muhly Grass
p. 224

Pampass Grass
p. 228

Patrinia
p. 230

Peacock Moss
p. 232

Penstemon
p. 234

Perennial Sunflower
p. 238

Phlox
p. 240

Pinks
p. 244

Pitcher Plant
p. 248

Plume Poppy
p. 252

Purple Coneflower
p. 254

Purple Loosestrife
p. 258

Ravenna Grass
p. 260

Red-Hot Poker
p. 262

Ribbon Grass
p. 264

Rosemary
p. 266

Russian Sage
p. 268

Salvia
p. 270

Sea Holly
p. 274

Sedum
p. 276

Shasta Daisy
p. 280

Soapwort
p. 282

Solomon's Seal
p. 284

Southern Shield Fern
p. 286

Spider Lily
p. 288

Spiderwort
p. 292

Stoke's Aster
p. 296

Thyme
p. 298

Toad-Lily
p. 302

Turtlehead
p. 304

Verbena
p. 306

Virginia Bluebells
p. 312

Veronica
p. 310

Wild Ginger
p. 314

Yarrow
p. 318

Introduction

PERENNIAL GARDENING IN GEORGIA IS A YEAR-ROUND ACTIVITY throughout the state. The content and bloom times of perennial gardens from the coastal plain to the piedmont and mountains will be slightly different, but our weather never entirely shuts down a perennial garden. Georgia's zones, from 6b in the mountains to 8b along the coast and the Florida border, are a gift to gardeners.

However, along with the gift comes a challenge. The challenge is that the arrival of the first frost in fall and the last frost in spring varies by three to four weeks within each zone and micro-climate. We can have a beautiful Indian summer week of weather, with temperatures in the high 70s to low 80s. This weather can be abruptly halted by the arrival of a hard first freeze, killing some of the growth on your perennials, though not the plant itself. The variation also makes it difficult to say when, exactly, any perennial will bloom. Some years your yarrow may begin to bloom in mid- to late April, others in mid- to late May. Always remember—plants don't read books.

Generally, perennials are herbaceous (non-woody) plants that live for three or more years. These perennials generally die back to the ground at the end of the growing season and start fresh with new shoots each spring. In Georgia, many perennials, such as echinacea, veronica and dianthus, are started from seed in fall. They grow during winter, bloom the following summer and then die back to the ground the following winter. Some plants grouped with garden perennials do not die back completely; the subshrubs, such as butterfly bush, fall into this category. Other plants remain green all winter; for example, dianthus, hellebores and some daylilies are evergreen perennials.

Georgia Gardening Environment

Climate, geography and soil type influence what types of perennials grow and thrive in any specific area. Generally, Georgia experiences a humid, subtropical climate. We have mild winters and hot, humid summers. In winter, the prevailing wind blows from the northwest and can bring down cold Arctic air from Canada. February is the most difficult weather month for gardeners in Georgia. Several sunny, 68° F days and nights above freezing can be followed by a 4° F night causing many plants that have broken dormancy during the warm period to have their new growth killed by the frigid night. Average January temperatures range from 36° F in the north to 53° F in the south. There are usually fewer than 30 days along the coast where the temperature drops below freezing (32° F) but over 120 days below freezing in some of the northeastern mountainous areas. In summer, the prevailing wind is from the southwest, bringing warm, humid air from the Gulf of Mexico. Average July temperatures range from 70° F along the North Carolina border to 84° F in the south. Southern Georgia often has more than 90 days when the temperature rises above 90° F, whereas there are fewer than

15 days above 90° F in the northeast. Summer temperatures can easily spike to over 90° F in the mountains and to over 100° F in the inland coastal plain.

The length of the growing season (from the last frost in spring to the first frost in fall) ranges from about 180 days in the northeast to over 270 along the coast. The last frost in spring usually occurs in late February along the coast and in early May in the mountains. The first frost date in fall is in early October in the northeast and early December along the southern part of the coast.

Georgia often receives enough rainfall in a year to take care of the needs of most plants. Rainfall amounts range from around 45" in the interior Southern Coastal Plain to over 80" in some spots in the mountainous northeast. January to March are the wettest months and October is the driest. Rain can also be intense in July when we experience our share of thunderstorms, especially in the southwest corner of the state. Average annual snowfall usually amounts to less than 3" per year for most of the state, ranging from 12" of snow on some of the northeast mountaintops to no snow along the coast. We do get the occasional large snowstorm, such as the 1993 storm that deposited nearly 24" of snow across the northern regions of the state.

Other climatic influences and events we need to be aware of include the effects of El Niño and La Niña, the yearly threat of hurricanes and tornadoes and the possibility of lightning and hail from thunderstorms.

Hardiness Zones and Geography

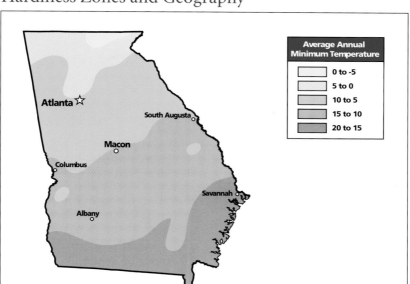

Average Annual
Minimum Temperature

- 0 to -5
- 5 to 0
- 10 to 5
- 15 to 10
- 20 to 15

Atlanta ☆
South Augusta ○
Macon ○
Columbus
Savannah ○
Albany ○

Georgia is divided into three distinct geographic regions that span from sea to sky: the Coastal Plains, the Piedmont and the Mountains. The United States Department of Agriculture (USDA) plant hardiness map—the basis for the map above—is based on average lowest winter temperatures and divides our state into three hardiness zones (6,7 and 8) that closely reflect our various geographic regions.

Naturally, the mountain areas of the state are the coldest in the winter. Zone 6b dips into northern Georgia, encompassing most of the Blue Ridge, and has average coldest winter temperatures ranging from -5° to 0° F. This area also receives the most rainfall and snowfall in the state. The spring storm fronts that cross Georgia have the most effect on this area.

Zone 7a has the lowest average winter temperatures from 0° to 5° F. This zone includes the lower mountain elevations, loops down around Cobb County, then swings north to take in the northern portion of the Ridge and Valley and all of the Appalachian Plateau. This area has more days above 90° F in the summer than the higher elevations of the Blue Ridge in zone 6b, but it often experiences just as many days (70–90) when the temperature drops below the freezing mark.

Zone 7b (5° to 10° F) includes the Piedmont, the rest of north Georgia, the Fall Line, a large part of Stewart County and the border area of Burke and Jenkins Counties. There is more rain and fewer days above 90° F in the northern Piedmont than in the south.

Zone 8a (10° to 15° F) encompasses most of the Southern Coastal Plain (the East Gulf Coastal Plain). This area has the warmest summers in all of Georgia. Zone 8b encompasses the Atlantic Coast Flatwoods (the Atlantic Coastal Plain) and the southern counties in the Southern Coastal Plain. Summertime temperatures do not rise as high as they do inland, but winters are very mild due to the moderating effects of the Atlantic Ocean.

A heat zone map is available for determining heat stress on plants. It was developed by the American Horticultural Society, and it is based on the average number of days that the temperature rises above 86° F. That heat combined with our high summer humidity can really stress plants. Moisture is transpired more rapidly, leaving the plant searching for more water in the rootzone or trying to cope when it can't find any. This is one of the reasons peonies prefer northern climates—Georgia is too hot for too long for their beautiful blooms to reach peak performance.

Georgia soil is predominantly sandy, acidic and of low to medium fertility. The percentage of sand in the soil decreases as you move north and west. The Atlantic Coast Flatwoods have a wide variety of soils that are generally poorly drained. The Southern Coastal Plain has a mix of sandy loam and sandy clay, and most of our agricultural crops are grown here. These soils are generally deep and well drained. The deep, sandy soils along the Fall Line are often infertile and do not have a good water holding capacity. Piedmont soils are dominated by clay subsoil that has been exposed by erosion. The remaining topsoils are low in fertility, well drained and acidic. The valley soils of the Blue Ridge and Ridge and Valley are also low in fertility and very acidic. (See "Getting Started," p. 19, for more information on assessing conditions in your garden.)

Don't feel intimidated or limited by the information on large-scale climate zone maps, perennial hardiness indicators and soil patterns. Hardiness zone divisions, for example, are guidelines based mostly on the average lowest winter temperatures. As well, local topography in the garden creates microclimates, small areas that may be more or less favorable for growing different plants. Microclimates may be created, for example, in the shelter of a nearby building, in a low, cold hollow, at the top of a windswept knoll or along the shoreline of one of Georgia's many lakes.

Microclimates give gardeners almost anywhere in Georgia the possibility of growing that one perennial that everyone says won't grow here. Part of the fun of growing perennials is the challenge of gardening with plants that are borderline hardy, so don't stop experimenting.

Be aware of the heat island effect. Urbanization of the country has produced many more buildings and paved areas that effectively trap solar energy, releasing the heat only very slowly each night. Temperatures in the center of large cities are often a few degrees warmer than the surrounding area.

Many enthusiastic and creative people, both amateur and professional, are involved in gardening in Georgia. Individual growers, breeders, societies, schools, publications and public gardens provide information, encouragement and fruitful debate for the gardener. Georgia gardeners possess a knowledge of planting and propagation methods and a plethora of opinions on what is best for any patch of ground. Outstanding garden shows, public gardens, arboretums and private gardens in our state attract crowds of people all year long. These events and locations are sources of inspiration as well as valuable information.

Perennials are relatively inexpensive and are easy to share with friends and neighbors. The more varieties you try, the more likely you will be to discover what loves to grow in your garden. Our advice: "Dig in and just grow for it!"

Perennial Gardens

PERENNIALS CAN BE INCLUDED IN ANY TYPE, SIZE OR STYLE OF garden. From the riot of color in a cottage garden or the cool, soothing shades of green in a woodland garden to a welcoming cluster of pots on a front doorstep, perennials open up a world of design possibilities for even the inexperienced gardener.

Perennials can stand alone in a garden or combine with other plants. They form a bridge between the permanent structure provided by woody plants and the temporary color provided by annuals. Perennials often flower longer and grow to mature size more quickly than shrubs, and in many cases they require less care and are less prone to pests and disease than annuals.

It is very important when planning your garden to decide what you like. If you enjoy the plants in your garden, you will be more likely to give them proper care. Visit garden centers to see the range of plants available and to discuss possibilities with the staff. Decide what style of garden you like. Think about the ones you have most admired in your neighborhood, in books or while visiting friends. Use these ideas as starting points for planning your own garden.

Foliage Plants

A good perennial garden can be interesting throughout the year. Try to select perennials that bloom at different times to have some part

Many coral bells have attractive, colorful foliage.

of your garden flowering all season. Each perennial entry in this book indicates blooming seasons; you will also find the Quick Reference Chart on p. 322 handy when selecting plants that bloom at different times.

Consider the foliage of the perennials you want to use. Leaves can be bold or flimsy, coarse or fine in texture, big or small, light or dark; their color can vary from any multitude of greens to yellow, gray, blue or purple; and they can be striped, splashed, edged, dotted or mottled. Their surfaces can be shiny, fuzzy, silky, rough or smooth. The famous white gardens at Sissinghurst, England, did not simply showcase a haphazard collection of white flowers. Rather, they were designed to remove the distraction of color and allow the eye to linger on the foliage, to appreciate its subtle appeal. Flowers come and go, but a garden planned with careful attention to foliage will always be interesting. Most gardeners begin with an attraction to flowers and expand that attraction to include the seductive array of foliage available.

As well, consider the size and shape of the perennials you choose. Use a variety of forms to make your garden more diverse. The size of your garden influences these decisions, but you do not have to limit a small garden to small perennials or a large garden to large perennials. Use a balanced combination of plant sizes that are in scale with their specific location. (See individual entries and Quick Reference Chart, p. 322.)

We tend to focus on color because it is often the first thing we notice in a garden. Choose a variety of flower and foliage colors, keeping in mind that different colors have different effects on our senses. Cool colors, such as blue, purple and green, are soothing and make small spaces seem bigger. Warm colors, such as red, orange and yellow, are more stimulating and appear to fill large spaces. (See individual entries and Quick Reference Chart, p. 322.)

Textures can also create a sense of space. Large leaves are coarsely textured. Their visibility from a greater distance makes spaces seem smaller and more shaded. Small leaves, or those that are finely divided, are considered finely textured. They create a sense of greater space and light. Many gardens have been designed solely on the basis of texture.

Finally, decide how much time you have to devote to your garden. With good planning and preparation, you can enjoy a relatively low-maintenance perennial garden. Try to use plants that perform well with little maintenance and those that are generally pest and disease free.

Coarse-textured Perennials
- Black-eyed Susan
- Bloodroot
- Canna Lily
- Hardy Hibiscus
- Hosta
- Plume Poppy
- Purple Coneflower
- Red-hot Poker
- Sedum 'Autumn Joy'

Black-eyed Susan

Hosta

Fine-textured Perennials
- Astilbe
- Bleeding Heart
- Boltonia
- Bluestar
- Columbine
- Coreopsis
- Ferns
- Gaura
- Meadow Rue
- Muhly Grass
- Pinks
- Rosemary
- Russian Sage
- Yarrow

Low-maintenance Perennials
- Aster
- Barrenwort
- Beebalm
- Black-eyed Susan
- Bluestar
- Coral Bells
- Coreopsis
- Daylily
- Eulalia Grass
- Feather Reed Grass
- Hosta
- Kalimeris
- Pinks
- Russian Sage
- Shasta Daisy

Columbine

Getting Started

ONCE YOU HAVE SOME IDEAS ABOUT WHAT YOU WANT IN YOUR garden, consider the growing conditions. Plants grown in ideal conditions, or conditions as close to ideal as possible, are healthier and less prone to pest and disease problems than plants growing in stressful conditions. Some plants considered high maintenance become low maintenance when grown in the right conditions.

Avoid trying to make your garden match the growing conditions of the plants you like. Instead, choose plants to match your garden conditions. The levels of light, type of soil and amount of exposure in your garden provide guidelines that make plant selection easier. A sketch of your garden, drawn on graph paper, may help you organize the various considerations you want to keep in mind as you plan. Knowing your growing conditions can prevent costly mistakes—plan ahead rather than correct later.

Light

There are four categories of light in a garden: full sun, partial shade, light shade and full shade. Available light is affected by buildings, trees, fences and the position of the sun at different times of the day and year. Knowing what light is available in your garden will help you determine where to place plants adapted to different light levels.

Full sun locations, such as south-facing walls, receive direct sunlight at least six hours per day. Partial shade (partial sun) locations, such as east- or west-facing walls, receive direct sunlight for part of the day (four to six hours) and shade for the rest. Light shade locations receive shade most or all of the day, although some sunlight does filter through to ground level. The ground under a small-leaved tree, such as birch, is often considered to be in light shade. Full shade locations, such as the north side of a house, receive no direct sunlight.

It is important to remember that the intensity of full sun can vary. For example, heat can become trapped and magnified between buildings, baking all but the most heat-tolerant plants in a concrete oven. Conversely, that shaded, sheltered hollow that protects your heat-hating plants in the humid summer heat may become a frost trap in winter, killing tender plants that should otherwise survive.

Plant your perennials where they will grow best. For hot, dry areas and for low-lying, damp sections of the garden, select plants that prefer those conditions.

Perennials for Full Sun

Artemisia
Black-eyed Susan
Blanket Flower
Blazing Star
Blue Lyme Grass
Butterfly Weed
Candytuft
Canna Lily
Chrysanthemum
Crocosmia
Daylily
Hardy Hibiscus
Pampas Grass
Pinks
Ravenna Grass
Red-hot Poker
Russian Sage
Sea Holly
Verbena
Yarrow

Crocosmia

Foamflower

Perennials for Full Shade

- Astilbe
- Barrenwort
- Bleeding Heart
- Bloodroot
- Cardinal Flower
- Christmas Fern
- Christmas Rose
- Foamflower
- Green and Gold
- Hardy Begonia
- Hosta
- Northern Maidenhair Fern
- Solomon's Seal
- Toad-Lily

Soil

Plants and the soil they grow in have a unique relationship—many important plant functions go on underground. Soil holds air, water, nutrients, organic matter and a variety of beneficial organisms. Plants depend upon these resources for their nutritional needs, and their roots use the soil as an anchor. In turn, plants influence soil development by breaking down large clods with their roots, and they increase soil fertility by releasing by-products during their growth and by being recycled by soil microorganisms when they die.

Soil is made up of particles of different sizes. Sand particles are the largest. Sand has lots of air space and doesn't compact easily, so water drains quickly out of sandy soil and nutrients are quickly washed away. Clay particles are the smallest and are visible only through a microscope. Water penetrates and drains from clay very slowly. Clay holds the most nutrients, but there is little room for air so it compacts easily. Silt particles are smaller than sand particles but larger than clay particles. Most soil is made up of a mixture of different particle sizes. Soil with a balanced mix of these three particle sizes is called loam.

The organic portion of the soil includes living and dead components. The dead components are the residues, metabolites and waste products of plants, animals and microorganisms. The living components are composed of bacteria, fungi, nematodes, protozoa, arthropods and earthworms. These organisms decompose organic compounds, including plant and animal residues and wastes, pesticides and other pollutants. They trap and store nitrogen and other nutrients in their bodies, and they produce hormones that plants use. Their activities enhance soil structure, allowing for better air and water movement into the soil and less runoff. They compete with and prey on plant pests, and they provide food for aboveground animals. The living soil organisms, the dead organic matter components, the plants and the aboveground animals make up what is known as the soil food web.

Soil structure is the arrangement of the mineral and organic components into stable aggregates. The aggregation process is aided by roots pushing through the soil and the substances the roots secrete, by wetting and drying, by freezing and thawing and especially by soil microorganisms in their search for food.

The soil's particle size and the degree the land slopes influence the drainage properties of your soil. Rocky soil on a hillside will probably drain very quickly and should be reserved for those plants that prefer a very well-drained soil. Low-lying areas retain water longer, and some areas may rarely drain at all. Moist areas suit plants that require a consistent water supply, and areas that stay wet can be used for plants that prefer boggy conditions.

Drainage can be improved in very wet areas by adding organic matter or granite grit to the soil, by installing some form of drainage tile or by building raised beds. Use caution when adding sand to clay soils. Doing so can easily make your soil as hard as concrete; consult with landscape professionals to prevent potential problems. If you have to use sand, use builder's sand, which has the largest particle size for sand. Avoid play sand, which is the worst. Water retention in sandy soil can be improved through the addition of organic matter.

Another aspect of soil to consider is its pH—the measure of acidity or alkalinity. A pH of 7 is neutral; higher numbers (up to 14) indicate alkaline conditions, and lower numbers (down to 0) indicate acidic conditions. Soil pH influences nutrient availability for plants. Although some plants prefer acid or alkaline soils, most grow best in a mid-range pH of between 5.5 and 7.5.

Soils tend to become acidic in areas where rainfall is plentiful. Soil can be made more alkaline by adding horticultural lime, which is a very common practice in Georgia. For more acidic soil, add pine needles, sulfur, alfalfa pellets or chopped oak leaves. Altering the pH of your soil takes a long time, often many years, and is not easy. If there are only one or two plants you are trying to grow that require a soil with a different pH from your existing soil, consider growing them in a container or raised bed where it will be easier to control and amend the pH as needed.

Test your soil if you plan to amend it. There are two types of soil tests that will let you know exactly what is happening in your soil. A standard soil test measures pH level, nutrient content (amount and forms) and how much organic matter is present. Standard soil tests provide suggestions on how to alter the soil's characteristics (pH, mineral content, percentage of organic matter) to grow the plants you want to grow. Your local County Extension Office will do a standard soil test, including soil pH, for a small fee. If your local office does not offer soil testing, it will know who does.

The other type of test is a food-web assay. This test counts total and active bacteria, total and active fungi, numbers and types of protozoa and numbers and types of nematodes. It also assesses whether the sample is aerobic or anaerobic, identifies the kind and amount of beneficial mycorrhizal colonization on the roots (if you include roots in the sample) and determines how much of the plant surface is covered with microorganisms. The foodweb assay provides suggestions on how to attain the soil life balance and diversity needed to grow the plants you want to grow.

Perennials for Sandy Soil

Artemisia
Blazing Star
Blue Lyme Grass
Coreopsis
False Indigo
Penstemon
Red-hot Poker
Spotted Beebalm

Perennials for Clay Soil

Black-eyed Susan
Blanket Flower
Blazing Star
Foamflower
Hosta
Sedum
Turtlehead

Perennials for Moist Soil

Astilbe
Autumn Fern
Barrenwort
Beebalm
Bleeding Heart
Bluestar
Cardinal Flower
Christmas Rose
Hardy Hibiscus
Iris
Japanese Painted Fern
Pitcher Plant
Purple Loosestrife
Swamp Milkweed
Southern Shield Fern

Perennials for Dry Soil

Artemisia
Blue Lyme Grass
Carolina Lupine
Coreopsis
Evening Primrose
False Sunflower
Goldenrod
Pampas Grass
Penstemon
Russian Sage
Salvia
Sedum
Yarrow

Artemisia

Blazing star

Astilbe

Evening primrose

Exposure

Exposure is another important environmental influence in your garden. Wind, heat, cold and rain are some of the elements your garden is exposed to, and different plants are better adapted than others to withstand the potential damage of these forces. Buildings, walls, fences, hills, hedges and trees can all influence your garden's exposure.

Wind in particular can cause extensive damage to your plants. Plants become dehydrated in windy locations if they aren't able to draw water out of the soil fast enough to replace what is lost through the leaves. Tall, stiff-stemmed perennials can be knocked over or broken by strong winds. Some plants that do not require staking in a sheltered location may need to be staked in a more exposed one.

Use plants that are recommended for exposed locations, or temper the effects of the wind with a hedge or trees. A solid wall creates wind turbulence on the downwind side, while a looser structure, such as a hedge, breaks up the force of the wind and protects a larger area.

No matter what conditions you have in your garden, there are perennials that will flourish and provide you with a variety of colors, sizes and forms.

Salt-tolerant Perennials
- Muhly Grass
- Red-hot Poker
- Swamp Sunflower

Perennials for Exposed Locations
- Artemesia
- Black-eyed Susan
- Blanket Flower
- Blue Lyme Grass
- Butterfly Weed
- Candytuft
- Columbine
- Eulalia Grass
- Evening Primrose
- Pampas Grass
- Penstemon
- Pinks
- Russian Sage
- Sedum (groundcover species)
- Shasta Daisy
- Thyme
- Yarrow

Red-hot poker

Sedum (groundcover species)

Preparing the Garden

BEFORE YOU PLANT YOUR PERENNIALS, TAKE TIME TO PROPERLY prepare the garden. Doing so will save you time and effort later on. Many gardening problems can be avoided with good preparation and maintenance. Start with as few weeds as possible and with well-prepared soil that has had organic material added to give your plants a good start.

Turning compost into beds

Always remove weeds and debris before planting.

First, loosen the soil with a large garden fork and remove the weeds. Avoid working the soil when it is very wet or very dry because you will damage the soil structure by breaking down the pockets that hold air and water.

Next, you'll want to amend the soil with organic matter.

Organic Soil Amendments

Organic matter is an important component of soil that Georgia soils are generally low in. All soils, from the heaviest clay to the lightest sand, benefit from the addition of organic matter. Not only does this material contribute nutrients, but it also improves the structure of soil. Organic matter improves heavy clay soils by loosening them and allowing air and water to penetrate. It

improves sandy or light soils by binding together the large particles and increasing their ability to retain water, which allows plants to absorb nutrients before they are leached away.

Common organic additives for your soil include grass clippings, shredded leaves, pine straw, well-rotted manure, alfalfa pellets, mushroom compost and garden compost. Alfalfa pellets supply a range of nutrients including trace elements. They also contain a plant growth hormone. Granulated, composted chicken or barnyard manure, available from suppliers of organic gardening products, is a wonderful product. Composted horse manure is also an excellent additive and is usually available from stables, often in a seemingly endless supply. If you have access to fresh manure, compost

Wooden compost bins.

it first or use it sparingly because roots that come in contact with fresh manure will suffer fertilizer burn. Incorporate the manure into beds at least two weeks before—or better yet, the season before—planting. Avoid using fresh manure in vegetable beds to prevent the potential spread of fecal-borne diseases.

Work your organic matter into the soil with a garden fork, spade or power tiller. If you are adding just one or two plants and do not want to prepare an entire bed, dig holes twice as wide and deep as the root-ball of each plant. Add a slow-release organic fertilizer, compost or composted manure to the backfill of soil that you spread around the plant. Fresh chicken or barnyard manure can also be used to improve small areas, but it should not be placed in the planting hole. Place only a small amount on top of the soil where it can leach into the soil. This way you will not expose the tender roots of the plant to fertilizer burn.

Within a few months, earthworms and other decomposer organisms will break down the organic matter, releasing nutrients for plants. At the same time, the activities of these decomposers will help keep the soil from compacting.

Composting

In forests and meadows, organic debris, such as leaves and other plant bits, breaks down on the soil surface,

A variety of manufactured plastic compost bins.

and the nutrients are gradually made available to the plants growing there. In the garden, pests and disease may be a problem, and untidy debris isn't practical. Still, we can easily acquire the same nutrient benefits by composting. Compost is a great regular additive for your perennial garden, and good composting methods will help reduce pest and disease problems.

Green and brown materials for composting

Compost can be made easily in a pile, a wooden box or a purchased compost bin. The process is not complicated. A pile of kitchen scraps (no dairy or meat), grass clippings and fall leaves will eventually break down if simply left alone. Such "passive," or cool, composting may take one to two seasons for all the materials to break down. You can speed up the process and create an "active," or hot, compost pile by following a few simple guidelines.

Use dry as well as fresh materials, with a higher proportion of dry matter than fresh green matter. Appropriate dry matter includes chopped straw, shredded leaves, newspaper and sawdust. Green matter may consist of kitchen scraps, grass clippings and pulled weeds that haven't formed seed heads, in case your compost pile doesn't heat up enough to kill the weed seeds. If the weeds have seedheads, remove the seedheads before the weeds go into the compost pile. The green matter breaks down quickly and produces nitrogen, which composting organisms use to break down dry matter. Again, do not include any meat or dairy products with your kitchen scraps.

Spread the green materials evenly throughout the pile by layering them between dry materials. Mix in small amounts of soil from your garden or previously finished compost to introduce beneficial microorganisms. If the pile seems dry, sprinkle some water between the layers—the compost should be moist but not soaking: about as wet as a wrung-out sponge. Adding nitrogen, like that found in fertilizer, speeds up decomposition. Avoid strong concentrations of nitrogen, or you may kill beneficial organisms.

An active (hot) compost process

Finished compost ready for the garden

once the temperature drops. Turning and aerating the pile will stimulate the process to heat up again. The pile can be left to sit without turning and will eventually be ready to use if you are willing to wait several months to a year.

Avoid adding diseased or pest-ridden materials to your compost pile. If the damaging organisms are not destroyed, they could spread throughout your garden. If you must add questionable material to the pile, place it near the center, where the temperature is highest. Never add tomato vines from the garden because they often harbor diseases.

Turn the pile over or poke holes in it with a pitchfork every week or two. Air must get into the pile to speed up decomposition. A well-aerated compost pile will generate a lot of heat, reaching temperatures up to 160° F. At this high temperature, weed seeds are destroyed and many damaging soil organisms are killed. Most beneficial organisms will not be killed unless the temperature exceeds 160° F. To monitor the temperature of the compost near the middle of the pile, you will need a thermometer that is attached to a long probe, similar to a large meat thermometer. Turn your compost

When you can no longer recognize the matter that you put into the compost bin, and the temperature no longer rises upon turning, your compost is ready to be mixed into your garden beds. The process may take as little as one month, and it will leave you with organic material that is rich in nutrients and beneficial organisms.

If you do not wish to make your own compost, it can be purchased from most garden centers.

Compost worms

Selecting Perennials

PERENNIALS CAN BE PURCHASED AS PLANTS OR SEEDS. PURCHASED plants may begin flowering the same year they are planted, while plants started from seed may take two to three years to mature. Starting from seed is more economical if you want large numbers of plants. (See "Propagating Perennials," p. 45, to learn how to start perennials from seed.)

Get your perennials from a reputable source, and check to make sure the plants are not diseased or pest-ridden. Garden centers, mail-order catalogs and even friends and neighbors are excellent sources of perennials. A number of garden societies promote the exchange of seeds and plants, and many public gardens sell seeds of rare plants. Gardening clubs are also a great source of rare and unusual plants.

Better nurseries have Georgia Certified Plant Professionals available to assist you. These people have passed stringent tests administered by the Georgia Green Industry Association. It will be helpful to them if you bring

Plant on left is rootbound, plant on right is healthy.

a sketch of the area you intend to plant (see "Getting Started," p. 19). Be sure to mark shaded areas, wet areas, windy areas and so forth on the sketch so that the nursery professionals can help you choose plants for each location. You will also find it convenient to take our book to the nursery with you. You'll have information about the plants and photos of them at your fingertips as you browse.

Purchased plants come in two main forms. Potted perennials are growing in pots, usually the ones they were raised in. Bare-root perennials consist of pieces of root packed in moist peat moss or sawdust. These roots are typically dormant, although some of the previous year's growth may be evident or there may be new growth starting. Sometimes the roots appear to have no evident growth, past or present. Both potted and bare-root perennials are good purchases, and in each case there are things to look for to make sure that you are getting a plant of the best quality.

Potted plants come in many sizes. Although a larger plant may appear more mature, a smaller one will suffer less from the shock of being transplanted. Most perennials grow quickly once they are planted in the garden, so the better buy may well be the smaller plant. Select plants that seem to be a good size for the pot they are in. When a plant is tapped lightly out of the pot, the roots should be visible but should not be winding and twisting around the inside of the pot.

The leaves should be a healthy color. If they appear to be chewed or damaged, check carefully for diseases or insects. Do not purchase a diseased plant. If you find insects on the plant, you may not want to purchase it unless you are willing to cope with the hitchhikers you are taking home. Remember to look under the leaves for insect pests. To avoid spreading the pest, deal with any pest problems before you move the plant into the garden.

Once you get your potted plants home, water them if they are dry and keep them in a lightly shaded location until you plant them. Remove any damaged growth and discard it. This can be done at the nursery before you bring the plant home. Plant your new perennials as soon as possible.

Bare-root plants are most commonly sold through mail order, but some are available in garden centers, usually in spring. If you're buying from a garden center, look for roots that are dormant (without top growth). A bare-root plant that has been trying to grow in the stressful conditions of a plastic bag may have too little energy to recover, or it may take longer to establish once planted.

Cut off any damaged parts of the roots with a very sharp knife. Bare-root perennials will dehydrate quickly out of soil, so they need to be planted more quickly than potted plants. Soak the roots in lukewarm water for one to two hours to rehydrate them. Do not leave them in water longer than that, or you may encourage root or crown rot. Plant the roots either directly in the garden or into pots with good-quality potting soil until they can be moved to the garden.

It may be difficult to distinguish the top from the bottom of some bare-root plants. Usually there is a telltale dip or stub from which the plant previously grew. If you can't find any distinguishing characteristics, lay the root in the ground on its side and the plant will send the roots down and the shoots up.

Root mass of rootbound plant.

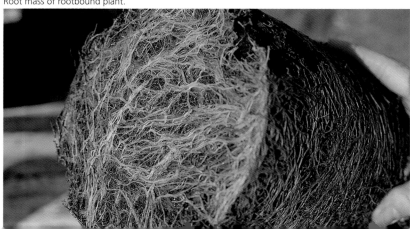

Planting Perennials

ONCE YOU HAVE PLANNED YOUR GARDEN, PREPARED THE SOIL and purchased your perennials, it's time to plant. If the perennials came with identification tags, be sure to poke them into the soil next to the new plants. Next spring, when most of your perennial bed is nothing but a few stubs of green, the tags will help you with identification and remind you that there is indeed a plant in that patch of soil. Most of these tags include information on what care the plant needs. A diagram of your garden showing the plants' positions is also helpful, in case the tags get lost.

Potted Perennials

Perennials in pots are convenient because you can arrange them across the bed before you start to plant. Once you have the collection organized, you can begin planting. To prevent the roots from drying out, do not unpot the plants until immediately before you transplant.

To plant potted perennials, start by digging a hole about the width and depth of the pot. Remove the perennial from the pot. If the pot is small enough, you can hold your hand across the top of the pot, letting your fingers straddle the stem of the plant, and then turn it upside down. Never pull on the stem or leaves to get a plant out of a pot. It is better to cut a difficult pot off rather than risk damaging the plant.

If you have taken advantage of an end-of-season sale, you will probably have to deal with root-bound plants. Before planting them, you will need to tease apart the roots if they are winding around the rootball. If the roots have become densely wound around the inside of the pot, cut into or score the root mass with a sharp knife to encourage new growth. If there is a solid mat at the bottom of the rootball, remove it. Such roots will not be able to spread out and establish themselves in the soil; the new root tips will only become trapped in the existing mass.

Gently spread out the roots as you plant, teasing a few roots out of the soil ball to get the plant growing in the right direction. The process of cutting into the bottom half of the rootball and spreading the two halves of the mass outward like a pair of wings is called "butterflying." It is an effective way to promote fast growth of pot-bound perennials when transplanting.

Place the plant in the prepared hole. It should be planted at the same level that it was at in the pot, or a little higher, to allow for the soil to settle. If the plant is too low in the ground, it may rot when rain collects around the crown. Fill the soil in around the roots and firm it down. Sometimes you will have soil left over, but, on occasion, there will not be enough soil. Some gardeners say this is due to planting at the waxing or waning of the moon. Water the plant well as soon as you have planted it and keep watering regularly until the plant has become established.

Support the plant as you remove the pot (above).

Loosen the rootball a little before planting (above).

Bare-root Perennials

During planting, bare-root perennials should not be spaced out across the bed unless you previously planted them in temporary pots. Roots dry out very quickly if you leave them lying about waiting to be planted. If you want to visualize your spacing, you can poke sticks into the ground or put rocks down to represent the locations of your perennials.

If you have been keeping your bare-root perennials in potting soil, you may find that the roots have not grown enough to knit the soil together and that all the soil falls away from the root when you remove it from the pot. Don't be concerned. Simply follow the regular root-planting instructions. If the soil does hold together, plant the root the way you would a potted perennial.

The type of hole you need to dig depends on the type of roots the bare-root perennial has. Plants with fibrous roots will need a mound of soil in the center of the planting hole over which the roots can be spread out evenly. The hole should be dug as deep as the longest roots. Mound the soil into the center of the hole up to ground level. Spread the roots out around the mound and cover them with loosened soil.

Plants with a taproot need a hole that is narrow and about as deep as the root is long. Use a trowel to open up a suitable hole, then tuck the root into it and fill it in again.

Some plants have what appear to be taproots, but the shoot seems to be growing off the side of the root rather than upward from one end. These 'roots' are actually modified underground stems called rhizomes. Many irises, for example, grow from rhizomes. Rhizomes should be planted horizontally in a shallow hole and covered with soil.

In most cases, you should try to get the crown of the plant at or just above soil level and loosen the soil that surrounds the planting hole. Keep the roots thoroughly watered until the plants are well established.

Whether the plants are potted or bare-root, leave them alone for a while to let them recover from the stress of planting. In the first month, you will need only to water the plant regularly, weed around it and watch for pests. A layer of mulch no more than 2" thick spread on the bed and around your plants will keep in moisture and control weeds.

If you have prepared your beds properly, you probably won't have to fertilize in the first year. If you do wish to fertilize, wait until your new plants have started healthy new growth, and apply only a weak organic fertilizer to avoid damaging the sensitive new roots.

Planters

Perennials can also be grown in planters for portable displays that can be moved around the garden as needed. Planters can be used on patios or decks, in gardens with very poor soil or in yards where children and dogs might destroy a traditional perennial bed.

Always use a good quality potting mix intended for containers. Soil from your garden and cheaply priced planting soil (essentially top-soil in a bag), quickly lose their

Golden Hakone grass

structure when used in a container. They soon become a solid lump, preventing air, water and roots from penetrating into the soil. Perennials will never thrive in a container if planted in soil from the garden. At the very least, mix half garden or planting soil with half potting mix, and blend the two together well. Be warned, though, that trying to extend your potting mix with garden soil often leads to disappointment.

Many perennials, such as hostas and daylilies, can grow in the same container without any fresh potting mix for five or six years. Be sure to fertilize and water perennials in planters more often than those growing in the ground. Dig your finger deep into the soil around the perennial to check that it really

needs water. Too much water in the planter causes root rot.

When designing a planter garden, you can keep one type of perennial in each planter and display many different planters together, or mix different perennials in large planters with annuals and bulbs. The latter choice results in a dynamic bouquet of flowers and foliage. Keep tall, upright perennials, such as yarrow, in the center of the planter; rounded or bushy types, such as coreopsis, around the sides; and low-growing or draping perennials, such as candytuft, along the edges. Perennials with long bloom times or attractive foliage work well in planters.

Choose hardy perennials that tolerate difficult conditions. Planters can be exposed to extreme weather,

Rosemary

drying out quickly in hot weather and becoming waterlogged after a couple of rainy days. Large containers are easier to maintain than small containers because they don't dry out as quickly. Lightweight fiberglass or foam containers are good because you have no worries about winter freezing and breakage. Also, they are easy to wheel to other parts of the garden for a quick change.

Some of the more invasive perennials make good choices for planters because they are tough to kill, and their otherwise aggressive spread is kept in check by the container.

Perennials for Planters

Blazing Star
Blue Lyme Grass
Candytuft
Golden Hakone Grass
Mondo Grass
Peacock Moss
Penstemon
Pinks
Ribbon Grass
Rosemary
Salvia
Thyme
Toad-Lily
Verbena
Yarrow

Caring for Perennials

MANY PERENNIALS REQUIRE LITTLE CARE BUT ALL BENEFIT FROM a few maintenance basics. Weeding, mulching, watering, fertilizing and grooming are some of the chores that, when done on a regular basis, keep major work to a minimum.

Weeding is an important maintenance task.

Weeding

Controlling weeds is one of the most important things you will do in your garden. Weeds compete with perennials for light, nutrients and space, and they can also harbor pests and diseases.

Many weed seeds, especially those of annual weeds, need light to germinate. Therefore, try to prevent weeds from germinating by blocking their access to light with a layer of mulch. As your garden matures,

some perennials will themselves suppress weeds by blocking the light.

Pull out weeds that do germinate while they are still small—before they have a chance to flower, set seed and start a whole new generation of problems. Weeds can be pulled out by hand or with a hoe. Quickly scuffing across the soil surface with the hoe will pull out small weeds and sever larger ones from their roots.

Mulching

Mulch is an important gardening tool. As mentioned above, it prevents weed seeds from germinating by blocking out the light, and small weeds that do pop up in a mulched bed are very easy to pull. Soil temperatures remain more consistent, and more moisture is retained under a layer of mulch. Mulch also prevents soil erosion during heavy rain or strong winds.

Organic mulches include compost, bark chips, shredded leaves and grass clippings. These mulches are desirable because they improve the soil and add nutrients as they break

Mulch helps keep soil moist and weeds at bay.

down. Shredded newspaper also makes good mulch. Shredding is important for leaves and newspaper because large pieces may keep too much moisture close to the crown of the plant. Unshredded newspaper may also block air movement and gas exchange in the soil and will attract slugs.

In spring, spread a 2–2$^1/_2$" layer of mulch over your perennial beds around your plants. Keep the area immediately around the crown or stem of each plant clear. Mulch that is too close to plants can trap moisture and prevent good air circulation, encouraging disease. If the layer of mulch disappears into the soil over summer, replenish it.

Watering

Watering is another basic of perennial care. Once established, many perennials need little supplemental watering if they have been planted in their preferred conditions and are given a moisture-retaining mulch. Planting perennials with similar water requirements together makes watering easier.

Water infrequently and thoroughly. Ensure the water penetrates at least 4" into the soil. Plants given a light sprinkle of water every day will develop roots that stay close to the soil surface, making the plants vulnerable to heat and drought. Watering deeply once a week encourages plants to develop a deeper root system. In hot, dry weather, they will be able to seek out the water trapped deep in the ground.

Do most of your watering in the morning. In the heat of the day, much of the water is lost to evaporation. Late in the day, moisture left on the plant may not dry and will encourage fungal diseases to develop.

Avoid overwatering. Check the soil for dryness by poking your finger into the top 1–2". You can also try rolling a bit of the soil from around the plant into a ball. If the soil forms a ball, it is moist and needs no extra water.

Remember that perennials in containers or planters usually need to be watered more frequently than those growing in the ground. The smaller the container, the more often the plants will need watering. Containers may need to be watered twice daily during hot, sunny weather. If the soil in your container dries out, you will have to water several times to make sure water is absorbed throughout the planting medium. Dig into the soil, and if it is dry at all, water more.

Fertilizing

If you prepare your beds well and add new compost to them each spring, you should not need to add extra fertilizer. If you have a limited amount of compost, you can mix a slow-release organic fertilizer into the soil around your perennials in spring. Some plants, such as rose mallow, are heavy feeders that need additional supplements throughout the growing season. In the garden, it is best to use organic fertilizers to minimize any disruption of the soil microorganisms. Chemical fertilizers are acceptable for container grown plants because the potting soil is most often sterile.

Watering wand

Many organic and chemical fertilizers are available at garden centers. Most fertilizer instructions recommend a higher rate than is necessary for good plant growth. Never use more than the recommended quantity because too much fertilizer will do more harm than good. Fertilizer that is applied in high concentrations can burn the plant roots. Problems are more likely to be caused by chemical fertilizers because they are more concentrated than organic types.

For perennials, it is important to support good root development in the first year or two of growth. Phosphorus is the fertilizer that promotes root growth, so if you lack compost, look for fertilizers high in phosphorus while plants are establishing. The typical fertilizer formula is N : P : K (Nitrogen : Phosphorus : Potassium). After plants are established, nitrogen becomes important for leaf development and potassium for flower and seed development.

Deadheading often promotes more blooms!

Grooming

Many perennials benefit from grooming. Resilient plants, plentiful blooms and compact growth are the signs of a well-groomed garden. Thinning, trimming, disbudding, deadheading and staking are grooming techniques that can enhance the beauty of a perennial bed. The methods are simple, but you may have to experiment to get the right effect in your own garden.

Thinning is done to clump-forming perennials such as black-eyed Susan, purple coneflower and beebalm early in the year, when shoots have just emerged. These plants develop a dense clump of stems that allows very little air or light into the center of the plant. Remove half of the shoots when they first emerge to increase air circulation and prevent diseases such as powdery mildew. The increased light encourages compact growth and more flowers. Throughout the growing season, thin any growth that is weak, diseased or growing in the wrong direction.

Pinching or trimming perennials is a simple procedure, but timing it correctly and achieving just the right look can be tricky. Early in the year, before the flower buds have appeared, pinch the plant to encourage new side shoots. Remove the plant tip and some stems just above a leaf or pair of leaves. You can pinch stem by stem with your fingers, or, if you have a lot of plants, you can trim off the tops with your hedge shears to one-third of the height you expect the plants to reach. The growth that begins to emerge can be trimmed again. Beautiful layered effects can be achieved by staggering the trimming times by a week or two.

Give plants enough time to set buds and flower. Continual pinching or trimming will encourage very dense growth but also delay flowering. Most spring-flowering plants cannot be pinched back or they will not flower. Early-summer or mid-summer bloomers should be pinched only once, as early in the season as possible. Late-summer and fall bloomers can be pinched several times but should be left alone past July 4. Don't pinch a plant if flower buds have formed—it may not have enough energy or time left in the year to develop a new set of buds. Experimenting and keeping detailed notes will improve your pinching skills.

Perennials to Pinch Early in the Season

- Aster
- Beebalm
- Black-eyed Susan
- Cardinal Flower
- Chrysanthemum
- Penstemon
- Purple Coneflower
- Rough Verbena
- Shasta Daisy
- Tall Verbena

Perennials to Shear Back After Blooming

- Bluestar
- Candytuft
- Creeping Phlox
- False Sunflower
- Hardy Geranium
- Perennial Sunflower
- Soapwort
- Spiderwort
- Yarrow

Disbudding is the removal of some flower buds to encourage the remaining ones to produce larger flowers. This technique is popular with rose and camellia growers and with gardeners who enter plants in fairs or similar flower competitions.

Aster

Bluestar

Deadheading, the removal of flowers once they have finished blooming, serves several purposes. It keeps plants looking tidy; it prevents the plant from spreading seeds, and therefore seedlings, throughout the garden; it often prolongs blooming; and it helps prevent pest and disease problems.

Flowers can be removed by hand or snipped off with hand pruners. Bushy plants with many tiny flowers, and particularly plants with a short bloom period, such as candytuft, can be more aggressively pruned back with garden shears once they have finished flowering. For some plants, such as creeping phlox, shearing will promote new growth and possibly more blooms later in the season.

Deadheading is not necessary for every plant. Some plants have attractive seedheads that can be left in place to provide interest in the garden over winter and attract birds. Other plants are short-lived, and leaving some of the seedheads in place encourages future generations to replace the old plants. Foxglove is one example of a short-lived perennial that reseeds. In some cases the self-sown seedlings do not possess the attractive features of the parent plant. Deadheading may be required in these cases.

Perennials with Interesting Seedheads

Astilbe
Black-eyed Susan
Blackberry Lily
False Indigo
Feather Reed Grass
Hardy Geranium
Plume Poppy
Purple Coneflower
Ravenna Grass
Sea Holly
Sedum 'Autumn Joy'

Perennials that Self-Seed

Astilbe
Black-eyed Susan
Blackberry Lily
Bleeding Heart (variable seedlings)
Bloodroot
Cardinal Flower
Christmas Rose
Columbine
Evening Primrose
Foxglove
Gaura
Goldenrod
Patrinia
Pinks
Plume Poppy
Purple Loosestrife
Ravenna Grass
Tall Verbena

Sea holly

Pinks

Staking

Staking, the use of poles, branches or wires to hold plants erect, can often be avoided by astute thinning and trimming, but a few plants always need support to look their best. Three types of stakes are used for the different growth habits that need support.

Plants that develop tall spikes, such as some foxgloves, require each spike to be staked individually. A strong, narrow pole, such as a bamboo stick, can be pushed into the ground early in the year and the spike tied to the stake as it grows. Ensure the plant is securely fastened with plant-friendly ties of a soft, stretchable material or with strips of thin plastic, such as plastic grocery bags or plastic wrap. A forked branch can also be used to support single-stemmed plants.

Many plants get top heavy as they grow and tend to flop over once they reach a certain height. A wire hoop, sometimes called a peony ring, is the most unobtrusive way to hold up such a plant. When the plant is young, the legs of the peony ring are pushed into the ground around it, and as the plant grows, it is supported by the wire ring. At the same time, the bushy growth hides the ring.

Other plants, such as coreopsis, form a floppy tangle of stems. These plants can be given a bit of support with twiggy branches inserted into the ground around young plants; the plants then grow up into the twigs.

Along with thinning and trimming, there are other steps you can take to reduce the need for staking. First,

Spiral stakes work well for supporting tall, single stems.

grow plants in the right conditions. Don't assume a plant will do better in a richer soil than is recommended. Very rich soil causes many plants to produce weak, leggy growth that is prone to falling over. Similarly, a plant that likes full sun will become stretched out and leggy if grown in shade. Second, use other plants for support. Grow plants that have a stable structure between plants that need support. The weaker plants may still fall over slightly, but only as far as their neighbors will allow. Many plants are available in compact varieties that don't require staking.

Winter Protection for Tender Perennials

To protect a tender perennial during winter, or a perennial you know is planted outside its zone, don't cut it back until early spring. Cutting back a tender perennial leaves stems that are open on the top and can fill with moisture. The moisture travels down to the base of the plant, freezes and expands during a cold night, often killing the entire plant. Do not cut any perennials back until you see new growth begin in late winter to early spring.

Drought before a hard freeze can kill tender and hardy perennials. If the roots and soil are dry before a hard freeze, the roots can dehydrate within hours if it is cold enough, which can kill the entire plant. If a hard freeze is expected and your soil is dry, water around your perennials to protect them from dehydration.

Some salvias (above) and spiderworts (below) are tender perennials.

Propagating Perennials

PROPAGATING YOUR OWN PERENNIALS IS AN INTERESTING AND challenging aspect of gardening that can save you money, but it also requires time and space. Seeds, cuttings and division are the three methods of increasing your perennial population. Each method has advantages and disadvantages.

Shade cloth covering a cold frame (below)

A cold frame is a wonderful gardening aid regardless of which method of propagation you use. It can be used to protect tender plants over winter, to start vegetable seeds early in spring, to harden plants off before moving them to the garden, to protect fall-germinating seedlings and young cuttings or divisions and to start seeds that need a cold treatment. This mini-greenhouse

Filling cell packs

Using folded paper to plant small seeds
Spray bottle provides gentle mist

structure is built so that ground level on the inside of the cold frame is lower than on the outside, so the soil around the outside insulates the plants within. The angled, hinged lid is fitted with glass. The lid lets light in to collect some heat during the day, and it prevents rain from damaging tender plants. If the interior gets too hot, the lid can be raised for ventilation.

Seeds

Starting perennials from seed is a great way to propagate a large number of plants at a relatively low cost. You can purchase seeds or collect them from your own or a friend's perennial garden. The work involved in growing plants from seed is worth it when you see the plants you raised from tiny seedlings finally begin to flower.

Propagating from seed has some limitations. Some cultivars and varieties don't pass on their desirable traits to their offspring. Other perennials have seeds that take a very long time to germinate, if they germinate at all, and may take even longer to grow to flowering size. Many perennials, however, grow easily from seed and flower within a year or two of being transplanted into the garden.

Specific propagation information is given for each plant in this book, but there are a few basic rules for starting all seeds. Some seeds can be started directly in the garden (direct sown), but it is easier to control temperature and moisture levels and to provide a sterile environment if you start the seeds indoors. Seeds can be started in pots or, if you need a lot of plants, flats. Use a sterile soil mix intended for starting seeds. The mix will generally need to be kept moist but not soggy. Most seeds germinate in moderately warm temperatures of about 57°–70° F.

Seed-starting supplies are available at garden centers. Many supplies aren't necessary, but some, such as seed-tray dividers, are useful. These dividers, often called plug trays, are made of plastic and prevent the roots of seedlings from tangling and being disturbed during transplanting. Heating coils or pads can also come in handy. Placed under the pots or flats, they keep the soil at a constant temperature.

A prepared seed tray with cover

Fill your pot or seed tray with the soil mix and firm it down slightly—not too firmly or the soil will not drain. Wet the soil before planting your seeds because they may wash into clumps if the soil is watered immediately afterward.

Medium-sized to large seeds can be planted individually and spaced out in pots or trays. If you have divided inserts for your trays, plant one or two seeds per section. Lightly cover medium-sized seeds with soil. Press large seeds into the soil before lightly covering them. Do not cover seeds that need to be exposed to light to germinate.

Small seeds may have to be sprinkled onto the soil. Fold a sheet of paper in half and place the seeds in the crease. Gently tap the underside of the fold to bounce or roll the seeds off the paper in a controlled manner. Some seeds are so tiny that they look like dust. These tiny seeds can be mixed with a small quantity of very fine sand and spread on the soil surface. Small and tiny seeds may not need to be covered with any more soil.

Plant only one type of seed in each pot or flat. Each species has a different rate of germination, and the germinated seedlings will require different conditions than the seeds that have yet to germinate.

Water the seeds using a very fine spray if the soil starts to dry out. A hand-held spray bottle will moisten the soil without disturbing the seeds. To keep the environment moist, place pots inside clear plastic bags. Change the bags or turn them inside out once condensation starts to build up and drip. Plastic bags can be held up with stakes or wires poked in around the edges of the pot. Many seed trays come with clear plastic covers that can be placed over the flats to keep moisture in. The plastic can be removed once the seeds have germinated.

The amount and timing of watering is critical to successfully growing

perennials from seed. Most germinated seeds and young seedlings will
perish if the soil is allowed to dry
out. Strive to maintain a consistently
moist soil, which may mean watering lightly two to three times a day.
As the seedlings get bigger, cut
back on the number of times you
water, but water a little heavier
each time. A handy guideline to
follow: when the seedlings have
their first true leaves, you can cut
back to watering once a day.

Seeds generally do not require a
lot of light to germinate, so pots or
trays can be kept in any warm, out-
of-the-way place. Once the seeds
have germinated, place them in a
bright location out of direct sun.
Seedlings should be transplanted
to individual pots once they have
three or four true leaves. True
leaves are the ones that look like
the mature leaves. (The first one or
two leaves are actually part of the
seed; they are called seed leaves, or
cotyledons.) Plants in plug trays
can be left until neighboring leaves
start to touch each other. At this
point the plants will be competing
for light and should be transplanted to individual pots.

Young seedlings do not need to be
fertilized. The seed itself provides all
the nutrition the seedling will need.
Fertilizer causes seedlings to produce
soft, spindly growth that is susceptible to attack by insects and diseases.
A fertilizer diluted to one-quarter or
one-half strength can be used once
seedlings have four or five true
leaves. Organic fertilizers are safer to
use because they do not burn and
need to be used less often.

All seedlings are susceptible to a
problem called damping off, which
is caused by soil-borne fungi. An
afflicted seedling looks as though
someone has pinched the stem at
soil level, causing the plant to topple
over. The pinched area blackens and
the seedling dies. Sterile soil mix,
good air circulation and evenly
moist soil will help prevent damping
off. It also helps to spread a $1/4$" layer
of peat moss over the seedbed.

Perennials to Start from Seed

Beebalm
Blackberry Lily
Blanket Flower
Blue Lyme Grass
Candytuft
Columbine
Coreopsis
Foxglove
Hardy Begonia
Hardy Hibiscus
Muhly Grass
Pampas Grass
Perennial Sunflower
Purple Coneflower
Verbena
Yarrow

Foxglove

Many seeds sprout easily as soon as they are planted. Some, however, have protective devices that prevent them from germinating when conditions are not favorable or from germinating all at once. Some seeds bear thick seed coats, some produce chemicals that prevent germination and some are programmed for staggered germination. In the wild, such strategies improve the chances of survival, but you will have to lower the defenses of these types of seeds before they will germinate.

Scratching the seed coats with sandpaper

Soaking seeds in a glass of water

Seeds can be tricked into thinking the conditions are right for sprouting. Some thick-coated seeds can be soaked for a day or two in a glass of water to promote germination. The soaking mimics the beginning of the rainy season, which is when the plant would germinate in its natural environment. The water softens the seed coat and in some cases washes away the chemicals that have been preventing germination. Hardy hibiscus is an example of a plant with seeds that need to be soaked before they will germinate.

Other thick-coated seeds need to be scratched (scarified) to allow moisture to penetrate the seed coat and prompt germination. In nature, birds scratch the seeds with the gravel in their craws and acid in their stomachs. You can mimic this process by nicking the seeds with a knife or file, or by gently rubbing them between two sheets of sandpaper. Leave the scratched seeds in a dry place for a day or so before planting them, to give them a chance to prepare for germination before they are exposed to water. Anemones have seeds that need their thick coats scratched.

Plants from northern climates often have seeds that wait until spring before they germinate. These seeds must be given a cold treatment, which mimics winter, before they will germinate. Yarrow has seeds that respond to cold treatment.

One method of cold treatment is to plant the seeds in a pot or tray and place them in the refrigerator for up to two months. Check the container regularly and don't allow the seeds to dry out. This method is fairly simple but not very practical if your refrigerator is crowded.

Mixing seeds with moist peat moss for cold treatment

Cuttings

Cuttings are an excellent way to propagate varieties and cultivars that you really like but that don't come true from seed or don't produce seed at all. Each cutting will grow into a reproduction (clone) of the parent plant. Cuttings are taken from the stems of some perennials and the roots or rhizomes of others.

Stem cuttings are generally taken in spring and early summer. During this time plants produce a flush of fresh, new growth, either before or after flowering. Avoid taking cuttings from plants that are in flower. Plants that are blooming or about to bloom are busy trying to reproduce; plants that are busy growing, by contrast, are already full of the right hormones to promote quick root growth. If you do take cuttings from plants that are flowering, be sure to remove the flowers and the buds to divert the plant's energy back into growing roots and leaves.

Because cuttings need to be kept in a warm, humid place to root, they are prone to fungal diseases. Providing proper sanitation (sterile soil mix, clean tools and containers) and encouraging quick rooting will increase the survival rate of your cuttings, but be sure to plant a lot of them to make up for any losses. Dusting with soil sulfur will also help reduce the incidence of fungal disease.

Generally, stem cuttings are more successful and quicker to grow if you include the tip of the stem in the cutting. Debate exists over what length of stem to cut below the tip. Some gardeners claim that smaller

A less space-consuming method is to mix the seeds with some moistened sand, peat moss or sphagnum moss. Place the mix in a sealed sandwich bag and pop it in the refrigerator for up to two months, again being sure the sand or moss doesn't dry out. The seeds can then be planted into a pot or tray. Spread the seeds and the moist sand or moss onto the prepared surface and press it all down gently.

As noted in certain entries in this book, some plants have seeds that must be planted when freshly ripe. These seeds cannot be stored for long periods of time.

Remove lower leaves

Dip the cut end in rooting hormone.

Firm the cutting into the soil.

Newly planted cuttings

Healthy roots on cuttings

cuttings are more likely to root and root more quickly. Other gardeners claim that larger cuttings develop more roots and become established more quickly once planted in the garden. You may wish to try different sizes to see what works best for you. Generally, a small cutting is 1–2" long and a large cutting is 4–6" long.

Perennials to Propagate from Stem Cuttings

Bluestar
Coreopsis
Dwarf Plumbago
Coreopsis
Penstemon
Pinks
Rosemary
Salvia 'Indigo Spires'
Sedum 'Autumn Joy'
Thyme
Turtlehead
Yarrow

Penstemon

Size of cuttings is partly determined by the number of leaf nodes on the cutting. You will want at least three or four nodes on a cutting. The node is where the leaf joins the stem, and it is from here that the new roots and leaves grow. The base of the cutting will be just below a node. Strip the leaves gently from the first and second nodes and plant them below the soil surface. Retain the leaves on the top part of the cutting above the soil. Some plants have a lot of space between nodes, so your cutting may be longer than the 1–2" or 4–6" guideline. Other plants have almost no space at all between nodes. Cut these plants according to the length guidelines, and gently remove the leaves from the lower half of the cutting. Plants with closely spaced nodes often root quickly and abundantly.

Always use a sharp, sterile knife to take cuttings. (To sterilize a knife, dip it in denatured alcohol or a 10% bleach solution.) Make cuts straight across the stem. Once you have stripped the leaves, dip the end of the cutting into a rooting-hormone powder intended for softwood cuttings. Sprinkle the powder onto a piece of paper and dip the cutting into it. Discard any extra powder left on the paper to prevent the spread of disease. Tap or blow the extra powder off the cutting. Cuttings caked with rooting hormone are more likely to rot than to root, and they don't root any faster than those that are lightly dusted.

Most gardeners plant their cuttings directly into a sterile soil mix. Other gardeners prefer to keep their cuttings in water until they show root growth and then plant them. If you choose to place cuttings in

Yarrow

water, use dark containers instead of clear containers for the best results.

The sooner you plant your cuttings or place them in water, the better. The less water the cuttings lose, the less likely they are to wilt and the more quickly they will root.

Cuttings can be planted in a similar manner to seeds. Use a sterile soil mix intended for seeds or cuttings. You can also root cuttings in sterilized sand, perlite, vermiculite or a combination of the three. Firm the soil down and moisten it before you start planting. Poke a hole in the soil with a pencil or similar object, tuck the cutting in and gently firm the soil around it. Make sure the lowest leaves do not touch the soil. The cuttings should be spaced far enough apart that adjoining leaves do not touch each other.

Cover the pots or trays with plastic to keep in the humidity. The rigid plastic lids that are available for trays may not be high enough to fit over cuttings, in which case you will have to use a plastic bag. Push stakes or wires into the soil around the edge of the pot so that the plastic will be held off the leaves.

Keep the cuttings in a warm place, about 65°–70° F, in bright, indirect light. Keep the soil moist using a hand-held mister. Turn the bag inside out when condensation becomes heavy. A couple of holes poked in the bag will create some ventilation.

Most cuttings require one to four weeks to root. After two weeks, give the cutting a gentle tug. You will feel resistance if roots have formed. If the cutting feels as though it can pull out of the soil, gently push it back down and leave it longer. New growth is also a good sign that your cutting has rooted. Some gardeners simply leave the cuttings alone until they can see roots through the holes in the bottoms of the pots. Uncover the cuttings once they have developed roots.

When the cuttings are showing new leaf growth, apply a foliar feed using a hand-held mister. Plants quickly absorb nutrients through the leaves, and by feeding that way you can avoid stressing the newly formed roots. Your local garden center should have foliar fertilizers and information about applying them.

Turtlehead

Once your cuttings have rooted and have had a chance to establish, they can be potted individually. If you rooted several cuttings in one pot or tray, you may find that the roots have tangled together. If gentle pulling doesn't separate them, take the entire tangled clump and try rinsing some of the soil away. Doing so should free enough roots to allow you to separate the plants.

Pot the young plants in sterile potting soil. They can be moved into a sheltered area of the garden or a cold frame and grown in pots until they are mature enough to fend for themselves. The plants may need some protection over the first winter in the coldest areas of the state. Keep them in the cold frame if they are still in pots, or give them an extra layer of mulch if they have been planted out.

Daylily

Basal cuttings involve removing the new growth from the main clump of a plant and rooting it in the same manner as stem cuttings. Many plants send up new shoots or plantlets around their bases. Often, the plantlets will already have a few roots growing. Once separated, these young plants develop quickly and may even grow to flowering size the first summer.

Perennials to Start from Basal Cuttings
Daylily
Phlox
Purple Loosestrife
Sedum

Treat these cuttings as you would a stem cutting. Use a sterile knife to cut out the shoot. You may have to cut back some of the top growth of the shoot because the tiny, developing roots may not be able to support all of it. Sterile soil mix and humid conditions are best. Pot plants individually, or place them in soft soil in the garden until new growth appears and roots have developed; then you can transplant them to any desired location.

Root cuttings can also be taken from some plants. Dandelions are often inadvertently propagated this way: even the smallest piece of root left in the ground can sprout a new plant, foiling attempts to eradicate them. But there are desirable perennials that share this ability.

Cuttings can be taken from the fleshy roots of certain perennials that do not propagate well from stem cuttings. These cuttings

Sedum

should be taken in early or mid-spring when the ground is just starting to warm and the roots are about to break dormancy. At this time, the roots of the perennials are full of nutrients that the plants stored the previous summer and fall, and hormones are initiating growth. You may have to wet the soil around the plant so that you can loosen it enough to get to the roots.

You do not want very young or very old roots. Very young roots are usually white and quite soft; very old roots are tough and woody. The roots you should use will be tan and still fleshy.

To prepare your root, cut out the section you will be using with a sterile knife. Cut the root into pieces 1–2" long. Remove any side roots before planting the sections in pots or planting trays. Roots must be planted in a vertical position, and they need to be kept in the orientation they held when attached to the parent plant. People use different tricks to help them remember which end is up. One method is to cut straight across the tops and diagonally across the bottoms.

You can use the same type of soil mix as you would for seeds and stem cuttings. Poke the pieces vertically into the soil, leaving a tiny bit of the end sticking up out of the soil. Remember to keep the pieces the right way up. Keep the pots or trays in a warm place out of direct sunlight. The root cuttings will send up new shoots once they have rooted and can be planted in the same manner as stem cuttings (see p. 50).

The main difference between starting root cuttings and starting stem cuttings is that the root cuttings must be kept fairly dry; they can rot very easily. Keep the cuttings slightly moist, but not wet, while you are rooting them and avoid overwatering as they establish.

Perennials to Propagate from Root Cuttings

- Blanket Flower
- Black-eyed Susan
- Columbine
- Phlox
- Sea Holly
- Sedum
- Virginia Bluebells

Columbine

Wild ginger

Rhizome cuttings are the easiest means of propagating plants from underground parts. In addition to true roots, some plants have rhizomes, which are thick, fleshy modified stems that grow horizontally underground. A rhizome sends up new shoots at intervals along its length, and in this way the plant spreads. It is easy to take advantage of this feature.

Perennials to Propagate from Rhizomes

- Barrenwort
- Blackberry Lily
- Bloodroot
- Canna Lily
- Hardy Ageratum
- Iris
- Solomon's Seal
- Wild Ginger

Iris

Dig up a rhizome when the plant is growing vigorously, usually in late spring or early summer. If you look closely at the rhizome, you will see that it appears to be growing in sections. The places where these sections join are called nodes. It is from these nodes that small, stringy feeder roots extend downward and new plants sprout upward. You may even see small plantlets already sprouting.

Cut your chunk of rhizome into pieces. Each piece should have at least one of these nodes in it.

Fill a pot or planting tray to about 1" from the top with perlite, vermiculite or seeding soil. Moisten the soil and let the excess water drain away. Lay the rhizome pieces flat on top of the mix, and almost cover them with more of the soil mix. If you leave a small bit of the top exposed to the light, it will encourage the shoots to sprout. The soil does not have to be kept wet. To avoid rot, let your rhizome dry out between waterings.

Once your rhizome cuttings have established, they can be potted individually and grown in the same manner as stem cuttings (see p. 50).

Stolons are very similar to rhizomes except that they grow horizontally on the soil surface. They can be treated in the same way as rhizomes.

Division

Division is perhaps the easiest way to propagate perennials. As most perennials grow, they form larger and larger clumps. Dividing this clump periodically will rejuvenate the plant, keep its size in check and provide you with more plants. If a plant you really want is

expensive, consider buying only one, because within a few years you may have more than you can handle.

How often or whether a perennial should be divided varies. Some perennials, such as astilbes, need dividing every three to four years to keep them vigorous. Other perennials

Digging up perennial clump for division (above, center)

Clump of stems, roots & crowns (below)

are content to be left alone for a long time, though they can be successfully divided for propagation if desired. Still others should never be divided. They may have a single crown from which the plants grow, or they may simply dislike having their roots disturbed.

Pulling the clump apart

Cleanly cut tuberous and rhizomatous perennials when dividing (above). Rhizome sections ready for planting (below)

Perennials that do not like to be divided can often be propagated by basal or stem cuttings.

Each entry in this book gives recommendations for division. In general, watch for these signs that indicate a perennial may need dividing:
- the center of the plant has died out
- the plant is no longer flowering as profusely as it did in previous years
- the plant is encroaching on the growing space of other plants sharing the bed

It is relatively easy to divide perennials. Begin by digging up the entire clump and knocking any large clods of soil away from the rootball. The clump can then be split into several pieces. A small plant with fibrous roots can be torn into sections by hand. A large plant can be pried apart with a pair of garden forks inserted back-to-back into the clump. Square-bladed spades made specifically for slicing through root masses are widely available. Plants with thicker, tuberous or rhizomatous roots can be cut into sections with a sharp, sterile knife. In all cases, cut away any old sections that have died out and replant only the newer, more vigorous sections.

Once your clump has been divided, replant one or two of the sections into the original location. Take the opportunity to work organic matter into the soil before replanting. The other sections can be moved to new spots in the garden or potted and given to gardening friends and neighbors.

Get the sections back into the ground as quickly as possible to prevent the exposed roots from drying out. Plan where you are going to plant your divisions and have the spots prepared before you start digging up. Plant your perennial divisions in pots if you aren't sure where to put them.

The larger the sections of the division, the more quickly the plant will re-establish and grow to blooming size again. For example, a perennial divided into four sections will bloom sooner than the same one divided into eight sections. Very small divisions may benefit from being planted in pots until they are bigger and better able to compete in the garden.

Newly planted divisions will need extra care and attention. Keep them well watered until they have re-established. For the first few days after planting, give them shade from direct sunlight. A light covering of burlap or damp newspaper should be sufficient to shelter them for this short period. Divisions that have been planted in pots should be kept in a shaded location.

There is some debate about the best time to divide perennials. Some gardeners prefer to divide perennials while they are dormant, whereas others believe they establish more quickly if divided when they are growing vigorously. You may wish to experiment with dividing at different times of the year to see what works best for you. If you do divide perennials while they are growing, you will need to cut back one-third to one-half of the growth to avoid stressing the roots while they are repairing the damage done to them.

Sometimes when the center of a perennial dies out, it can be rejuvenated without digging up the whole plant. Dig out the center of the plant, ensuring you remove all of the dead and weak growth. Replace the soil you removed with fresh planting mix, and sprinkle a small amount of alfalfa pellets on top of the mix. The center of the plant should fill in quickly.

Perennials that Should Not be Divided

Butterfly Weed
Carolina Lupine
Christmas Rose
False Indigo
Gaura
Russian Sage

Butterfly weed (above), false indigo (below)

Problems & Pests

PERENNIAL GARDENS ARE BOTH AN ASSET AND A LIABILITY WHEN it comes to pests and disease. Perennial beds often contain a mixture of different plant species. Because many insects and diseases attack only one species of plant, mixed beds make it difficult for pests and diseases to find their preferred hosts and establish a population. At the same time, because the plants are in the same spot for many years, any problems that do develop can become permanent. Luckily, if allowed, beneficial insects, birds and other pest-devouring organisms can also develop permanent populations. Plants selected for this book are generally less susceptible to problems. Included are a few native plants that have survived the conditions in Georgia for millennia.

For many years pest control meant spraying or dusting to eliminate every pest in the landscape. A more moderate approach advocated today is known as IPM (Integrated Pest Management or Integrated Plant Management). The goal of IPM is to reduce pest problems to levels at which only negligible damage is done.

You must determine what degree of damage is acceptable to you. Consider whether a pest's damage is localized or covers the entire plant. Will the damage kill the plant or is it only affecting the outward appearance? Are there methods of controlling the pest without chemicals? Many universities, especially the Cooperative Extension departments, have information about IPM. The University of Illinois Extension has a good overview of IPM at <www.ipm.uiuc.edu/ipm/index. html>. Georgia specific information can be found at <www.gaipm.org>.

IPM includes learning about your plants and the conditions they need for healthy growth, what pests might affect your plants, where and when to look for those pests and how to control them. Keep records of pest damage because your observations can reveal patterns useful in spotting recurring problems and in planning your maintenance regime.

An effective, responsible pest management program has four steps. Cultural controls are the most important. Physical controls should be attempted next, followed by biological controls. Resort to chemical controls only when the first three possibilities have been exhausted.

Cultural controls are the gardening techniques you use in the day-to-day care of your garden. It is very important to keep your soil healthy with plenty of organic matter. A healthy soil foodweb is very effective in keeping pest organisms in check. It is also important to grow perennials in the conditions for which they are adapted.

Other cultural controls are equally simple and straightforward. Choose resistant varieties of perennials that are not prone to problems. Space your plants so that they have good air circulation in and around them and are not stressed from competing for light, nutrients and space. Remove plants that are decimated by the same pests every year. Dispose of diseased foliage and branches. Prevent the spread of disease by keeping your gardening tools clean and by tidying up fallen leaves and dead plant matter at the end of every growing season.

Physically removing weeds and pests is an effective control strategy.

Physical controls are generally used to combat insect and mammal problems. An example of such a control is picking insects off plants by hand, which is not as daunting as it may seem if you catch the problem when it is just beginning. Large, slow insects such as Japanese beetles are particularly easy to pick off. Other physical controls include traps, barriers, scarecrows and natural repellants that make a plant taste or smell bad to pests. Garden centers offer a wide array of such devices. Physical control of diseases usually involves removing the infected plant or parts of the plant to keep the problem from spreading.

Biological controls make use of populations of natural predators. Birds, snakes, frogs, spiders, lady beetles and certain bacteria and

Frogs eat many insect pests.

The green lacewing is a garden good guy.

fungi help keep pest populations at a manageable level. Encourage these creatures to take up permanent residence in your garden. A birdbath and birdfeeder will encourage birds to enjoy your yard and feed on a wide variety of insect pests. Many beneficial insects are probably already living in your garden, and you can encourage them to stay and multiply by planting appropriate food sources. For example, many beneficial insects eat nectar from flowers such as yarrow and daisies.

One form of biological control is the naturally occurring soil bacterium *Bacillus thuringiensis* var. *kurstaki,* or *B.t.* for short. It breaks down the gut lining of some insect pests and is available in garden centers. However, *B.t.* can harm or kill many beneficial insects in your lawn, so large applications of it are not a good idea. Very small, targeted applications of very minute amounts may be acceptable.

Chemical controls should be used only as a last resort because they can do more harm than good. The main drawback to using any chemical is that the substance may also kill the beneficial insects you have been trying to attract. Another drawback is that chemicals tend to strip away the protective coating of bacteria and fungi that live on the plant surface. Once this layer has been removed, the plant is vulnerable to attack by pest organisms. If, however, you have tried cultural, physical and biological methods and still wish to take further action, call your local University of Georgia Extension office to obtain a list of chemicals recommended for particular diseases or insects. Try to use "organic" types, available at most garden centers. Organic sprays are no less dangerous than chemical ones, but they will at least break down into harmless compounds eventually. Always choose the least toxic option that has the shortest residual activity. Consumers are demanding effective pest products that do not harm the environment, and less toxic, more precisely targeted pesticides are becoming available. See also the environmentally friendly alternatives listed on p. 70.

When using pesticides, follow the manufacturer's instructions carefully. NEVER overuse any pesticide. A large amount of pesticide—organic or not—is no more effective in controlling pests than the recommended amount. Also note that if a particular pest is not listed on the package, it will not be controlled by that product. Any treatment you choose should be applied when the pest is most vulnerable to the treatment and only when the action threshold has been reached. Only spray the infected area (spot spray), rather than applying blanket coverage. Proper and early identification of pests is vital to finding a quick solution.

Glossary of Pests & Diseases

Anthracnose
Fungus. Yellow or brown spots on leaves; sunken lesions and blisters on stems; can kill plant.
What to Do: Choose resistant varieties and cultivars; keep soil well drained; thin out stems to improve air circulation; avoid handling wet foliage. Remove and destroy infected plant parts; clean up and destroy debris from infected plants at end of growing season. Liquid copper spray can prevent spread to other susceptible plants.

Aphids
Tiny, pear-shaped insects, winged or wingless; green, black, brown, red or gray. Cluster along stems, on buds and on leaves. Suck sap from plants; cause distorted or stunted growth. Sticky honeydew forms on surfaces and encourages sooty mold growth.
What to Do: Squish small colonies by hand; dislodge them with water spray; spray serious infestations with insecticidal soap, horticultural oil or neem oil (see p. 71

and package directions); encourage predatory insects and birds that feed on aphids.

Aster Yellows
see Viruses

Beetles
Many types and sizes; usually rounded with hard, shell-like outer wings covering membranous inner wings. Some are beneficial, e.g., ladybird beetles ("ladybugs"). Others, e.g., Japanese beetles, flea beetles, blister beetles, leaf skeletonizers and weevils, eat plants. Larvae: see Borers, Grubs. Leave wide range of chewing damage: make small or large holes in or around margins of leaves; consume entire leaves or areas between leaf veins ("skeletonize"); may also chew holes in flowers.
What to Do: Pick beetles off at night and drop them into an old coffee can half filled with soapy water (soap prevents them from floating); spread an old sheet under plants and shake off beetles to collect and dispose of

Aphids

Adult ladybird beetle

them. Use a hand-held vacuum cleaner to remove them from plant. Parasitic nematodes are effective if the beetle goes through part of its growing cycle in the ground.

Blight
Fungal or bacterial diseases, many types; e.g., leaf blight, snow blight, tip blight. Leaves, stems and flowers blacken, rot and die.

What to Do: Thin stems to improve air circulation; keep mulch away from base of plants; remove debris from garden at end of growing season. Remove and destroy infected plant parts.

Borers
Larvae of some moths, wasps, beetles; among the most damaging plant pests. Worm-like; vary in size and get bigger as they bore through plants. Burrow into stems, leaves and/ or roots, destroying conducting tissue and weakening stems to cause breakage. Leaves will wilt; may see tunnels in leaves, stems or roots; rhizomes may be hollowed out entirely or in part.
What to Do: May be able to squish borers within leaves. Remove and destroy bored parts; may need to dig up and destroy infected roots and rhizomes.

Green stink bug

Budworms
Moth larvae $1/2$" to $3/4$" long; striped; green, yellow-green, tan, dull red. Examples: geranium budworm, tobacco budworm. Bore into buds, eating from inside out; may also eat open flowers and new leaf growth. Buds and new leaves appear tattered or riddled with holes.
What to Do: Pick off by hand daily and drop in soapy water. Remove infested plants and destroy. Can apply preventive spray of *B.t.* on mature plants. Don't replant susceptible varieties.

Bugs (True Bugs)
Small insects, up to $1/2$" long; green, brown, black or brightly colored and patterned. Many beneficial; a few pests, such as lace bugs, pierce plants to suck out sap. Toxins may be injected that deform plants; sunken areas left where pierced; leaves rip as they grow; leaves, buds and new growth may be dwarfed and deformed.
What to Do: Remove debris and weeds from around plants in fall to destroy overwintering sites. Pick off by hand and drop into soapy water. Use parasitic nematodes if part of bug's growth cycle is in the ground. Spray plants with insecticidal soap or neem oil (see p. 71 and package directions).

Canker
Swollen or sunken lesions, often on stems, caused by many different bacterial and fungal diseases. Most canker-causing diseases enter through wounds.
What to Do: Maintain plant vigor; avoid causing wounds; control borers and other tissue-dwelling pests. Prune out and destroy infected plant parts. Sterilize pruning tools before and after use.

Caterpillars
Larvae of butterflies, moths, sawflies. Examples: budworms (see Budworms), cutworms (see Cutworms), leaf rollers, leaf tiers, loopers. Chew foliage and buds; can completely defoliate plant if infestation severe.
What to Do: Removal from plant is best control. Use high-pressure water and soap, or pick caterpillars off by hand. Control biologically using *B.t.* It

is very important to know your butterfly caterpillars and their host plants before automatically eradicating the caterpillars, as many are beneficial species.

Cutworms
Larvae (caterpillars) of some moths. About 1" long, plump, smooth-skinned; curl up when poked or disturbed. Usually affect young plants and seedlings, which may be completely consumed or chewed off at ground level.

What to Do: Pick off by hand. Use old toilet tissue rolls to make barrier collars around plant bases; push tubes at least halfway into ground. Or, put three toothpicks around each plant, making sure toothpicks are right up against stem.

Damping Off
see p. 48

Galls
Unusual swellings of plant tissues that may be caused by insects, such as Hemerocallis gall midge, or by diseases. Can affect leaves, buds, stems, flowers, fruit. Often a specific gall affects a single genus or species.

What to Do: Cut galls out of plant and destroy them. Galls caused by insects usually contain the insect's eggs and juvenile stages. Prevent such galls by controlling insects before they lay eggs; otherwise, try to remove and destroy infected tissue before young insects emerge. Galls caused by insects generally more unsightly than damaging to plant. Galls caused by diseases often require destruction of plant. Avoid placing other plants susceptible to same disease in that location.

Gray Mold (*Botrytis* Blight)
Fungal disease. Leaves, stems and flowers blacken, rot and die.

What to Do: Thin stems to improve air circulation; keep mulch away from base of plant, particularly in spring when plant starts to sprout; remove debris from garden at end of growing season; do not overwater. Remove and destroy any infected plant parts. Use horticultural oil as a preventive measure. Compost tea is also effective.

Caterpillar eating flowers

Grubs
Larvae of different beetles, commonly found below soil level; usually curled in C-shape. Body white or gray; head may be white, gray, brown or reddish. Problematic in lawns; may feed on plant roots. Plant wilts despite regular watering; may pull easily out of ground in severe cases.

What to Do: Toss any grubs found while digging onto a stone path or patio for birds to devour; apply parasitic nematodes.

Leaf Blotch
see Leaf Spot

Leafhoppers & Treehoppers
Small, wedge-shaped insects; can be green, brown, gray or multi-colored. Jump around frantically when disturbed. Suck juice from plant leaves, cause

Spittlebug froth

distorted growth, carry diseases such as aster yellows.

What to Do: Encourage predators by planting nectar-producing species such as yarrow. Wash insects off with strong spray of water; spray with insecticidal soap or neem oil (see p. 71 and package directions).

Leaf Miners

Tiny, stubby larvae of some butterflies and moths; may be yellow or green. Tunnel within leaves leaving winding trails; tunneled areas lighter in color than rest of leaf. Unsightly rather than health risk to plant.

Leaf miner galleries in leaf

What to Do: Remove debris from area in fall to destroy overwintering sites; attract parasitic wasps with nectar plants such as yarrows. Remove and destroy infected foliage; can sometimes squish by hand within leaf. Floating row covers prevent eggs from being laid on plant. Bright blue sticky cards, available in most nurseries and through mail order, attract and trap adult leaf miners.

Leaf Spot

Two common types: one caused by bacteria and the other by fungi. Bacterial: small, brown or purple speckles grow to encompass entire leaves; leaves may drop. Fungal: black, brown or yellow spots; leaves wither; e.g. scab, tar spot, leaf blotch.

What to Do: Bacterial infection more severe; must remove entire plant. For fungal infection, remove and destroy infected plant parts. Sterilize removal tools; avoid wetting foliage or touching wet foliage; remove and destroy debris at end of growing season. Spray plant with liquid copper. Compost tea or a mixture of baking soda and citrus oil (p. 70) also works in most instances.

Mealybugs

Tiny, crawling insects related to aphids; appear to be covered with white fuzz or flour. More often found on houseplants than in the garden. Sucking damage stunts and stresses plant. Mealybugs excrete honeydew, promoting sooty mold.

What to Do: Remove by hand from smaller plants; wash off plant with soap and water; wipe off with alcohol-soaked swabs; remove heavily infested leaves; encourage or introduce natural predators such as mealybug destroyer beetle and parasitic wasps; spray with insecticidal soap. Note: larvae of mealybug destroyer beetle look like very large mealybugs. Always check plants for mealybugs before buying.

Mildew

Two types, both caused by fungus, but with slightly different symptoms. Downy mildew: yellow spots on upper sides of leaves and downy fuzz on undersides; fuzz may be yellow, white or gray. Powdery mildew: white or gray powdery coating on leaf surfaces that doesn't brush off.

What to Do: Choose resistant cultivars; space plants well; thin stems to encourage air circulation; tidy any debris in fall. Remove and destroy infected leaves or other parts. Spray compost tea or highly diluted fish emulsion (1 tsp. per qt. of water) to control downy and powdery mildew. Control powdery mildew by spraying foliage with mixture of horticultural oil and baking soda in water (see p. 71). Three applications one week apart needed.

Mites

Tiny, eight-legged relatives of spiders without their insect-eating habits. Examples: spider mites, rust mites, thread-footed mites. Invisible or nearly invisible to naked eye; red, yellow, green or translucent; usually found on undersides of plant leaves. Suck juice out of leaves; may see their fine webs on leaves

and stems; may see mites moving on leaf undersides; leaves become discolored and speckled in appearance, then turn brown and shrivel up.

What to Do: Wash off with a strong spray of water daily until all signs of infestation are gone; predatory mites are available through garden centers; apply insecticidal soap, horticultural oil or neem oil (see p. 71 and package directions).

Nematodes

Tiny worms that give plants disease symptoms. One type infects foliage and stems; the other infects roots. Foliar: yellow spots that turn brown on leaves; leaves shrivel and wither; problem starts on lowest leaves and works up plant. Root-knot: plant is stunted; may wilt; yellow spots on leaves; roots have tiny bumps or knots.

What to Do: Mulch soil, add organic matter, clean up debris in fall; don't touch wet foliage of infected plants. Can add parasitic nematodes to soil. Remove infected plants in extreme cases.

Powdery mildew

Rot

Several different fungi or bacteria that affect different parts of plant and can kill plant. Bacterial soft rot: enters through wounds; begins as small, water-soaked lesions on roots and leaves. As lesions grow, their surfaces darken but remain unbroken, while underlying tissue becomes soft and mushy. Lesions may ooze if surface broken. Black rot: bacterial; enters through pores or small wounds. Begins as V-shaped lesions along leaf margins. Leaf veins turn black and eventually plant dies. Crown rot (stem rot): fungal; affects base of plant, causing stems to blacken and fall over and leaves to yellow and wilt. Root rot: fungal; leaves yellow and plant wilts; digging up plant shows roots rotted away.

What to Do: Keep soil well drained; don't damage plant when digging around it; keep mulches away from plant base. Remove infected plants.

Rust

Fungi. Pale spots on upper leaf surfaces; orange, fuzzy or dusty spots on leaf undersides. Examples: blister rust, hollyhock rust, white rust.

What to Do: Choose varieties and cultivars resistant to rust; avoid handling wet leaves; provide plant with good air circulation; use horticultural oil to protect new foliage; clean up garden debris at end of season. Remove and destroy infected plant parts. Do not put infected plants in compost pile.

Scale Insects

Tiny, shelled insects that suck sap, weakening and possibly killing plant or making it vulnerable to other problems. Scale appears as tiny bumps typically along stems or on undersides of foliage. Once female scale insect has pierced plant with

Snail climbing foliage

mouthpart, it is there for life. Juvenile scale insects are called crawlers.

What to Do: Wipe off with alcohol-soaked swabs; spray with water to dislodge crawlers; prune out heavily infested branches; encourage natural predators and parasites; spray horticultural oil in spring before bud break.

Slugs & Snails

Both mollusks; slugs lack shells whereas snails have a spiral shell; both have slimy, smooth skin. Can be up to 8" long; gray, green, black, beige, yellow or spotted. Leave large, ragged holes in leaves and silvery slime trails on and around plants.

What to Do: Remove slug habitat, including garden debris or mulches around plant bases. Use slug-repellant mulches. Increase air circulation. Pick off by hand in the evening and squish with boot or drop in can of soapy water. Spread diatomaceous earth (available in garden centers; do not use the kind meant for swimming pool filters) on soil around plants to pierce and dehydrate the soft slug or snail

bodies. Commercial slug and snail baits are effective; some new formulations nontoxic to pets and children. Beer in a shallow dish may be effective. Attach strips of copper to wood around raised beds or to small boards inserted around susceptible groups of plants; slugs and snails get shocked if they touch copper surfaces.

Smut

Fungus that affects any aboveground plant parts including leaves, stems and flowers. Forms fleshy, white galls that turn black and powdery.

What to Do: Remove and destroy infected plants. Avoid placing same plants in that spot for next few years.

Sooty Mold

Fungus. Thin black film forms on leaf surfaces and reduces amount of light getting to leaf surfaces.

What to Do: Wipe mold off leaf surfaces; control insects such as aphids, mealybugs, whiteflies (honeydew left on leaves encourages mold).

Spider Mites

see Mites

Thrips

Tiny insects, difficult to see; may be visible if you disturb them by blowing gently on an infested flower. Yellow, black or brown with narrow, fringed wings. Suck juice out of plant cells, particularly in flowers and buds, causing gray-mottled petals and leaves, dying buds and distorted, stunted growth.

What to Do: Remove and destroy infected plant parts; encourage native predatory insects with nectar plants such as yarrows; spray severe infestations with insecticidal soap or with horticultural oil at 5 tbsp. per gallon of water. Use sticky blue cards to attract and trap adults.

Viruses

Plant may be stunted and leaves and flowers distorted, streaked or discolored. Examples: aster yellows, mosaic virus, ringspot virus.

What to Do: Viral diseases in plants cannot be treated. Destroy infected plants; control insects such as aphids, leafhoppers and whiteflies that spread disease.

Weevils

see Beetles

Whiteflies

Tiny, white, moth-like flying insects that flutter up into the air when the plant is disturbed. Live on undersides of leaves and suck juice out, causing yellowed leaves and weakened plants; leave sticky honeydew on leaves, encouraging sooty mold.

What to Do: There are few organic alternatives for whiteflies; usual and most effective remedy is to remove infested plant so insects don't spread to rest of garden. Destroy weeds where insects may live. Attract native predatory beetles and parasitic wasps with nectar plants such as yarrows. Spray severe cases with insecticidal soap (see p. 71). Use yellow sticky cards available from garden centers or make your own sticky trap: mount tin can on stake, wrap can with yellow paper and cover with clear, small, plastic bag smeared with petroleum jelly; replace bag when full of flies. Plant sweet alyssum in immediate area. Make spray from old coffee grounds (see p. 71).

Mosiac virus

Wilt

If watering hasn't helped a wilted plant, one of two wilt fungi may be at fault. *Fusarium* wilt: plant wilts, leaves turn yellow then die; symptoms generally appear first on one part of plant before spreading to other parts. *Verticillium* wilt: plant wilts; leaves curl up at edges, turn yellow then drop off; plant may die.

What to Do: Both wilts difficult to control. Choose resistant plant varieties and cultivars; clean up debris at end of growing season. Destroy infected plants; solarize (sterilize) soil before replanting—contact local garden center for assistance.

Worms

see Caterpillars, Nematodes

Pest Control Alternatives

The following common-sense treatments for pests and diseases allow the gardener some measure of control without resorting to harmful chemical fungicides and pesticides.

Ant Control

Mix 3 c. water, 1 c. white sugar and 4 tsp. liquid boric acid in a pot. Bring this mix just to a boil and remove from heat. Let the mix cool. Pour small amounts of the cooled mix into bottlecaps or other very small containers and place them around the ant-infested area. You can also try setting out a mixture of equal parts powdered borax and icing sugar (no water).

Antitranspirants

These products were developed to reduce water transpiration, or loss of water, in plants. The waxy polymers surround fungal spores, preventing the spread of spores to nearby leaves and stems. When applied according to label directions, these products are environmentally friendly.

Baking Soda & Citrus Oil

This mixture treats both leaf spot and powdery mildew. In a spray bottle, mix 4 tsp. baking soda, 1 tbsp. citrus oil and 1 gal. water. Spray the foliage lightly, including the undersides. Do not pour or spray this mix directly onto soil.

Beneficial predatory ground beetle

Baking Soda & Horticultural Oil

This mixture is effective against powdery mildew. In a spray bottle, mix 4 tsp. baking soda, 1 tbsp. horticultural oil and 1 gal. water. Spray foliage lightly, including undersides. Do not pour or spray this mix directly onto soil.

Coffee Grounds Spray

Boil 2 lb. coffee grounds in 3 gal. water for about 10 minutes. Allow to cool; strain the grounds out. Apply as a spray to reduce problems with whiteflies.

Fish Emulsion / Seaweed (Kelp)

These products are usually used as foliar nutrient feeds but appear to also work against fungal diseases either by preventing the fungus from spreading to noninfected areas or by changing the growing conditions for the fungus.

Garlic Spray

This spray is an effective, organic means of controlling aphids, leafhoppers, whiteflies and some fungi and nematodes. Soak 6 tbsp. finely minced garlic in 2 tsp. mineral oil for at least 24 hours. Add 1 pt. of water and $1^1/_2$ tsp. of liquid dish soap. Stir and strain into a glass container for storage. Combine 1–2 tbsp. of this concentrate with 2 c. water to make a spray. Test spray on a couple of leaves and check after two days for any damage. If no damage, spray infested plants thoroughly, ensuring good coverage of foliage.

Horticultural Oil

Mix 5 tbsp. horticultural oil per 1 gal. of water and apply as a spray for a variety of insect and fungal problems.

Insecticidal Soap

Mix 1 tsp. of mild dish detergent or pure soap (biodegradable options are available) with 1 qt. of water in a clean spray bottle. Spray the surfaces of insect-infested plants and rinse well within an hour of spraying to avoid foliage discoloration.

Milk Spray

Milk spray helps prevent and control powdery mildew. It has been tested on roses and a variety of vegetables, with moderate success. Mix 1 part milk with 9 parts water and apply as a spray every five to seven days for a total of three applications. Low-fat milk is recommended for less odor.

Neem Oil

Neem oil is derived from the neem tree (native to India) and is used as an insecticide, miticide and fungicide. It is most effective when used preventively. Apply when conditions are favorable for disease development. Neem is virtually harmless to most beneficial insects and microorganisms.

Sulfur and Lime-Sulfur

These products are good as preventive measures for fungal diseases. You can purchase ready-made products or wettable powders that you mix yourself. Do not spray when the temperature is expected to be 90° F or higher or you may damage your plants.

About This Guide

THE PERENNIALS IN THIS BOOK ARE ORGANIZED ALPHABETICALLY by their most familiar common names. Additional common names and scientific names appear after the primary reference. The illustrated Flowers at a Glance section at the beginning of the book allows you to become familiar with the different flowers quickly, and it will help you find a plant if you're not sure what it's called.

Height and spread ranges, flower colors, blooming times and hardiness zones are clearly indicated at the beginning of each entry. At the back of the book, you will find a Quick Reference Chart that summarizes different features and requirements of the plants; this chart comes in handy when planning diversity in your garden.

Each entry gives clear instructions and tips for planting and growing the perennial, and it recommends many of our favorite species and varieties. Note: If height or spread ranges or hardiness zones are not given for a recommended plant, assume these values are the same as the ranges at the beginning of the entry. Keep in mind, too, that many more hybrids, cultivars and varieties are often available. Check with your local greenhouses or garden centers when making your selection.

Pests or diseases commonly associated with a perennial, if any, are also listed for each entry. Consult the "Problems & Pests" section of the introduction for information on how to solve these problems.

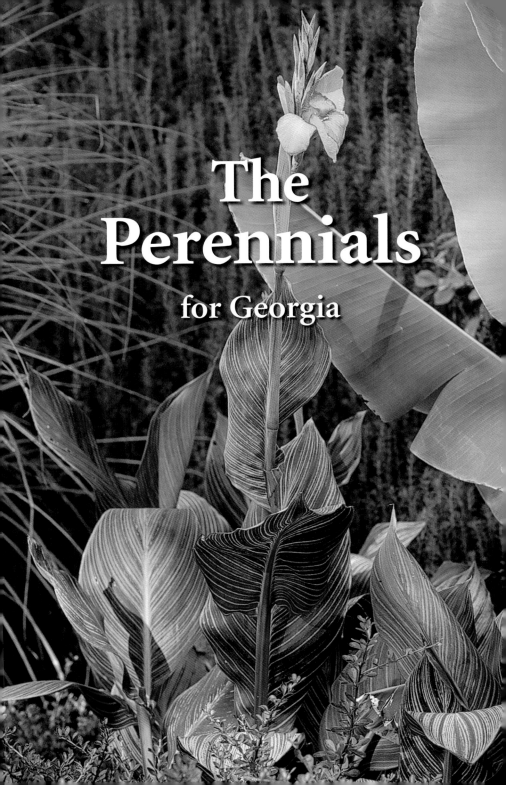

The Perennials

for Georgia

Artemisia

Wormwood, Sage

Artemisia

Height: 6–36" **Spread:** 10"–6' **Flower color:** gray, white, yellow, generally inconspicuous; plant grown for foliage **Blooms:** late summer, mid-fall **Zones:** 3–8

ARTEMISIAS ARE WORKHORSES IN YOUR GARDEN, EASILY recognized because of their silvery foliage. First, every garden must have silver foliage. Silver makes all the various foliage shades of green, blue-green, yellow-green, burgundy, etc, become more intense. Second, artemisia reflects light off of itself on rainy days and under a full moon, transcending mere ordinariness. I have read poetry after midnight, in my garden, by the light of only a full moon and several artemisias. Third, artemisia has foliage that acts as filler for its companion plants, creating the effect of a giant, enchanted floral arrangement.

Planting

Seeding: Not recommended

Planting out: Spring, summer or fall

Spacing: 10–36"

Growing

Artemisias grow best in **full sun**. The soil should be of **average to high fertility** and **well drained**. These plants dislike wet, humid conditions.

Artemisias respond well to pruning in late spring. If you prune too early, before new growth appears at the base of the plant, frost may kill any new growth.

A. schmidtiana 'Nana' (above), *A. stelleriana* 'Silver Brocade' (below)

A. 'Powis Castle' (above & below)

There are almost 300 species of Artemisia distributed around the world.

Whenever artemisias begin to look straggly, cut them back hard to encourage new growth and maintain a neater form. Divide every two or three years when plants appear to be thinning in the center.

Tips

The silvery gray foliage of artemisias makes them good backdrop plants behind brightly colored flowers, and they are useful for filling in spaces between other plants in rock gardens and borders. Smaller forms may also be used to create knot gardens.

Some species can become invasive. If you want to control horizontal spreading of an artemisia, plant it in a container sunk into the ground. Maintain good drainage by completely removing the bottom of the container.

Recommended

A. **'Powis Castle'** is one of the finest artemisias, with long, lacy, silvery foliage. It grows 24–36" tall and 3–6' wide. Its flowers are inconspicuous. (Zones 6–8)

A. schmidtiana (silver mound) is a low, dense, mound-forming perennial. It grows 12–24" tall and spreads 12–18". The silvery gray foliage is feathery and hairy. **'Nana'** (dwarf silver mound) is very compact and grows only half the size of the species. This cultivar is extremely hardy and is more commonly grown than the species.

A. stelleriana (beach wormwood, old woman, dusty miller) is an upright to sprawling plant that grows 12–24" tall and 24–36" wide and spreads by rhizomes. It has coarse-textured, gray, woolly foliage similar to annual dusty miller (*Senecio cineraria*), and inconspicious yellow flowers that are produced in summer. This plant is tolerant of seaside conditions. **'Silver Brocade'** is a low, somewhat spreading cultivar about 6" tall and up to 18" wide. Its soft, pale gray leaves have rounded lobes. This cultivar is extremely intolerant of wet conditions. (Zones 3–7)

Problems & Pests

Rust, downy mildew and other fungal diseases are possible problems for artemisias.

The genus name may honor either Artemisia, a botanist and medical researcher from 353 BC and the sister of King Mausolus, or Artemis, Goddess of the Hunt and the Moon in Greek mythology.

A. schmidtiana 'Nana'

Aster

Aster

Height: 7"–13'   **Spread:** 18"–4'   **Flower color:** blue, purple, pink
Blooms: mid-summer to mid-fall   **Zones:** 3–10

WHEN IN BLOOM ASTERS ARE POSITIVELY DRENCHED IN DAISY-LIKE flowers, a virtual billboard shouting, "Be Happy!" To get the maximum happiness factor from your asters, make sure they are planted in full sun in well-drained soil and are clipped back by several inches once or twice before July 4, which will almost double the number of flowers. Clipping back your asters will also help tidy up their foliage, which can look a bit like a weed growing along the railroad tracks. Many asters attract multitudes of butterflies. Imagine your garden filled with these mid- to late summer flowers, oodles of color and a bounty of movement with the butterflies. Wonderful!

These old-fashioned flowers were once called "starworts" because of the many petals that radiate out from the center of the flowerhead.

Planting

Seeding: Not recommended

Planting out: Spring or fall

Spacing: 18–36"

Growing

Asters prefer **full sun** but benefit from some afternoon shade to keep them from suffering in the summer heat and humidity. The soil should be **fertile, moist** and **well drained.** *A. divaricatus* prefers **partial to full shade** and **moderately fertile** soil. Pinch or shear asters back in early summer to promote dense growth and reduce disease problems. Divide every two to three years to maintain vigor and control spread, or the plants will decline rapidly. The tall selections require staking.

Tips

Asters can be used in the middle or at the back of borders and in cottage gardens. These plants can also be naturalized in wild gardens.

The genus *Aster* has gone through a major upheaval over the last decade. The genus has been split into numerous genera based on morphology and

A. novae-angliae

DNA sequencing. Apparently there are no true asters native to North America. Most North American asters are now listed under the genus *Symphyotrichum* or *Eurybia.*

Recommended

A. carolinianus (*Ampelaster carolinianus,* climbing Carolina aster) is a lanky, semi-evergreen subshrub with arching stems that can die to the ground in a cold winter. It can climb to 10–13' with support and spreads 3–4' wide. The medium green foliage often turns red-purple in fall. The pale pink to purple, mildly fragrant

A. novae-angliae (in back) *and A. novi-belgii* (in front)

flowers bloom from late summer through fall. When not trained to climb, it tends to sprawl. Do not cut the stems back in spring unless they were winter killed. (Zones 6–10)

A. divaricatus (*E. divaricata*, white wood aster) is a clump-forming perennial that spreads by rhizomes. It has arching, black-purple stems, attractive medium green foliage and loose clusters of yellow-centered, white flowers that bloom from mid-summer to mid-fall. The yellow flower centers fade to purple with age. This north-Georgia native grows 24–36" tall and wide. (Zones 4–8)

A. novae-angliae (*S. novae-angliae*, New England aster) is an upright, clump-forming perennial that grows 5' tall and spreads 24" or more. It bears yellow-centered, purple flowers that bloom from late August to frost. **'Alma Potschke'** bears rose-colored flowers that last up to five

A. novi-belgii (above), *A. tataricus* (below)

weeks. It grows 3–4' tall and 24" wide. **'Purple Dome'** is a spreading dwarf with dark purple flowers. It grows 18–24" tall and 24–30" wide. This cultivar is resistant to mildew. (Zones 3–8)

A. novi-belgii (*S. novi-belgii*, Michaelmas daisy, New York aster) is a dense, upright, clump-forming perennial. It grows 3–5' tall, spreads 18–36" and produces more purple flowers than its relatives. **'Pink Bouquet'** sports pink blooms on plants 7–12" tall. **'Professor Anton Kippenburg'** grows 15" tall and 24" wide. It blooms in September with semi-double, medium blue flowers. (Zones 3–8)

A. tataricus (Tatarian daisy) is an upright, clump-forming perennial that bears abundant yellow-centered, purple flowers. Individual plants grow 6–7' tall and 3–4' wide, but clumps can grow wider as the plant spreads from its thick rhizomes. The paddle-shaped, rough-textured, dark green leaves are 24" long and 6" wide. **'Jin-Dai'** grows 4–5' tall and 24–36" wide and bears light lavender blue flowers. It is not as hardy as the species.

Problems & Pests

Powdery mildew, aster wilt, aster yellows, aphids, mites, slugs and nematodes can cause trouble.

What looks like a single flower of an aster—or of any daisy-like plant—is actually a cluster of many tiny flowers. Look closely at the center of the flowerhead, and you will see all the individual flowers.

A. tataricus

Astilbe

Astilbe

Height: 1–5'   **Spread:** 18–36"   **Flower color:** white, cream, pink, peach, purple, red   **Blooms:** late spring, early, mid- or late summer   **Zones:** 3–9

WHEN IN BLOOM, ASTILBE DRAWS YOUR EYE IMMEDIATELY TO its cone-shaped blossoms. If you've chosen a pink blooming astilbe, you have planted a flower that looks like a tapered confection of cotton candy on a stick. Astilbe foliage is almost fern-like. If you're gardening in shade, this plant proves that you can still have interest and color that rivals a sunny perennial border. One drawback of astilbe is that it needs a well-prepared soil that is moist yet well drained. In the right situation there is nothing more stunning than a grouping of flowering astilbe beside a blooming mophead hydrangea.

In late summer, transplant seedlings found near the parent plant for plumes of color throughout the garden.

A. chinensis 'Pumila'

Planting

Seeding: Not recommended; seedlings do not come true to type.

Planting out: Spring

Spacing: 18–36"

Growing

Astilbe enjoys **light or partial shade** and tolerates full shade, though flowering is reduced in deep shade. The soil should be **fertile, humus rich, acidic, moist** and **well drained**. Astilbe likes to grow near water sources, such as ponds and streams, but it dislikes standing in water. Provide a mulch in summer to keep the roots cool and moist. Divide every three years in spring or fall to maintain plant vigor.

Tips

Astilbe can be grown near the edges of bog gardens or ponds and in woodland gardens and shaded borders.

The root crown of an astilbe tends to lift out of the soil as the plant grows bigger. This problem can be solved by applying a top dressing of rich soil as a mulch when the plant starts lifting or by replanting the entire plant deeper into the soil.

Astilbe flowers fade to various shades of brown, and the flowerheads look interesting and natural well into fall. Deadheading will not extend the bloom, so the choice is yours whether to remove the spent blossoms. Astilbe self-seeds easily, but self-seeded plants are unlikely to look like the parent plant.

A. x arendsii cultivar (above & below)

Recommended

A. x *arendsii* (astilbe, false spirea, false goat's beard) grows 18"–4' tall and spreads 18–36". Many cultivars are available from this hybrid group, including the following popular selections. **'Bridal Veil'** is an upright variety whose pinkish white blooms fade to cream when mature. It can grow 3' tall. **'Cattleya'** grows to 4' tall and bears reddish pink flowers in mid-summer.

A. *chinensis* (Chinese astilbe) is a dense, vigorous perennial that tolerates dry soil better than other astilbe species. It grows about 24" tall, spreads 18" and has deeply cut, dark green foliage. It bears fluffy white, pink or purple flowers in late summer. **'Pumila'** (var. *pumila*) is more commonly found than the species. This plant forms a low groundcover 12" tall and up to 18" wide if grown in moist areas. It bears dark pink flowers. **Var. *taquetii* 'Superba'** grows

3–5' tall, producing fluffy, rosy purple flowers in a long, narrow spike from late summer to fall. It works well as an accent plant near water.

A. simplicifolia (star astilbe) is a compact astilbe with glossy, dark green leaves. The flower plumes are more airy and open than those of the other species and hybrids. **'Sprite'** is an upright variety that forms spreading clumps and may reach 14" in height. A one-time Perennial Plant of the Year, 'Sprite' produces silvery pink blooms in airy clusters above rich green foliage in May and June.

A. x arendsii cultivar

Problems & Pests

A variety of pests, such as whiteflies, black vine weevils and Japanese beetles, can occasionally attack astilbe. Powdery mildew, bacterial leaf spot and fungal leaf spot are also possible problems.

Astilbes make great cut flowers, and if you leave the plumes in a vase as the water evaporates, you'll have dried flowers to enjoy all winter.

Autumn Fern
Wood Fern, Shield Fern
Dryopteris

Height: 24–40" **Spread:** 24–40" **Flower color:** grown for foliage; *D. erythrosa* has conspicuous red spore structures **Blooms:** spore structures form in summer **Zones:** 5–9

IF YOU SEE THIS FERN ON A GARDEN TOUR, YOU WILL PROBABLY seek its name, then seek the nursery selling it. From the lacey silhouette of its fronds to its graceful, arching form, autumn fern can only be classed as elegant. It combines well with blooming shade perennials, acting almost as a ring setting to their showier blooms. Once established, this fern is almost Wagnerian in its toughness. Autumn fern is mostly evergreen, and though late February freezes will turn its foliage ratty, new shoots arrive quickly, and elegance is restored.

The genus Dryopteris *is made up of 225 species of moisture-loving ferns native to shady woodlands in temperate regions around the world.*

Planting

Seeding: Sow spores into warm soil as soon as they are ripe.

Planting out: Spring or fall

Spacing: 18–36"

Growing

These ferns grow best in **partial shade** but tolerate full sun (with afternoon shade, in consistently moist soil) or deep shade (with almost the same vigor). The soil should be **fertile, humus rich, moist** and **well drained**. Divide plants in spring to control spread and to propagate them.

Tips

These large, impressive ferns are useful as specimens or grouped in a shaded area or a woodland garden. They are ideal for an area that stays moist but not wet, and they beautifully complement other shade-loving plants, including hostas and coral bells.

Recommended

D. erythrosora (autumn fern, Japanese red shield fern) is an upright, evergreen perennial fern that spreads slowly by thick rhizomes and grows 24" tall and wide. The large, slightly arching, bronzy green to dark green fronds are a bright bronzy red hue when young. The large, red spore structures on the undersides of the fronds are conspicuous. If an extreme late frost kills the plant to the ground, it will recover and send up new growth. (Zones 5–9)

D. filix-mas (male fern) forms a clump of lacy fronds that grows 30–40" tall and 24–40" wide. This fern spreads by rhizomes. Cultivars with frond variations are available. (Zones 4–8)

Problems & Pests

Occasional problems with leaf gall, fungal leaf spot and rust may arise. Crown rot can occur in poorly drained soils.

D. erythrosora

Barrenwort
Bishop's Cap
Epimedium

Height: 6–12" **Spread:** 12" **Flower color:** white, pink, red, purple, yellow **Blooms:** mid- to late spring **Zones:** 4–8

IF YOU ARE TRYING TO GARDEN IN A WOODLAND WITH MANY aboveground tree roots that are seemingly gleeful in their efforts to thwart you intentions, barrenworts are a pretty, low-maintenance solution. I am careless in my love for barrenworts; each year when they bloom, I'm always surprised, realizing that, because they perform so effortlessly, I had forgotten about them. Poor performance of any plant in my garden is always duly noted. Now, if I could stop pine needles from piercing the barrenworts' foliage, I would be a magician.

Planting
Seeding: Start seed in a cold frame in fall. Some cultivars can only be propagated from divisions or rhizome cuttings.

Planting out: Spring

Spacing: 12"

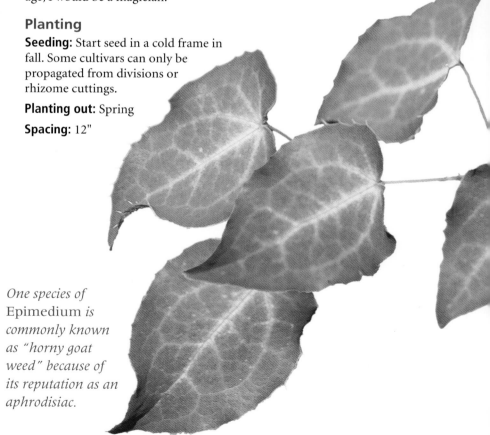

One species of Epimedium *is commonly known as "horny goat weed" because of its reputation as an aphrodisiac.*

Growing:

Barrenworts grow best in **light or partial shade** but tolerate full shade. The soil should be **fertile, humus rich** and **moist**. Provide shelter from the wind. Cut old foliage back in spring to encourage new growth and plentiful flowers. Divide after flowering or in fall, when the clump centers appear to be thinning or dying out.

Tips

These moisture-loving plants make great groundcovers in any shady situation. Use them in a low-lying rock garden, near a pond, in a border or in a woodland garden.

Recommended

E. grandiflorum (longspur barrenwort) forms a low, mounding clump. It grows 8–12" tall and spreads about 12". In spring, large clusters of pendant white, yellow, purple or pink flowers are held above the foliage. The young leaves are often bronzy purple.

E. x *rubrum* (red barrenwort) forms a spreading mound. It grows 8–12" tall and spreads about 12". Red flowers, sometimes flushed with yellow,

E. x youngianum 'Niveum' (above & below)

are borne in spring. This hybrid tolerates the most shade.

E. x *versicolor* forms mounds of finely divided foliage that grow 12" tall and wide. Young foliage is coppery red, fading to green with age. The small flowers are a deep reddish-pink with yellow petals.

E. x *youngianum* (Young's barrenwort) forms a low clump. It grows 6–8" tall and spreads about 12". Small clusters of white or pink flowers are produced in spring. **'Niveum'** bears white flowers.

Problems & Pests

Rare problems with vine weevils or mosaic virus can occur.

Beebalm
Bergamot
Monarda

Height: 1–4'   **Spread:** 12–36"   **Flower color:** red, pink, purple, white, yellow   **Blooms:** mid- to late summer   **Zones:** 3–9

THE BEAUTY OF A MATURE CLUMP OF BEEBALM WILL SEDUCE YOU into wanting it as a foliage plant. If you see it in bloom, you'll want to have it for the blooms. If you see the myriad butterflies attracted by it, you'll want to have the butterflies. If you smell the wind-raked foliage, you will want to have that fragrance in your garden. Foliage, bloom, butterflies and fragrance make beebalm a tour de force on the gardening stage. The only drawback to beebalm is its tendency to get powdery mildew, but this problem is easily corrected by thinning out the stems for greater airflow.

Planting

Seeding: Start seeds outdoors in a cold frame or indoors in early spring.

Planting out: Spring or fall

Spacing: 18–36"

Growing

Beebalm grows well in **full sun, partial shade** or **light shade**. The soil should be of **average fertility, humus rich, moist** and **well drained**. Dry conditions encourage mildew and loss of leaves, so regular watering is a must.

Beebalm spreads by creeping rhizomes that form large clumps; divide every two or three years in spring just as the new growth emerges.

To extend the flowering period and encourage compact growth, cut back some of the stems by half in June.

Tips

Use beebalm beside a stream or pond or in a lightly shaded, well-watered border. It spreads in moist,

M. didyma (above & below)

fertile soils, but, as with most other members of the mint family, the shallow roots can be removed easily.

The fresh or dried leaves may be used to make a refreshing, minty, citrus-scented tea. Put a handful of fresh leaves in a teapot, pour boiling water over them and let steep for at least five minutes. Sweeten the tea with honey to taste.

Beebalm attracts bees, butterflies and hummingbirds. Avoid using pesticides, which can seriously harm or kill these creatures and prevent you from using the plant for culinary or medicinal purposes.

M. didyma (above),
M. didyma 'Marshall's Delight' (below)

Recommended

M. didyma (common beebalm) is a bushy, mounding plant that forms a thick clump of stems with red or pink flowers. Some of the cultivars listed below are hybrids with *M. fistulosa* (wild beebalm), which bears pale pink to purple flowers. **'Beauty of Cobham'** grows 36" tall and 18" wide. It has purple-tinged, green foliage and lilac pink to pale pink flowers with purple bracts. It blooms from mid-summer to early fall. **'Blue Stocking'** ('Blaustrumph') is a heat- and drought-tolerant plant that bears vibrant, deep violet flowers with purple bracts. It grows 2–4' tall and 24–36" wide. **'Gardenview Scarlet'** bears large scarlet flowers, grows 36" tall and is resistant to powdery mildew. **'Jacob Cline'** grows 3–4' tall, bears deep red flowers and has good disease resistance. **'Marshall's Delight'** is mildew resistant in almost all gardens. It has bright, medium pink flowers and shiny, dark green leaves on plants 3–4' tall. It doesn't come true to type from seed and must be propagated by cuttings or divisions. **'Petite Delight'** is a compact, upright plant that grows 12–15" tall and 12–18" wide. It bears large, bright pink flowers. **'Panorama'** is a seed-propagated group of hybrids with flowers in scarlet, pink or salmon that grow to 30" tall. (Zones 3–8)

The genus name honors Spanish botanist and physician Nicholas Monardes (1493–1588).

M. punctata (spotted beebalm, dotted horsemint) is an upright, branched, spreading perennial that grows 12–36" tall and 12–24" wide, with hairy stems and foliage. The foliage has a wonderful thyme scent. In summer, this perennial bears tiered clusters of small, purple-spotted, pale yellow flowers with pink to white bracts. It is native to the coastal plains of our state and prefers sandy soils. (Zones 4–9)

M. didyma

Problems & Pests

Powdery mildew is the worst problem, but rust, leaf spot and leafhoppers can cause trouble. To help prevent powdery mildew, thin the stems in spring. If mildew strikes after flowering, cut the plants back to 6" to increase air circulation. Don't allow the plant to dry out for extended periods.

The alternative common name bergamot comes from the similarity of this plant's scent to that of Italian bergamot orange (Citrus bergamia), which is used in aromatherapy and to flavor Earl Grey tea.

M. didyma 'Petite Delight'

Black-Eyed Susan
Rudbeckia

Height: 2–8'   **Spread:** 18–36"   **Flower color:** yellow or orange, with brown or green centers   **Blooms:** mid-summer to fall   **Zones:** 3–9

DON'T MAKE THE MISTAKE OF SHUNNING BLACK-EYED SUSAN just because she is so common. It would be a shame not to have this tough perennial in your garden. Black-eyed Susan blooms in late summer when not much else is coming into fresh bloom. Boldly entering August's merciless Georgia heat in shocking shades of gold, your garden will appear to throw disdain at heat and humidity. Enjoy the whimsy of where black-eyed Susan spreads or simply compost the seedlings. Often, black-eyed Susan will place itself better than you originally did. Let the flowers whither in place, because the seedheads will attract birds throughout fall.

Planting

Seeding: Indoors in early spring or outdoors in a cold frame; soil temperature 61°–64° F

Planting out: Spring

Spacing: 12–36"

Growing

Black-eyed Susan grows well in **full sun** in **well-drained** soil of **average fertility**. Several *Rudbeckia* species are touted as 'claybusters' for their tolerance of fairly heavy clay soils. Established plants are somewhat drought tolerant but prefer to have regular water. Divide in spring or fall every three to five years, and don't hesitate to consign a few to the compost heap. Pinch plants in June to encourage shorter, bushier growth.

Tips

Use black-eyed Susan in wildflower or naturalistic gardens, in borders and in cottage-style gardens. It is best when planted in masses and drifts. The flowers last well when cut for arrangements.

Deadheading early in the flowering season keeps the plant flowering vigorously, but leave some seedheads in place later in the season for winter interest and as food for birds in fall and winter.

Recommended

R. fulgida var. *sullivantii* '**Goldsturm**' is an upright, spreading plant. It grows 24–36" tall and spreads 18–24". The large, bright golden yellow to orange-yellow flowers have brown centers.

R. fulgida var. *sullivantii* 'Goldsturm'

R. laciniata (cutleaf coneflower) forms a large, open clump. It grows 4–8' tall and spreads 24–36". The yellow flowers have green centers. '**Goldquelle**' has double yellow flowers on a plant 24–36" tall.

R. nitida (shining coneflower) is native to the southeastern U.S. It is an upright, spreading plant that grows 3–6' tall and spreads 24–36". The yellow flowers have green centers. '**Herbstsonne**' grows to 7' and has bright, golden yellow ray flowers with a green center.

Problems & Pests

Rare problems with slugs, aphids, rust, smut and leaf spot are possible.

R. laciniata

Blackberry Lily

Belamcanda chinensis

Height: 24–36" **Spread:** 12–18" **Flower color:** bright yellow to orange **Blooms:** early summer **Zones:** 5–9

WHEN NOT IN BLOOM, BLACKBERRY LILY LOOKS LIKE AN IRIS, WITH beautiful foliage suitable for any garden. When in bloom, from a distance it looks more like a freesia. Blackberry lily thrives with plenty of sun, good drainage and little care. My plants have not been long lived, but their talent for self-seeding (though they are not heavy self-seeders) has kept them in my garden continuously for almost two decades. The seedpods that form after the plant has bloomed look like the blackest, juiciest berries you have ever seen, but they are only for show and are not edible. You'll have difficulty deciding what you prefer the most about this perennial—the foliage, the blooms or the berries.

B. chinensis 'Mixed Colors'

Planting

Seeding: Sow seeds directly outdoors in fall, because a cold period is required for germination.

Planting out: Spring or fall

Spacing: 12–36"

Growing

Blackberry lily grows well in **full sun** or **partial shade,** in **moist, well-drained** soil of **average fertility** with **lots of organic matter** mixed in. It can adapt to sandy soils and some clay soils, as long as a lot of organic matter has been added. Plants grown in rich soil may need staking.

Blackberry lily can be propagated by dividing the rhizomes in spring, or it can easily be grown from seed.

Tips

Blackberry lily is used to provide a vertical element in mixed beds and borders.

Blackberry lily is actually not a lily but a member of the iris family. The seeds are **poisonous** *and should not be eaten.*

Recommended

B. chinensis forms clumps of sword-shaped, green foliage arranged in fans like those of iris plants. It spreads slowly from thick rhizomes. Clusters of star-shaped, yellow to orange flowers with red or maroon spots rise above the foliage in early summer. The individual flowers last only one day but are produced in succession over a long period. In fall, the fruit splits open to reveal shiny black berries.

Problems & Pests

Blackberry lily is mostly pest free. It may suffer from crown rot in wet soils. The foliage may scorch if the soil is allowed to dry out too much.

Blanket Flower

Gaillardia

Height: 12–36"   **Spread:** 12–24"   **Flower color:** combinations of red and yellow   **Blooms:** early summer to early fall   **Zones:** 3–9

WHEN I FIRST SAW IT GROWING ON A SUNNY, COMPACTED GEORGIA red clay slope next to a black asphalt driveway, blanket flower instantly told me, "You must have me for your toughest locations." In addition to thriving in horrific conditions, this flower bloomed for three months. It's not often that a beautiful flower will demand the toughest conditions your garden can produce. Blanket flower has a long blooming season with blooms showy enough to be seen from many yards away, but this plant has a short lifespan, perhaps two to four years. And if placed in the wrong environment for its personality, it becomes prone to problems.

Almost all Gaillardia *species are native to the U.S. and are usually found growing wild on the prairies.*

Planting

Seeding: Start seeds indoors or in the garden in early spring; leave uncovered because the seeds need light to germinate

Planting out: Spring

Spacing: 18"

Growing

Blanket flower prefers **full sun** in **well-drained, poor to moderately fertile** soil. It tolerates drought and heat but does not overwinter in heavy, wet soil. Deadheading encourages the plants to bloom all summer. Propagate by division or root cuttings in spring.

Cut the plants back to within 6" of the ground in late summer to encourage new growth and promote the longevity of these often short-lived plants.

Tips

Blanket flower looks at home in an informal cottage garden, wildflower garden or meadow planting. It is also attractive when planted in clumps of three or four in a mixed or herbaceous border. Dwarf varieties make good container plantings.

Because it is drought tolerant, blanket flower is ideal for neglected or rarely watered areas. Overwatering will increase pest or disease problems. Plant blanket flower where it will not get watered with other plants. Once this plant is established, the less water it receives, the better it does.

Recommended

G. x *grandiflora* is a bushy, upright plant 24–36" tall and 12–24" in spread. It bears daisy-like flowers

G. x *grandiflora* 'Kobold'

all summer and into early fall. The petals have yellow tips and red bases. **'Kobold'** ('Goblin') is a compact cultivar that grows only 12" tall. The flowers are variegated red and yellow, like those of the species.

Problems & Pests

Powdery mildew, downy mildew, leaf spot, rust, aster yellows and leafhoppers are possible, but rarely cause much trouble.

G. x *grandiflora*

Blazing Star
Spike Speedwell, Gayfeather
Liatris

Height: 24–36"   **Spread:** 18–24"   **Flower color:** purple, white, pink, blue
Blooms: summer, fall   **Zones:** 3–9

AS A CHILD, YOU PROBABLY FIRST SAW THIS FLOWER IN A FLORIST arrangement sent as a gift. A long green spike with a feathery blossom, it was typically the prettiest flower in those sometimes dreadful arrangements. Shockingly, blazing star grows well in Georgia. Good perennials with strong, spiky shapes are rare and much needed in the perennial border. Spike-shaped flowers make all the round and flat-topped flowers seem more round and more flat-topped. With plenty of sun and planted shallowly in amended soil, blazing star will accent differently shaped flowers for many years.

Planting

Seeding: Direct sow in fall. Plants may take two to four years to bloom from seed.

Planting out: Spring

Spacing: 18–24"

Growing

Blazing star prefers **full sun**. The soil should be of **average fertility, sandy, well drained** and **humus rich**. Water well during the growing season, but don't allow the plants to stand in water during cool weather. Mulch during summer to prevent moisture loss. Divide every three or four years in fall, when the clump appears crowded.

Trim off the spent flower spikes to promote a longer blooming period and to keep blazing star looking tidy.

Tips

Use this plant in borders and meadow plantings. Plant in a location that has good drainage to avoid root rot in winter. Blazing star does well in planters. Mix the spikes of blazing star with daisy-shaped flowers for added

L. spicata 'Floristan White'

drama. The spikes make excellent, long-lasting cut flowers.

Recommended

L. spicata is an erect, clump-forming plant with pinkish purple or white flowers. **'Floristan White'** grows 36" tall and has creamy white flowers. **'Kobold'** has deep purple flowers, multiple spikes and grows 24–36" tall.

Problems & Pests

Slugs, stem rot, root rot, leaf spot and rust are possible problems. New transplants are favorites of rabbits and deer.

L. spicata 'Kobold'

Bleeding Heart
Dicentra

Height: 1–13' **Spread:** 18"–4' **Flower color:** pink, white, purple, red, yellow **Blooms:** spring, summer **Zones:** 3–9

THE SWEET, HEART-SHAPED BLOSSOMS OF COMMON AND FRINGED bleeding hearts are expertly placed along their leafy stems, as if by a couturier. Their pink, white, or pink and white color is easily seen in the woodland from a distance. The arching habit and moist, succulent appearance of bleeding hearts creates a sense of the tropics in Georgia. The yellow-green foliage and stem contrast well with neighboring plants in a shady perennial garden. If your plants die back completely during an extremely hot summer, wait until spring—they will most likely send up new growth. Place your bleeding hearts near the dark green foliage of hellebores and the combination will delight for years.

These delicate plants are the perfect addition to a moist woodland garden. Plant them next to a shaded pond or stream.

Planting

Seeding: Start freshly ripened seed in a cold frame. Plants self-seed in the garden.

Planting out: Spring or fall

Spacing: 18–36"

Growing

Bleeding hearts prefer **light shade** but tolerate partial or full shade. *D. scandens* requires more sun than the other species but still appreciates afternoon shade. The soil should be **humus rich, moist** and **well drained**. Although bleeding hearts prefer to remain evenly moist, they tolerate drought quite well as long as the weather isn't too hot. Very dry summer conditions cause the plants to die back, but they will revive in fall or the following spring. Bleeding hearts must remain moist while blooming to prolong the flowering period. They rarely need dividing, but it can be done with care in spring.

D. eximia

Tips

Bleeding hearts can be naturalized in a woodland garden or grown in a border or rock garden. They do well near a pond or stream. Bleeding hearts also make excellent early-season specimen plants. Provide a trellis or some support for *D. scandens* to climb up, or you will have a mound of tangled stems.

D. spectabilis 'Alba'

D. spectabilis (above & below)

Recommended

D. eximia (fringed bleeding heart) forms a loose, mounded clump of lacy, fern-like foliage. It grows 15–24" tall and spreads about 18". The flowers are pink to lavender or, sometimes white, and they are borne mostly in spring but may be produced sporadically over summer. This species can take more sun than the common bleeding heart but needs to be kept well watered, or it will go dormant during hot, dry weather in summer.

***D.* hybrids** are often low-growing, mound-forming, floriferous plants. The foliage is green or gray-green to blue-green. Flowers come in many shades of pink, purple, red or white. **'Adrian Bloom'** forms a compact clump of dark gray-green foliage. It grows about 12" tall and spreads about 18". Bright red flowers are produced in late spring and continue to appear intermittently all summer. **'Luxuriant'** is a low-growing hybrid with blue-green foliage and red-pink

flowers. It grows about 15" tall and spreads about 24". Flowers appear in spring and early summer.

D. scandens (climbing bleeding heart) is a delicate perennial that climbs by tendrils. It grows 3–13' tall and 3–4' wide and has lacy, mid-green to yellow-green foliage. Clusters of yellow to white flowers begin blooming in late spring and continue until the first frost. The flowers may be tipped with pink or purple. **'Athens Yellow'** is a more vigorous selection that bears bright yellow to golden flowers. (Zones 6–9)

D. spectabilis (common bleeding heart) forms a large, elegant mound up to 4' tall and 3' wide. It blooms in late spring and early summer. The inner petals are white and the outer petals are pink. This species prefers light, dappled shade. The foliage will last through summer if enough water is provided; otherwise, the foliage will die back.

D. scandens

Problems & Pests

Slugs, downy mildew, *Verticillium* wilt, viruses, rust and fungal leaf spot can cause occasional problems.

D. eximia

Bloodroot
Puccoon, Indian Paint
Sanguinaria

Height: 6–10" **Spread:** 12" **Flower color:** white with yellow center
Blooms: late winter to early spring **Zones:** 3–9

BLOODROOT IS ONE OF THE FIRST FLOWERS TO BLOOM IN MY woodland garden. In some years the timing is late winter; in others years it is early spring. Bloodroot's snow-white blossom arises from the leaf litter of a shady wood before its foliage appears. This plant doesn't mind competition from tree roots, and it is like a beautiful piece of sculpture when arising from a rug of dark green dwarf mondo grass. A hot, dry summer will cause the foliage of bloodroot to disappear before fall. When planting this species, begin with a little grouping of three plants. Once you see how charmingly snow-like they are, you will want a glade of them.

Planting

Seeding: Start seeds in a cold frame in fall. The species will self-seed in the garden to form large colonies.

Planting out: Spring

Spacing: 8–12"

Growing

Bloodroot prefers **partial to full shade** and **humus-rich, well-drained, moist, fertile** soil. The delicate flowers easily lose their petals, so make sure to provide shelter from the elements, especially the wind. Divide the rhizomes after flowering is completed.

Tips

Bloodroot does best in a shaded, sheltered woodland garden, and it may also be used effectively in a shady rock garden.

Do not ingest any part of this plant. It is **toxic**.

Recommended

S. canadensis is a woodland plant that grows from thickened, branched rhizomes. Each growing tip of a rhizome will produce a single leaf and flower. The large,

S. canadensis

variable, lobed foliage is a dull blue-green to gray-green. The flower has white petals and yellow stamens and blooms in late winter to early spring as the leaf unfolds. **'Multiplex'** ('Flore Pleno') is a sterile selection that bears double flowers. The flowers are much sturdier and last longer than those of the species, and they are less affected by the elements.

Problems & Pests

May be afflicted with various types of leaf spot.

The common name bloodroot refers to the blood red juice that is extracted from the reddish orange rhizomes.

S. canadensis 'Multiplex'

Blue Lyme Grass
Sea Lyme Grass, European Dune Grass
Leymus

Height: 2–5'   **Spread:** 24–36" to indefinite   **Flower color:** blue-green fading to tan; plant grown for foliage   **Blooms:** summer   **Zones:** 4–10

BLUE LYME GRASS PERFORMS BEST, AND WITH THE LEAST EFFORT on your part, on or near the coast. Not only is it pretty in those conditions, but it is also helpful for holding sandy soils together because of its spreading habit. It is a good plant to use as foliage filler for adjacent plants in a perennial garden or mixed shrub border. However, blue lyme grass is not nearly as vigorous in Georgia's red clay farther inland from the coast. I've seen blue lyme grass in poorly drained soil survive for many years, but it lacks vigor and is a sickly yellow-blue versus a showy blue. This grass emphasizes any greens, silvers and burgundies that are nearby.

L. arenarius

Planting

Seeding: Sow seeds directly into the garden or in a cold frame in mid-spring.

Planting out: Spring

Spacing: 8–12"

Growing

Blue lyme grass prefers **full sun** and **moderately fertile, moist, well-drained** soil. It tolerates partial or light shade, wet or dry soil and sandy conditions. Cut back the foliage in late fall or early spring. Divide this plant in spring or fall.

Tips

A modest grower in clay, blue lyme grass becomes invasive in moist, loose soils. It is excellent for binding soils such as beach sand and for erosion control. The linear, blue-green leaves add wonderful contrasting color and texture to beds and borders, even

Even though blue lyme grass spreads somewhat aggressively by rhizomes in sandy soils, it is fairly easy to keep under control in clay soils.

though the plant is somewhat invasive. This grass is great for growing in containers that can be moved around to wherever an accent is needed.

Recommended

L. arenarius is an upright, perennial grass that forms clumps 24–36" tall and wide. The long, wide, arching leaves are blue-green. Its spikes of blue-green flowers can reach 5' tall in summer and fade to tan by fall. The plant spreads by rhizomes.

Problems & Pests

Plants may suffer from root rot, leaf spot and ergot.

Bluestar

Amsonia

Height: 15"–4'   **Spread:** 2–5'   **Flower color:** shades of light blue, white
Blooms: May and June   **Zones:** 3–9

DEPENDING ON THE SPECIES, BLUESTAR BLOOMS IN SPRING OR
summer, displaying a blue that jumps forward from a distance, not receding
into the background like most blue flowers. Flexibility in its need for sunlight
makes bluestar a versatile choice, especially with repetition being such an
important garden design tool. The State Botanical Garden in Athens, Georgia, has the prettiest stand of bluestar I've ever seen, with seven to nine plants
growing at the edge where woodland meets meadow. Seeing bluestar growing
on a sloping bank near a culvert and receiving water only during rainstorms
informed me where this plant grows best.

A. hubrichtii

Planting

Seeding: Start seeds in a cold frame in fall or spring.

Planting out: Spring

Spacing: 3–4'

Growing

Bluestar grows well in **full sun, partial shade** or **light shade**. Too much shade can produce floppy plants. The soil should be of **average fertility, slightly acidic, moist** and **well drained**. *A. tabernaemontana* tolerates drought once established. Too rich a soil results in thin, open growth and not as many flowers. Light trimming after flowering may bring on a second flush of blooms.

Bluestar can be propagated from cuttings in late spring to early summer or from divisions of established clumps in spring.

Tips

Bluestar is a pretty plant with a fine, billowy appearance. To achieve the most stunning results, plant it in groups of three to five. Its willow-like foliage turns an attractive yellow in fall, and its love of moist soil makes it a beautiful addition to the side of a stream or pond as well as in a border.

This easy-to-grow and hardy perennial is an excellent woodland plant, growing naturally at the margins between forests and fields.

Be sure to wash your hands thoroughly after handling bluestar because some people find that the sap irritates their skin.

Recommended

*A. **hubrichtii*** (Arkansas bluestar) grows 3–4' tall and 4' wide. It produces light blue to white, star-shaped blooms in spring. This plant prefers moist soil. The narrow, feathery foliage turns yellow gold in fall. (Zones 5–9)

*A. **tabernaemontana*** (willow bluestar) prefers sun but does well in partial shade. It grows 24–36" tall and up to 5' wide, producing small, lavender blue flowers in May and June. **Var.** *salicifolia* has narrower foliage and more open clusters of flowers than the species.

Problems & Pests

May have occasional problems with rust.

A. hubrichtii (above & below)

Although the base of these plants reaches about 18" in diameter, the sprawling foliage and flowerheads fill out to much wider reach.

Bluestar is low maintenance and has few problems unless the plant is stressed for a period of time.

A. *tabernaemontana* (above & below)

Boltonia

Boltonia

Height: 3–6'   **Spread:** up to 4'   **Flower color:** white, purple, pink; yellow centers   **Blooms:** late summer and fall   **Zones:** 4–9

MOST OF GEORGIA'S GARDEN ENCHANTMENTS DURING LATE August and early September seem more like disenchantments because of the heat, humidity and mosquitoes. That is, until boltonia coolly comes into bloom. Innumerable sprays of small, snowy, baby's breath type blooms grace this bushy, sun-loving perennial for almost two months. When the blooms begin to fade and turn brown, grab a huge handful of flowers and lop them off with your pruners. You'll get rid of the brown and encourage a minor second bloom. Boltonia may be lanky if it experiences a wet spring. Cutting off a few inches encourages stockier growth.

Boltonia is native to the eastern and central U.S.

Planting

Seeding: Start seeds in a cold frame in fall.

Planting out: Spring or fall

Spacing: 36"

Growing

Boltonia grows best in **full sun** and tolerates partial shade. It prefers a **moist, well-drained** soil of **average fertility**. A highly fertile soil can lead to overly large, floppy plants. Boltonia is somewhat drought tolerant once established but provides the best show with regular water. Deadheading does not produce more flowers. Divide in fall or early spring when the clump is becoming overgrown or seems to be dying out in the middle.

Although this plant rarely requires staking, it may benefit from some support, particularly in somewhat shaded sites. Use a twiggy branch or a peony hoop, and install it while the plant is young so that, as the foliage grows, the leaves hide the stake. If the plants grow too tall for your liking, cut the stems back by one-third in June.

Tips

This large plant can be used in the middle or at the back of a mixed

B. asteroides (above & below)

border, in a naturalized or cottage-style garden or near a pond or other water feature. A good alternative to taller asters, boltonia is less susceptible to powdery mildew.

Recommended

B. asteroides (white boltonia) is a large, upright perennial with narrow, grayish green leaves. It grows 3–6' tall and 4' wide. It bears lots of white or slightly purple, daisy-like flowers with yellow centers. **'Snowbank'** is the best boltonia for Southern gardens. It has a denser, more compact habit, growing only 3–4' tall, and it bears more plentiful flowers than the species.

Problems & Pests

Boltonia has rare problems with rust, leaf spot and powdery mildew.

Butterfly Weed
Milkweed
Asclepias

Height: 18–36"   **Spread:** 12–24"   **Flower color:** orange, yellow, white, red, pink, light purple   **Blooms:** summer   **Zones:** 3–9

WHY DON'T WE SEE MORE BUTTERFLY WEED IN GEORGIA? ITS DEEP taproot guarantees a drought-tolerant perennial, and it attracts the monarch butterfly. Preferring prairies and meadows, butterfly weed shouts its need for full sun and good drainage. Perhaps we don't see more of this plant because we coddle it too much. However, amending Georgia red clay isn't considered coddling; it breaks up our water-retaining soil, providing the drainage this plant needs. Expect monarch butterfly caterpillars to eat your plants. Plan ahead, and plant enough butterfly weed for yourself and for them.

Planting

Seeding: Start fresh seed in a cold frame in early spring.

Planting out: Spring

Spacing: 12–24"

Be careful not to pick off or destroy the green-and-black-striped caterpillars that feed on butterfly weed and milkweed—they become beautiful monarch butterflies.

A. incarnata

Growing

Butterfly weed prefers **full sun**. *A. tuberosa* grows in any **well-drained** soil but prefers a **fertile** soil. It is drought tolerant once established, but enjoys some moisture in an extended drought. *A. incarnata* prefers a **moist** or **boggy, fertile** soil.

To propagate, remove the plantlets that sprout up around the base of the plants. The deep taproot makes division very difficult.

Deadhead to encourage a second bloom.

Tips

Use *A. tuberosa* in meadow plantings and borders, on dry banks, in neglected areas and in wildflower, cottage and butterfly gardens. Use *A. incarnata* in moist borders and in bog, pondside or streamside plantings.

Butterfly weed is slow to start in spring. Place a marker beside each plant in fall so you won't forget the plant is there and inadvertently dig it up.

Recommended

*A. **incarnata*** (swamp milkweed) grows about 36" tall and spreads up to 12". It bears clusters of pink, white or light purple flowers in late spring or early summer. Although it naturally grows in moist areas, it appreciates a well-drained soil. (Zones 4–9)

*A. **tuberosa*** (butterfly weed) forms a clump of upright, leafy stems and bears clusters of orange flowers in mid-summer to early fall. It grows 18–36" tall and spreads 12–24". (Zones 4–9)

Problems & Pests

Aphids and mealybugs can cause occasional problems. If left unchecked, aphids can kill the plants within two years.

Candytuft
Iberis

Height: 6–12" **Spread:** 10–15" **Flower color:** white **Blooms:** spring; sometimes again in fall **Zones:** 3–9

CANDYTUFT DOES WELL IN GEORGIA WHEN IT LIKES ITS LOCATION. I've noticed through many years that the candytuft some gardeners plant grows so profusely that they eventually get rid of it. The more common experience with this plant is luxuriant growth that spreads desirably to unexpected areas, with enough to give away to friends. A second, rare class of gardeners doesn't seem to be able to keep candytuft alive beyond two years. For the best results, try planting this low-growing evergreen where sun meets partial shade—it's where I've consistently seen the best results.

Planting
Seeding: Direct sow in spring.

Planting out: Spring

Spacing: 6–12"

Growing

Candytuft prefers **full sun**. The soil should be of **poor to average fertility, moist, well drained** and **neutral to alkaline**.

In spring, when the new buds begin to break, cut away any brown sections resulting from winter damage. As the stems spread outward, they may root where they touch the ground. These rooted ends may be cut away from the central plant and replanted in new locations. Division is rarely required.

To promote new, compact growth, shear candytuft back by about one-third once it has finished flowering. Every two or three years it should be sheared back by one-half to two-thirds to discourage the development of too much woody growth and to encourage abundant flowering.

Tips

Use candytuft as an edging plant, in borders and rock gardens, in the crevices of rock walls and as a companion for spring-blooming bulbs.

I. sempervirens (above & below)

Recommended

*I. **sempervirens*** is a spreading, evergreen plant that grows 6–12" tall. It bears clusters of tiny, white flowers. **'Alexander's White'** is more compact than the species and bears abundant flowers. **'Little Gem'** is a compact, spring-flowering plant that spreads 10". **'October Glory'** grows 8" tall and blooms in spring and again in fall.

Problems & Pests

Occasional problems with slugs, caterpillars, damping off, gray mold and fungal leaf spot are possible.

Canna Lily

Canna

Height: 18"–6'   **Spread:** 20–36"   **Flower color:** many shades of red, yellow, coral, pink, white, orange; some are bicolored   **Blooms:** mid-summer to frost   **Zones:** 8–11, some to zone 7

THIS PLANT IS EVOCATIVE OF THE ENTIRE SOUTH, NOT JUST Georgia. Most of us have childhood memories of thickets of red or golden-yellow cannas in backyards and along fences and property lines. Indeed, cannas are so ubiquitous that if new varieties were not available, it would be laughable to think someone would pay real money to have them. The term "pass-along-plant" must have originated with cannas. Planting new varieties with unusual foliage and bloom colors can revive any childhood memories you may have of cannas. If you don't know the sound of wind through canna foliage, you are missing a sound of the South.

Planting

Seeding: Start seed indoors early or outdoors in spring when the soil temperature is 70° F. Scarify seed or soak for 24 hours before sowing.

Planting out: Once soil has warmed and the risk of frost has passed

Spacing: 12–24"

Growing

C. x generalis cultivar (above & below)

Canna lilies grow best in **full sun** in **fertile, moist, well-drained** soil. Plants can be started early indoors in containers to get a head start on the growing season. Deadhead to prolong blooming. Do not cut off more than 6" of the flowering stem, because the new flowers arise from lower down on the stem.

Divide in spring. Allow the cut areas of the newly divided pieces to dry for a couple of days before planting. Ensure each piece has at least one noticeable growing point or 'eye.' Plant rhizomes 4–6" deep into warm soil with the 'eyes' facing up. Soak the area thoroughly.

In the mountains and cooler areas of the state the rhizomes can be lifted after the foliage is killed back in fall. Clean off any clinging dirt and allow the rhizomes to dry a few days, then store them in a cool, frost-free location in paper bags or cardboard boxes containing peat moss. Once they start to sprout, pot them and move them to a bright window until they can be moved outdoors. In the warmer parts of zone 7, plants can be cut back to about 2–3" after the foliage dies, then covered with a 2" layer of dry organic mulch.

Tips

Canna lilies can be grown in a bed or border. They make dramatic specimen plants and look great when included in large planters.

C. x *generalis* cultivar (above & below)

Recommended

C. **x generalis** is the name given to
a number of complex hybrids. They
range from giant 6'+ tall plants to
dwarf plants barely reaching 18".
The large, bold, often colorful
foliage may be green, blue-green,
purple, burgundy or bronze and
often has striped variegation. The
flowers are vividly colored and come
in a wide range of shades and combinations. **'Bengal Tiger'** has green-
and-yellow-striped foliage and
orange flowers. It grows 4–6' tall.
'Pink Sunburst' grows 24–36"
tall. It bears large, pink flowers and
dark green foliage with yellow, pink
and red stripes. **'Red King Humbert'**
(Roi Humbert) produces dark
bronzy purple foliage and bright red
flowers. It can reach 6' tall or more.
'Tropicana' grows 4–6' tall and bears
orange flowers and green, pink,
gold, red, burgundy and orange variegated foliage.

Problems & Pests

Diseases encountered include rust,
fungal leaf spot and bacterial blight.
Slugs, snails and spider mites can
also cause problems.

C. x *generalis* cultivar (above & below)

*Old-fashioned canna lilies are
prone to leaf rollers, which create
unsightly foliage by rolling up in
the leaf margins. Newer cultivars
have been bred for beauty and
resistance to leaf rollers. Try one of
the new cultivars for colorful and
exotic foliage; they mix well with
flowering shrubs or annuals.*

Cardinal Flower
Lobelia
Lobelia

Height: 2–5'   **Spread:** 12–24"   **Flower color:** red, white, blue, purple
Blooms: summer to fall   **Zones:** 3–9

CARDINAL FLOWER IS ONE OF THE TRUEST REDS you can experience in your perennial garden. Most bright red blooms are associated with sunny gardens, but, surprisingly, this plant does best in shade near water. Another surprise: hummingbirds are extremely attracted to it. Many National Forest areas in Georgia are teaming with cardinal flower along their streams, proof of the plant's deer resistance. A close relative, blue cardinal flower is just as showy. It also grows well in the shade near water and is valued for its blue blossoms. The Atlanta Botanical Garden has been liberal with its plantings of cardinal flower in its boggy woodland area.

Lobelia was named after the Flemish botanist Mathias de l'Obel (1538–1616).

Planting

Seeding: Direct sow into the garden or a cold frame in spring when soil temperature reaches 70° F.

Planting out: Spring

Spacing: 12–18"

Growing

Cardinal flower grows well in **partial to full shade** or in full sun if the soil is constantly moist. The soil should be **fertile, slightly acidic** and **moist**. Provide a mulch over winter to protect the plant. Divide annually in early fall by lifting the entire plant and removing the new rosettes growing at the base. Replant immediately.

Pinch the plant in early summer to produce compact growth. Deadheading may encourage a second set of blooms. If you deadhead, allow a few flower spikes to remain to spread their

L. cardinalis (above), L. siphilitica (below)

seeds. Don't worry too much, though—the lower flowers on a spike are likely to set seed before the top flowers finish opening.

Tips

Cardinal flower is best used alongside a stream or pond and may also be used in bog gardens.

Cardinal flower may require more acidic soil than other plants growing around a pond. In this case, plant it in a container of peat-based potting soil and sink it into the ground at the edge of the pond.

Recommended

L. cardinalis (cardinal flower) forms an erect clump of bronzy green leaves. It grows 2–4' tall and spreads 12–24". It bears spikes of bright red flowers from summer to fall. **'Alba'** has white flowers and is not as cold hardy as the species.

L. cardinalis cultivar (above), *L. cardinalis* (below)

L. siphilitica (great blue lobelia, blue cardinal flower) forms an erect clump with bright green foliage. It grows 2–4' tall and spreads 12–18". Spikes of deep blue flowers are produced from mid-summer to fall.

L. x speciosa (hybrid cardinal flower) is the most vigorous of the cardinal flowers. Plants grow 3–5' tall and 12" wide, bearing red, pink or purple-blue flowers from summer to fall. They are longer lived and are more tolerant of different soil and moisture than the parent plants (*L. cardinalis, L. fulgens* and *L. siphilitica*). **'Queen Victoria'** forms a clump of reddish stems with maroon foliage and scarlet flowers. It grows about 36" tall and spreads 12". (Zones 5–9)

Problems & Pests

Rare problems with slugs, rust, smut and leaf spot can occur.

L. cardinalis (above & below)

These lovely plants, members of the bellflower family, contain deadly alkaloids and have poisoned people who tried to use them as herbal medicine.

Carolina Lupine
Bush Pea, False Lupine
Thermopsis

Height: 3–5' **Spread:** 24" **Flower color:** dull to bright yellow
Blooms: mid- to late spring **Zones:** 5–9

CAROLINA LUPINE IS A PASS-ALONG PLANT THAT IS OFTEN CHOSEN, like I chose it, for its similarity to lupine (*Lupinus*), which does not grow well in Georgia. Although it likes full sun in cooler climates, such as in north Georgia, Carolina lupine needs partial shade in the rest of our state. The foliage becomes ratty after blooming and should be cut back, but once it is established, this is a tough plant, so don't let ratty foliage fool you into thinking it is not happy. You'll enjoy these pea flower blooms for a month every spring.

T. villosa

Planting

Seeding: Sow fresh seed in fall in a cold frame or outdoors in spring; can also be started indoors in early spring

Planting out: Spring; transplant seedlings to their permanent position

Spacing: 18–24"

Growing

Carolina lupine grows well in **full sun to partial or light shade** in **fertile, well-drained, loamy** soil, but it adapts to a variety of soil conditions. This plant is drought and heat tolerant when established. Staking may be required in windy sites. An organic mulch reduces rootzone moisture loss and helps keep the roots cool.

Carolina lupine dislikes being divided, moved or having its roots disturbed. Propagation is by seeds or by carefully moving the young seedlings that grow at the base of the mother plant. Break open dried seedpods in fall to collect the fresh seed.

Tips

This beautiful, native plant looks great when planted en masse. It is at home in a wild flower garden and also works well in the middle or at the back of perennial or mixed beds and borders. The flowers are excellent for cutting.

Recommended

T. villosa (*T. caroliniana*) is a clump-forming, long-lived, native perennial that spreads slowly by rhizomes. It has thick, minimally branched stems and attractive, pea-like medium green foliage. It bears lupine-like clusters of downy, dull to bright yellow pea flowers in mid- to late spring.

Problems & Pests

Carolina lupine is mostly pest free but may experience powdery mildew, leaf spot, aphids and slugs.

Christmas Fern

Polystichum

Height: 12–18" **Spread:** 18–36" **Flower color:** tan colored sori
Blooms: plant grown for foliage **Zones:** 3–9

A GREAT FERN WITH AN EASY-TO-REMEMBER NAME, CHRISTMAS fern should be in every shade garden. This evergreen fern is a force in the garden for 11 months, typically losing its aesthetic appeal during February's cold-warm-cold spells. This fern's toughness, deer resistance and ease of transplanting should tempt anyone to plant it. Spreading easily but not aggressively by spores, Christmas fern creates a glade from a small nucleus of nursery-bought plants. Hosta always needs an evergreen companion, so remember to pair it with Christmas fern.

Planting

Seeding: Not applicable.

Planting out: Spring

Spacing: 18–36"

The evergreen ferns of the Polystichum *genus provide greenery year-round, and the appearance of the fronds varies significantly from species to species.*

Growing

Christmas fern grows well in **partial to full shade**. The soil should be **fertile, humus rich** and **moist**. Christmas fern is mostly deer proof.

Divide this fern in spring to propagate it or to control its spread. Remove dead and worn fronds in spring before the new ones fill in. Plants can also be grown from spores produced in the sori on the undersides of the fertile fronds.

Tips

Christmas fern can be used in beds and borders, and it is a good choice for a pondside garden. It is better suited to moist rather than wet conditions. This fern thrives in Georgia's acidic soil, and you'll see it with beautiful mosses at its base in the wild. The use of the fronds as Christmas decorations gave the plant its common name.

Recommended

P. acrostichoides is a vase-shaped, evergreen, perennial fern that forms

P. acrostichoides (above & below)

a circular clump of arching, lance-shaped, dark green fronds. The fertile fronds are shorter and slightly wider than the sterile fronds.

Problems & Pests

Christmas fern is relatively problem free.

Christmas fern is native to a large swath of the East Coast from Canada to Florida and inland to the Mississippi River.

Christmas Rose
Lenten Rose, Hellebore
Helleborus

Height: 15–30" **Spread:** 15–30" **Flower color:** white, green, pink, purple, yellow **Blooms:** late winter to mid-spring **Zones:** 4–9

DEEPLY CUT LOBES ON THE EVERGREEN FOLIAGE OF CHRISTMAS rose are redolent of the tropics, but this perennial blooms from January to April even on snowy or icy days. With large, wide, bell-shaped flowers that hang upside-down, Christmas rose is perfect for planting along the edges of your shady paths or near shady windows and doors where the flowers can be enjoyed. This plant is a good self-seeder, and you'll be able to transplant the seedlings and create large drifts of Christmas rose for a groundcover. Deer resistance and drought tolerance, in addition to the attractive blooms and foliage, make this plant a good companion to hostas and ferns. Many gardeners like to cut the foliage off during the blooming season to increase the impact of the flowers.

Planting

Seeding: Not recommended; seed is very slow to germinate.

Planting out: Spring or late summer

Spacing: 15–30"

Growing

Christmas rose prefers **light, dappled shade to full shade** and a **sheltered** location, but it tolerates some direct sun if the soil stays evenly moist. The soil should be **fertile, humus rich** and **well drained**. Water while the plant is establishing and during periods of drought.

Christmas rose dislikes root disturbance and should not be divided. Trim out any winter-tattered foliage in spring. New foliage will take its place. If the foliage gets too thick and dense, cut some off to help display the blossoms. Deadheading does not produce new blooms.

H. orientalis (above & below)

H. foetidus (above & below)

Tips

Use this plant in a sheltered border or rock garden, or naturalize it in a woodland garden.

All parts of this plant are **poisonous** and may cause intense discomfort if ingested. The sap may aggravate skin on contact.

Recommended

H. foetidus (bear's-foot hellebore) grows 30" tall and wide. It bears dark green leaves and clusters of light green flowers with purplish red edges. Cultivars offer larger sizes and varied flower colors.

H. x *hybridus* plants grow about 18" tall, with an equal spread. They may be deciduous or evergreen, and they bloom in a wide range of colors. Cultivars offer deeper colored, double, spotted and picotee flowers.

H. *orientalis* is a clump-forming, evergreen perennial that grows 15–24" tall and wide. Many cultivars and hybrids are available. The single to double flowers come in a wide range of colors, including white and shades of green, pink, purple and yellow, often in combinations and with spots, streaks or blotches.

H. x *hybridus* cultivar

Problems & Pests

Slugs, aphids, crown rot, leaf spot or black rot can be problems.

The leaf edges can be sharp, so wear long sleeves and gloves when handling these plants.

H. x *hybridus* 'Double Pink'

Chrysanthemum
Fall Garden Mum, Hybrid Garden Mum
Chrysanthemum

Height: 18–36" **Spread:** 18–36" **Flower color:** orange, yellow, pink, red, purple, white, green **Blooms:** late summer and fall **Zones:** 4–9

SOME PLANTS HAVE EARNED THE NICKNAME 'GAS STATION PLANT.' Chrysanthemums have become 'the grocery store plant.' Fall's arrival is heralded by the garish cultivated colors of chrysanthemums. They are splashed at the doorway of most grocery stores and plant nurseries. Most human lives are too short to worry about keeping grocery store chrysanthemums past one season. However, an old-fashioned exception, *C. x rubellum* 'Clara Curtis' can't be found at your grocery store. Find her at a nursery, and enjoy a true beauty without the garishness. Cut her in half twice before July 4 to maximize the quantity of her blooms.

Planting

Seeding: Not recommended

Planting out: Spring, summer or fall

Spacing: 18–24"

Growing

Chrysanthemums grow best in **full sun** in **fertile, moist, well-drained** soil. Divide in spring or fall every two years to keep plants vigorous and to prevent them from thinning out in the center. Pinch plants back in early summer to encourage bushy growth. You can deadhead in late fall or early winter, but leave the stems intact to protect the plants' crowns.

Planting early in the season improves their chances of surviving the winter.

Tips

These plants often flower until the first hard frost. Dot or group them in borders or use them as specimen plants near the house or in large planters. Some gardeners buy mums in late summer to replace summer annuals.

Recommended

C x *morifolium* is a large group of bushy, upright to mound-forming hybrids that generally grow 18–36" tall and wide. From mid-summer to fall they bear clusters of colorful flowers in many shades of orange, yellow, pink, red, purple, white or green.

C. x *rubellum* 'Clara Curtis' is a mound-forming perennial that bears a plethora of long-lasting, single to semi-double, watercolor pink flowers with yellow centers all summer. Plants grow 18–30" tall and 18–24" wide. (Zones 6–9)

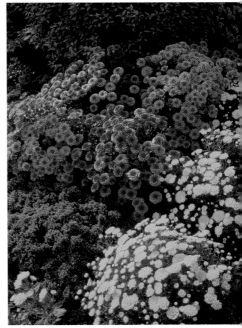

C. x *morifolium* hybrid

Problems & Pests

Aphids can be a true menace to these plants. Insecticidal soap can be used to treat the problem, but it should be washed off within an hour because it discolors the foliage when the sun hits it. Also watch for spider mites, whiteflies, leaf miners, leaf spot, powdery mildew, rust, aster yellows, blight, borers and rot.

C. x *rubellum* 'Clara Curtis'

Cinnamon Fern

Osmunda

Height: 2–5'   **Spread:** 2–4'   **Flower color:** cinnamon brown sporangia;
grown for foliage   **Blooms:** summer   **Zones:** 3–9

THESE TALL, COLORFUL FERNS SHOULD BE A STAPLE OF THE
shaded perennial garden. Changing from a light to rusty green as the fronds
mature, cinnamon ferns add a layer of interest during the changing seasons.
Their height, color and texture create a late-summer focal point of rusty foliage that contrasts well with its neighboring plants. Because they are herbaceous, these ferns are best used in combination with evergreen perennials
such as hellebore, but they are bold enough to be companions to the large,
southern indica azaleas.

Planting

Seeding: Sow fresh spores in 60° F soil. Spores are very short-lived.

Planting out: Spring

Spacing: 24–36"

Growing

Cinnamon ferns prefer **partial or light shade** but tolerate full sun in consistently moist soil. The soil should be **fertile, humus rich, acidic** and **moist**, but wet soils are tolerated. These ferns spread as off-sets form at the base of each plant. Divide established clumps in spring or fall when the plants are dormant.

Tips

These large ferns form an attractive mass when planted in large colonies. They can be included in beds and borders and make a welcome addition to a woodland garden or the edge of a pond.

Recommended

O. cinnamomea (cinnamon fern) has light green fronds that fan out in a circular fashion from a central point, making the whole plant resemble a badminton birdie. Produced in spring and standing straight up in the center of the plant, the leafless, bright green fertile fronds mature to a cinnamon brown.

O. regalis (royal fern) forms a dense clump of foliage. Feathery, flower-like, fertile fronds stand out among the sterile fronds in summer and mature to a rusty brown.

Problems & Pests

Rust may be a problem.

Cinnamon fern "flowers" are actually its conspicuous spore-producing sporangia.

O. regalis (above), *O. cinnamomea* (below)

Columbine
Aquilegia

Height: 7"–4'   **Spread:** 9–24"   **Flower color:** red, yellow, gold, pink, purple, blue, white; color of spurs often differs from that of petals   **Blooms:** spring, summer   **Zones:** 3–8

A DECEPTIVE-LOOKING FLOWER, COLUMBINE APPEARS DELICATE and hard to grow, yet is tough and enduring. The cultivars of columbine have a wide variety of heights and colors, but the native columbine, *A. canadensis,* should not be overlooked because of its showier relatives. Columbine foliage is blue-green and contrasts nicely with darker-foliaged plants. Although it is not a long-lived perennial, columbine readily self-seeds—typically in better locations than you or I could design. Keeping an organic garden includes tolerating the insignificant mildew and leaf-miner damage that columbine foliage attracts.

Columbine is a short-lived perennial that seeds freely, establishing itself in unexpected, and often charming, locations. If you wish to keep a particular form, you must preserve it carefully through frequent division or root cuttings.

Planting

Seeding: Direct sow in spring.

Planting out: Spring

Spacing: 15"

Growing

Columbine grows well in **light or partial shade** in **fertile, moist, well-drained** soil, but it adapts to most soil conditions. It can be grown in full sun if the soil remains moist. Division is not required but can be done to propagate desirable plants. The divided plants may take a while to recover because columbine dislikes having its roots disturbed.

Tips

Use columbine in a rock garden, in a formal or casual border or in a naturalized or woodland garden.

Columbine self-seeds, but it is in no way invasive. Each year a few new plants may turn up near the parent plant. If you have a variety of columbines planted near each other, you may even wind up with a new hybrid because these plants

A. x hybrida 'McKana's Giants'

crossbreed easily. A wide variety of flower colors is the most likely and interesting result. The new seedlings may not be identical to the parents, and there is some chance that they will revert to the original species. Any seedlings that turn up can be transplanted.

Recommended

A. alpina is an erect plant with nodding, blue and white or bright blue flowers. It grows 12–24" tall and 12–15" wide and blooms in early summer.

A. canadensis

A. chrysantha

red-orange spurs in spring and summer. **'Corbett'** grows 18–24" tall and bears light yellow flowers.

A. chrysantha (golden columbine) is more drought tolerant than other types. It reaches 2–4' in height, spreads 24" and produces yellow flowers with lighter spurs. It flowers from mid- to late spring.

A. x hybrida (A. x *cultorum*) (hybrid columbine) forms mounds of delicate foliage and has exceptional flowers. Many groups of hybrids have been developed for their showy flowers in a wide range of colors. When the exact parentage of a columbine is uncertain, it is grouped under this name. **'McKana's Giants'** (McKana Hybrids) are popular and bear flowers earlier than most columbines in yellow, pink, red, purple, mauve or white. They grow up to 30" tall.

A. canadensis (wild columbine, Canada columbine) is a native plant common in woodlands and fields. It grows 24–36" tall, spreads about 12–16" and bears yellow flowers with

A. x *hybrida* 'McKana's Giants'

A. **Music Series** are vigorous, compact plants that grow 18–24" tall and 9–12" wide. They produce a plethora of large flowers with large, wide petals and long spurs in a range of bicolors and solids in shades of white, blue, pink, red, yellow or gold.

A. **Songbird Series** are also compact plants with large, non-fading flowers held above the foliage. Plants in this series grow 12–24" tall and 12–16" wide with flowers in bright sky blue, blue and white, red and white, pure white, lavender and white, rose and white and pure, light yellow.

A. *vulgaris* (European columbine, common columbine, granny's bonnet) comes in a wide variety of colors, and this species has been used to develop many hybrids and cultivars. It grows only 12–24" tall with nodding, violet blooms whose spurs curve inward and end in small knobs. **'Nora Barlow'** has unique double flowers in a reddish hue with white tips.

A. Music Series

Problems & Pests

Mildew and rust can be troublesome during dry weather. Leaf miners can leave foliage with unsightly tunneling lines; remove any damaged foliage. Other problems include fungal leaf spot, aphids and caterpillars.

The common name, columbine, means "dove-like," and the flower was often depicted in medieval paintings to represent the dove of peace.

A. vulgaris 'Nora Barlow'

Coral Bells
Alum Root
Heuchera

Height: 1–4'   **Spread:** 12–18"   **Flower color:** red, pink, white
Blooms: spring, summer   **Zones:** 3–9

THE PAST 20 YEARS HAVE BEEN KIND TO CORAL BELLS, WITH MANY new cultivars making this desirable plant even more desirable. I first planted coral bells for their tall, airy blooms and have never been disappointed. Now I plant them for the incredible foliage that the newer cultivars provide—foliage that seems to be embroiled in a fantasy dream sequence of size, shape and color. When the environmental conditions are droughty during the blooming season, I cut off the blooms to preserve the beauty of the foliage. You can create a new relationship with shade-loving dwarf shrubs by planting coral bells at their base. *H. americana* 'Pewter Veil' with *Daphne* never ceases to delight.

Cut flowers of Heuchera *(hew-ker-uh) species can be used in arrangements.*

Planting

Seeding: Start from seed in spring in a cold frame; seedlings of cultivars and hybrids may not be true to type.

Planting out: Spring

Spacing: 12–18"

Growing

Coral bells grow best in **light or partial shade**. Foliage colors can bleach out in full sun, and plants become leggy in full shade. The soil should be of **average to rich fertility, humus rich, neutral to alkaline, moist** and **well drained**. Good air circulation is essential.

H. sanguinea

Remove spent flowers to prolong the blooming period. You can also remove the flowering stems as they appear if you feel they detract from the foliage. This does not hurt the plants.

Every two or three years, coral bells should be dug up to remove the oldest, woodiest roots and stems. Plants may be divided at this time,

if desired, then replanted with the crown at or just above soil level. Cultivars may be propagated by division in spring or fall.

Tips

Use coral bells as edging plants, clustered in woodland gardens or as groundcovers. Combine different foliage types for an interesting display.

Coral bells have a strange habit of pushing themselves up out of the soil. Mulch in fall if the plants begin heaving from the ground.

H. americana 'Plum Pudding'

H. x *brizioides* 'Firefly' (above)
H. Hybrids 'Crimson Curls' (below)

Recommended

Most of the cultivars available in nurseries and garden centers are actually hybrids developed from crosses between the various species. In the following list, the cultivars are grouped with one of their acknowledged parents.

H. americana is a mound-forming plant about 18" tall and 12" in spread. Its heart-shaped foliage is marbled and bronze-veined when it is young and matures to deep green. Cultivars have been developed for their attractive and variable foliage. **'Pewter Veil'** has silvery purple leaves with dark gray veins. Its flowers are white flushed with pink.

H. x *brizioides* is a group of mound-forming hybrids developed for their attractive flowers. They grow 12–30" tall and spread 12–18". **'Firefly'** has fragrant, bright pinkish red flowers. **'June Bride'** has thin stems with tiny, white to pinkish flowers.

H. **Hybrids** is a catchall category for the many new hybrids of complex or unknown parentage. Breeding continues at a blistering pace and includes species not listed here. Plants with more colorful foliage in varying shapes and sizes, larger and more colorful flowers and lengthened bloom times are available.

H. micrantha is a mounded, clump-forming plant up to 36" tall. The foliage is gray-green and the flowers are white. The species is not common in gardens, but many cultivars are commonly grown. BRESSINGHAM BRONZE ('Absi') grows 24" tall and 12–16" wide. It has very dark, shiny, crinkled, bronzy purple foliage and off-white flowers in late spring to mid-summer. **Var. *diversifolia* 'Palace Purple'** is one of the best-known coral bells. It has deep purple foliage and white blooms. It grows 18–20" tall and can be started from seed, but only some of the seedlings will be true to type.

H. sanguinea is the hardiest species. It forms a low-growing mat of foliage that is 12–18" tall, with an equal spread. The dark green foliage is marbled with silver. Red, pink or white flowers are borne in summer. **'Coral Cloud'** has pinkish red flowers and glossy, crinkled leaves. **'Frosty'** has red flowers and variegated silver foliage. **'Raspberry Regal'** is a larger plant, growing up to 4' high. The foliage is strongly marbled and the flowers are bright raspberry red.

Problems & Pests

Healthy coral bells have very few problems. In stressed situations, they can be afflicted with foliar nematodes, powdery mildew, rust or leaf spot.

H. micrantha var. *diversifolia* 'Palace Purple'

These delicate woodland plants enhance your garden with their bright colors, attractive foliage and airy sprays of flowers.

H. Hybrids *'Monet'*

Coreopsis
Tickseed
Coreopsis

Height: 12–32 "   **Spread:** 12–36 "   **Flower color:** yellow, pink, orange
Blooms: early to late summer   **Zones:** 3–9

REGULARLY ON ANY TOP-TEN PERENNIAL LIST FOR GEORGIA,
coreopsis performs to expectation. If you have problems with your coreopsis,
it is most likely because of not enough sun or not enough drainage. Once
you have prepared your soil and provided for this plant's sun and drainage
needs, coreopsis is a tough and showy performer in your garden. Shearing
once or twice per season keeps your plant vigorous. Don't think you must
prune each stem. Simply grab the largest handful of foliage you can; then cut
through the mass with sharp, top quality hand pruners. Yes, your plants
know the difference between top quality vs. cheap hand pruners.

Planting
Seeding: Direct sow in
spring, indoors in winter;
soil temperature 55°–61° F

Planting out: Spring

Spacing: 12–18"

Growing

This plant grows best in **full sun** or **partial shade**. The soil should be of **average fertility, sandy, light** and **well drained**. Moist, cool locations with heavy soil can promote crown rot. Too fertile a soil or too shaded a location encourages floppy growth.

Shear coreopsis by one-half in late spring for more compact growth. Deadhead to keep it blooming. Frequent division may be required to keep plant vigorous.

Tips

Coreopsis is a versatile plant, useful in formal and informal borders and in meadow plantings or cottage gardens. It looks best in groups.

Recommended

C. auriculata **'Nana'** (mouse-ear coreopsis) is low growing and well suited to rock gardens or the front of borders. It grows about 12" tall and spreads indefinitely, though slowly. It bears yellow-orange flowers in late spring.

C. verticillata (threadleaf coreopsis) is a mound-forming plant with attractive, finely divided foliage. It grows 24–32" tall and 18" wide, bearing bright yellow flowers in summer. **'Golden Showers'** has large, golden yellow flowers and ferny foliage. **'Moonbeam'** forms a compact mound of delicate foliage up to 36" wide. It bears creamy yellow flowers and does best with protection from the hot afternoon sun. **'Zagreb'** has deeper yellow flowers and grows 12" tall and wide.

C. verticillata 'Moonbeam'

Problems & Pests

Occasional problems with slugs, bacterial spot, gray mold, aster yellows, powdery mildew, downy mildew, crown rot and fungal spot are possible.

C. auriculata 'Nana'

Crocosmia
Montbretia
Crocosmia

Height: 18"–4' **Spread:** 12–18" **Flower color:** red, orange, yellow
Blooms: mid- to late summer **Zones:** 5–9

WITHOUT ITS BLOOM YOU MIGHT THINK CROCOSMIA IS AN IRIS. However, the distinctive, sword-like foliage is a bit thinner and more wrinkled than iris foliage. The blooms are used commercially in the florist trade. This plant performs beautifully in your garden with no fuss. It looks like an extremely dwarf version of gladiolus and is a member of the same plant family. Although it prefers full-sun, I've seen crocosmia do well in many gardens in partial shade, but always with good drainage. Also, keep an eye on its roots. Crocosmia likes to spread, making it a good pass-along plant. 'Lucifer' is the most commonly grown selection.

Planting

Seeding: Start seed indoors or out in early spring.

Planting out: Spring

Spacing: 8"

In the south, we know crocosmias by the older name montbretia. The newer name comes from the Greek words krokos, *"saffron," and* osme, *"smell," referring to the saffron-like scent of the dried flowers when placed in water.*

Growing

Crocosmia prefers **full sun**. The soil should be of **average fertility, humus rich, moist** and **well drained**. In the mountains, plant in a protected area and provide a good mulch of shredded leaves or other organic matter in fall to protect the roots from the fluctuating winter temperatures. When the clump is becoming dense, every two or three years, divide it in spring before growth starts. Overgrown clumps produce fewer flowers.

Tips

These attractive and unusual plants create a striking display when planted in groups in a herbaceous or mixed border. They look good when planted next to a pond, where the brightly colored flowers can be reflected in the water.

Recommended

C. x *crocosmiflora* is a spreading plant with long, strap-like leaves. It grows 18–36" tall and the clump spreads about 12". One-sided spikes

C. 'Norwich Canary'

of red, orange or yellow flowers are borne in mid- and late summer. **'Citronella'** ('Golden Fleece') bears bright yellow flowers.

C. **'Lucifer'** is the hardiest of the bunch and bears bright scarlet red flowers in mid- to late summer. It grows 3–4' tall, with a spread of about 18".

Problems & Pests

Occasional trouble with spider mites can occur. Hose the mites off as soon as they appear.

Hummingbirds will love you for planting the fiery 'Lucifer.'

C. 'Lucifer'

Daffodil

Narcissus

Height: 4–24" **Spread:** 4–12" **Flower color:** white, yellow, peach, orange,
pink; often bicolored **Blooms:** early to late spring **Zones:** 3–8

DON'T WORRY ABOUT FADING, YELLOWING OR BROWNING
daffodil foliage marring your garden; plant daffodils where their foliage
won't matter, such as in a meadow, at the base of large deciduous shrubs or
within a thick perennial border. Forsythia, quince and hydrangea are all bare
shrubs in spring, and they shout for a setting of blossoms. Once the daffodil
blossoms fade, the shrubs leaf out and hide any unsightly daffodil foliage.
Some experts say never to cut off daffodil foliage before it yellows, and others
say it doesn't hurt the plant to cut the foliage while still green. It might be
best to experiment and create your own rules.

Planting

Seeding: Difficult. Sow freshly ripened seed into a cold frame in fall. Plants can take 5–7 years to begin flowering.

Planting out: Plant bulbs in fall

Spacing: 3–6"

Growing

Daffodils grow best in **full sun** or **light, dappled shade** in **average to fertile** and **well drained** soil. Keep the soil moist during growth and flowering, but allow it to dry out a little when the plants are dormant. Divide plants in fall every 4–5 years or when flowers decrease in size and number.

Plant the bulbs when the weather cools in fall. As a guideline for how deeply to plant the bulb, measure it from top to bottom and multiply that number by three. Select the largest bulbs for the type you are growing. Ensure they are blemish-free with no soft spots.

Tips

Plant daffodils where they can be left to naturalize—in the light shade beneath a tree or in a woodland garden. In mixed beds and borders, the

N. hybrid (above & below)

faded leaves can be hidden by the summer foliage of other plants. Large-leafed perennials, such as large holly ferns, make fine companion plants.

Recommended

Many species, hybrids and cultivars of daffodils are available. Flowers may be borne solitarily or in clusters. They are often bicolored and come in shades of white, yellow, peach, orange and pink. There are 12 different flower form categories for cultivated daffodils. Choose dwarf varieties for small gardens.

Problems & Pests

Problems may arise from basal rot, bulb rot, nematodes, bulb scale mites, slugs and large narcissus bulb flies.

Daylily
Hemerocallis

Height: 1–6' **Spread:** 1–4' **Flower color:** every color except blue and pure white **Blooms:** summer **Zones:** 2–9

DAYLILIES HAVE SO MANY DIFFERENT CULTIVARS THAT THEY CAN create their own perennial border. Dwarf, medium or large varieties are available, and their foliage ranges from dark to light green with shades of blue. Blooms are shaped like fat trumpets or thread-like spider legs, all in an incredible array of colors. Daylilies' blooming season ranges from early to late summer. Planted by a moist pond edge or on a dry slope, daylilies perform happily. All they ask for is sun. When planted as groundcover, daylilies discourage competition, especially from weeds. And it doesn't matter if you purchase a daylily for hundreds of dollars, win one at a garden club plant raffle or perhaps dig some from a friend's garden—they are all wonderful.

Planting

Seeding: Not recommended; hybrids and cultivars don't come true to type.

Planting out: Spring

Spacing: 1–4'

Growing

Daylilies bear the most flowers in **full sun** but also grow in partial shade. The soil should be **fertile, moist** and **well drained,** but these plants adapt to most conditions and are hard to kill once established. Although daylilies can be left indefinitely without dividing, you can divide them every two to three years to keep them vigorous or to propagate them.

H. 'Luxury Lace'

The petals of daylilies are edible. Add them to salads for a splash of colour and a pleasantly peppery taste.

H. 'Stella D'oro'

Tips

Plant daylilies in borders and beds, on banks and in ditches to control erosion. They can be naturalized in woodland or meadow gardens. Small varieties look nice in planters.

Deadhead to prolong blooming. Be careful when deadheading purple-flowered daylilies because the sap can stain fingers and clothes. Once blooming is complete and the foliage begins turning yellow, daylilies can be pruned right to the ground for a second flush of beautiful growth until frost.

H. fulva 'Kwanzo Variegata' (above), *H.* 'Dewey Roquemore' (below)

Recommended

H. fulva (tawny daylily) grows 3–6'
tall and 4' wide. It bears rusty or
tawny orange blooms. This species
has become naturalized across most
of the country.

***H.* Hybrids** are clump-forming
plants with narrow, arching, strap-
like foliage. They grow 1–4' tall and
wide, depending on the hybrid,
and come in an almost infinite number of forms, sizes and colors. See
your local garden center or daylily
grower to find out what is available
and is most suitable for your garden.

Problems & Pests

Generally these plants are pest free.
Rare problems with rust, *Hemerocallis* gall midge, aphids, spider
mites, thrips and slugs are possible.

H. 'Janet Gayle'

*Derived from the Greek words for
day,* hemera, *and beauty,* kallos,
*the genus name, like the common
name, indicates that these lovely
blooms last only one day.*

H. fulva 'Flore Pleno'

Dwarf Plumbago
Blue Leadwort
Ceratostigma

Height: 7–12" **Spread:** 15" **Flower color:** blue **Blooms:** late summer and fall **Zones:** 5–9

BLUE IS A RECEDING COLOR IN THE LANDSCAPE; IT BACKS AWAY from you, making a small space appear larger. It is also a cool color, making hot days appear cooler. Those are design statements that dwarf plumbago only follows by half. The blue flowers of dwarf plumbago are cool looking on a hot day, but they are so bright that they jump forward at you. Don't think this plant is a flopping perennial; its habit is to grow wider than it does tall, making it a desirable groundcover base for asters, purple cone flowers, patrinia and more.

Dwarf plumbago can also be propagated in spring by digging up rooted suckers or by layering the branches.

Planting

Seeding: Not recommended

Planting out: Spring

Spacing: 15"

Growing

Dwarf plumbago grows best in **full sun** but survives with afternoon shade. It prefers **moist, well-drained** soil **high in organic matter**. This quick-growing plant is moderately drought tolerant once established and makes an excellent and tough ground-cover. Its hardiness is improved by a mulch in winter in zone 5 regions. Divide dwarf plumbago in spring. Cuttings may be started from new growth in early summer.

Tips

Dwarf plumbago makes a wonder-ful addition to a rock garden. It creeps happily between the rocks of a stone wall.

C. plumbaginoides (above & below)

Recommended

C. plumbaginoides is a woody plant with erect stems growing 7–12" tall and 15" wide. The foliage starts out as a lighter green highlighted with purple, becomes darker green as the outdoor temperature rises and turns bronzy red in fall. (Zones 5–8)

Problems & Pests

Powdery mildew may occur.

Eulalia Grass

Chinese Silver Grass, Japanese Silver Grass, Maiden Grass

Miscanthus

Height: 3–10'   **Spread:** 2–5'   **Flower color:** pink to red tinted plumes that fade to tan or silver   **Blooms:** late summer to fall   **Zones:** 5–9

POET AND AUTHOR MAY SARTON SAID, '…FLOWERS AND PLANTS are silent presences; they nourish every sense except the ear.' Eulalia grass is an exception—it does nourish the ear. Its dried winter foliage, blowing gracefully in the wind, delights the eye and sounds like a small, rocky, north Georgia stream. Most sunny perennial borders need the silhouette of at least one ornamental grass, and eulalia grass is a showy, low maintenance choice. It is also a good choice as a companion for evergreen shrubs. You can divide this plant every few years. Just dig it up and hack it in half.

M. sinensis 'Strictus'

Planting

Seeding: Start seeds in a cold frame in early-spring.

Planting out: Spring

Spacing: 2–4'

Growing

Eulalia grass prefers **full sun** in **fertile, moderately moist, well-drained** soil, but it tolerates a variety of conditions.

Tips

Eulalia grass creates a dramatic impact when massed in a naturalized area or mixed border, although varieties that grow quite large are best displayed as specimens. Tall varieties make effective temporary summer screens. If left alone in fall and winter, the dried foliage and showy plumes look very attractive.

Recommended

M. sinsesis is a clumping, perennial grass that spreads slowly from short, thick rhizomes. **'Andante'** has narrow, arching foliage with green and white vertical stripes and pink plumes that fade to silver with age. It grows 7–8' tall and 4' wide. **'Gracillimus'** (maiden grass) grows 6–8' tall and 4' wide and has long, fine-textured, arching leaves and reddish plumes. **'Morning Light'** (variegated maiden grass) grows 4–5' tall and 3' wide. This delicate plant has very narrow, green foliage with fine white leaf edges and pinkish plumes. **Var**. **purpurescens** (flame grass) has upright foliage that turns bright orange-red to burgundy red

M. sinensis 'Rigoletto' (above), *M. sinensis* 'Andante' (below)

in early fall. It grows 4–5' tall and 3' wide. **'Rigoletto'** grows 3–4' tall and 2–3' wide. It has narrow, creamy white and green vertically striped foliage and pinkish plumes. **'Strictus'** (porcupine grass) is a tall, stiff, upright selection with unusual horizontal yellow bands. It grows 6–7' tall and 5' wide. **'Variegatus'** has pale yellow and pale green vertically striped foliage and reddish pink plumes. It tends to flop in rich, moist soils. It grows 6–8' tall and 5' wide.

Problems & Pests

Eulalia grass is generally free of pests and disease, but may experience infrequent attacks from mealy bugs or fungal blight.

M. sinensis var *purpurescens*

The fan-shaped plumes of eulalia grass are ideal for cutting and for use in crafts and in fresh or dried arrangements.

Evening Primrose, Sundrops

Oenothera

Height: 6–18"   **Spread:** 8–18"   **Flower color:** yellow, pink, white
Blooms: summer, early fall   **Zones:** 3–10

SUNDROPS CAME TO ME AS A PASS-ALONG PLANT, AND I HAVE
been able to pass it along many times. Not readily available at nurseries, this
showy, easy-to-grow plant with lemon yellow blooms should enjoy a renais-
sance. Plant it in combination with iris and black-eyed Susan, and the trinity
will have something in bloom all summer, along with stunning foliage contrasts. Evening primrose is also easy to grow and not readily available. This
plant is probably the primrose you see blooming in pink or white along
sunny railroad tracks. Yes, sundrops and evening primrose do spread, but not
enough to consider them high maintenance. Just pull up and pass along or
compost what you don't want.

*The flowers of some
species of* Oenothera
*emit phosphorescent
light, giving rise to
another common
name—evening star.*

Planting

Seeding: Start seeds in a cold frame in mid-spring.

Planting out: Spring

Spacing: 12"

Growing

These plants prefer **full sun**. The soil should be of **poor to average fertility** and very **well drained**. In fertile soil, these plants can become invasive. They aren't bothered by hot, humid weather. Divide them in spring.

Tips

Use these plants in the front of a border and to edge borders and pathways. They brighten a gravelly bank or rock garden.

Evening primrose can be a bit invasive, self-seeding readily and finding its way into unexpected places.

Recommended

O. drummondii (beach evening primrose) is an erect to prostrate, hairy, silvery perennial that grows 6–12" tall and 8–15" wide. It bears large, bright yellow flowers that open in the evening. (Zones 7–10)

O. speciosa

O. fruticosa (sundrops) grows 12–18" tall and wide. It bears bright yellow flowers in summer. The foliage of this plant turns red after a light frost. **'Fireworks'** has red stems and yellow blooms that open from red buds. (Zones 3–8)

O. speciosa (showy evening primrose) is a lanky, upright or spreading plant. It grows 10–12" tall and wide. Its flowers can be pink or white. (Zones 3–8)

Problems & Pests

Rare problems with downy mildew, powdery mildew, leaf gall, rust and leaf spot are possible. Plants may develop root rot in poorly drained soil.

O. fruticosa

False Indigo

Baptisia

Height: 2–5' **Spread:** 2–4' **Flower color:** purple-blue, purple-white, white
Blooms: late spring, early summer **Zones:** 3–9

ELIZABETH LAWRENCE, THE DOYENNE OF SOUTHERN GARDEN
writers, mentions that false indigo (*B. australis*) "flourishes in the heavy
moist soil of the iris border." She wrote those words in 1942 and nothing has
changed. *B. australis* is still the best false indigo for southern gardens, it still
thrives in heavy, moist soil and it is still stunning in combination with iris.
Beautiful in bloom, this plant's blue-green foliage is showy and the dried
seedpods are preferred by many to the blooms. False indigo is long-lived.

*If you've had difficulties
with lupine, try the far
less demanding false
indigo instead.*

B. australis 'Purple Smoke'

Planting

Seeding: Sow indoors in early spring, or direct sow in late summer.

Planting out: Spring

Spacing: 24–36"

Growing

False indigo prefers **full sun** but tolerates partial shade; too much shade causes lank growth that flops over easily. The soil should be of **poor to average fertility, sandy** and **well drained**. Divide false indigo carefully in spring; it has a deep, fleshy taproot that does not like to be disturbed. Young plants need protection for the first winter.

The hard seed coats may need to be penetrated before the seeds can germinate. Scratch the seeds between two pieces of sandpaper before planting them.

Tips

False indigo can be used in an informal border or cottage-type garden. It is attractive when used in a natural planting, on a slope or in any well-drained, sunny spot in the garden.

Recommended

B. alba is an erect, bushy plant growing 2–4' tall and 24" wide. In early summer it produces spike-like, open clusters of creamy white flowers that sometimes have purple-tinged upper petals. (Zones 4–9)

B. australis is an upright or somewhat spreading, clump-forming plant that bears spikes of purple-blue flowers in early summer. The swollen seedpods provide interest in late summer and fall. **'Purple Smoke'** is a hybrid with *B. australis* as one of the parents. It has smoky, purple-white flowers.

B. tinctoria (wild yellow indigo) grows 24–36" tall and wide and has bright yellow flowers that bloom all summer. The flowers are followed by black seedpods.

Problems & Pests

Minor problems with mildew, leaf spot and rust can occur.

False Sunflower
Ox Eye, Orange Sunflower
Heliopsis

Height: 2–6'   **Spread:** 18"–4'   **Flower color:** yellow, orange
Blooms: mid-summer to mid-fall   **Zones:** 2–9

IF YOU DESIRE A SUNNY PERENNIAL GARDEN THAT DOESN'T require a lot of amendments during soil preparation, false sunflower should be at the top of your planting list. Rich soil or too much fertilizer produces spindly plants that grow more foliage than flowers. In addition to preferring a bland soil, false sunflower is also extremely drought tolerant. It is more than tough enough to handle a typical hot, humid southern summer; its constitution has been compared to *Gaillardia*. Because of improvements in cultivation, the cultivars of false sunflower are better to grow than the species.

The stems of false sunflower are stiff, making the blooms useful in fresh arrangements.

Planting

Seeding: Start seed indoors, or seed outdoors in spring; soil temperature 68° F

Planting out: Spring

Spacing: 24"

Growing

False sunflower prefers **full sun** but tolerates partial shade. If grown in an overly rich soil or in partial shade, the plants may need staking during the first year. The soil should be **average to fertile, humus rich, moist** and **well drained**. Most soil conditions are tolerated, including poor, dry soils, but the plant is not drought tolerant over long periods. Divide every two or so years.

Deadhead to prolong the blooming period. Cut plants back once flowering is complete.

Tips

Use false sunflower at the back or in the middle of perennial or mixed borders. This plant is easy to grow and is popular with novice gardeners.

H. helianthoides

Recommended

H. helianthoides forms an upright clump of stems and foliage and bears yellow or orange, daisy-like flowers. The species grows 3–6' tall. **'Loraine Sunshine'** ('Helhan') has attractive, green-and-white-variegated foliage and bright yellow flowers. It grows 24–30" tall and 24" wide. **'Summer Sun'** ('Sommersonne') grows 36" tall and bears single or semi-double flowers in bright golden yellow.

Problems & Pests

Occasional trouble with aphids, Japanese beetles and powdery mildew can occur.

H. helianthoides 'Lorraine Sunshine'

Feather Reed Grass

Calamagrostis

Height: 2–5' **Spread:** 18–36" **Flower color:** silvery pink or purple-red plumes fade to tan **Blooms:** mid-summer to fall **Zones:** 4–9

STRONGLY VERTICAL THROUGHOUT ITS ENTIRE form, feather reed grass contrasts in silhouette with most ornamental grasses by not having any of its rough leaves arching over. This is a tall, sun-loving grass that likes a pond's edge or a perennial border and always looks as if it arrived naturally in a garden instead of being bought and planted. The flowers of feather reed grass dry to a beautiful broom sedge brown at the end of summer. The leaves will become your wind vane, showing you the direction and strength of a passing breeze.

Planting

Seeding: Sow *C. arundinacea* var. *brachytricha* seed in situ in fall; *C.* x *acutiflora* cultivars are sterile.

Planting out: Spring

Spacing: 24"

Growing

Feather reed grass grows best in **full sun** in **fertile, moist, well-drained** soil, though heavy clay and dry soils are tolerated. This grass may be susceptible to rust in cool, wet summers or in areas with poor air circulation. Rain and heavy snow may cause it to flop temporarily, but it quickly bounces back. Cut it back to 2–4" in very early spring before growth begins. Divide it when it dies out in the center.

C. x acutiflora 'Karl Foerster' (above & below)

Tips

Whether it's used as a single, stately focal point, in small groupings or in large drifts, this is a desirable, low-maintenance grass. It combines well with late-summer- and fall-blooming perennials.

Recommended

C. x *acutiflora* **'Karl Foerster'** (Foerster's feather reed grass) forms a loose mound of green foliage, 3–5' tall and 24–36" wide, from which the airy bottlebrush flowers emerge in June. The flowering stems have a loose, arching habit when they first emerge but grow more stiff and upright over summer. The silvery pink flowers turn rich tan, and the green foliage turns bright gold in fall. Other cultivars include **'Overdam,'** a compact, more open, less hardy selection with white leaf edges, and **'Avalanche,'** which has a white center stripe.

C. arundinacea var. *brachytricha* (fall blooming reed grass) flowers much later with wider, fluffier heads than *C.* x *acutiflora* cultivars. It forms a v-shaped clump, 24–36" tall and 18–24" wide, bearing pinkish to purple-red plumes that fade to a silvery tan in late summer.

Problems & Pests

These plants are mostly problem free but may be susceptible to rust and fungal diseases, such as powdery mildew, in overly moist or damp conditions.

Foamflower

Tiarella

Height: 4–12"   **Spread:** 12–24"   **Flower color:** white, pink
Blooms: spring, sometimes to early summer   **Zones:** 3–8

FOAMFLOWER HAS SUCH A LONG BLOOMING SEASON—SIX WEEKS
each spring—that it's not unusual to picture it in your mind as always
blooming. The fat buds are pinkish white and open to a white that is showy
from a distance. Regardless of its bloom, you will want this diminutive flowering perennial for its evergreen groundcover attributes. Spreading by stolons, this groundcover is a nice frame for hostas and ferns. If planted at the
edge of a shaded, newly dug pond, foamflower will spread and give the illusion of age and naturalness within a short span of time.

Planting

Seeding: Start seed in a cold frame in spring or directly in the garden in fall.

Planting out: Spring

Spacing: 6–24"

*The starry flowers clustered
along the stems look like
festive sparklers.*

Growing

Foamflower prefers **partial, light or full shade** without afternoon sun. The soil should be **humus rich, moist** and **slightly acidic**. This plant adapts to most soils.

Divide foamflower in spring. If the foliage fades or rusts in summer, cut it partway to the ground and new growth will emerge. Deadhead to encourage re-blooming.

If the foliage fades or rusts in summer, cut it partway to the ground and new growth will emerge.

Tips

Foamflower is an excellent groundcover for shaded and woodland gardens. It can be included in shaded borders and left to naturalize in wild gardens.

Some foamflower plants spread by runners, which are easily pulled up to stop excessive spread.

Recommended

T. cordifolia (Allegheny foamflower) is a low-growing plant that bears spikes of foamy, white flowers in spring. The heart-shaped foliage turns bronze in fall and remains that

T. cordifolia (above & below)

color throughout winter. **'Oakleaf'** forms a dense clump of dark green, somewhat oak-shaped leaves and bears pink flowers. Its foliage turns bronzy red in fall.

T. **'Ink Blot'** has soft pink flowers and large, heart-shaped, dark green foliage with a very dark purple blotch in the center of each leaf.

T. **'Maple Leaf'** is a clump-forming hybrid with bronze-green, maple-like leaves and pink-flushed flowers.

T. **'Skeleton Key'** has white flowers and deeply cut, dark green, glossy foliage with purple tinges along the veins and midrib.

Problems & Pests

Rust and slugs are possible problems.

Foxglove

Digitalis

Height: 2–5' **Spread:** 12–24" **Flower color:** pink, purple, yellow, apricot, maroon, red, white **Blooms:** late spring and summer **Zones:** 3–8

FOXGLOVE IS ONE OF THE BEST FLOWERS TO USE FOR repetition throughout your partially shaded to sunny perennial garden, or your mixed flowering shrub and perennial garden. Foxglove presents a tall, spike shape with bell-like flowers, and it contrasts beautifully with whatever is near. Confident enough to partner with a blooming mophead hydrangea, foxglove claims bragging rights with the showiest of companions. Look for cell packs of foxglove at nurseries in fall. Fondly called 'dear old digitalis' in E. M. Forster's movie *Howard's End*, this plant is evergreen and will grow all winter, producing vigorous early-summer and summer blooms. You might first plant foxglove to show-off, but soon you'll plant it because you've fallen in love with it.

Planting

Seeding: Direct sow or start in a cold frame in early spring. Seeds need light to germinate. Flowering is unlikely the first year.

Planting out: Spring

Spacing: 12–24"

Foxglove is extremely **poisonous***; simply touching the plant has been known to cause rashes, headaches and nausea.*

Growing

Foxglove grows best in **partial or light shade** but tolerates full sun in good soil. The soil should be **fertile, humus rich** and **moist**. This plant adapts to most soils that are neither too wet nor too dry.

Division is unnecessary for purple or yellow foxglove because they do not live long enough to be divided. They continue to occupy your garden by virtue of their ability to self-seed. Strawberry foxglove can be divided in spring or fall.

D. grandiflora

You can deadhead foxglove once it has finished flowering, but it is a good idea to leave some of the spikes in place to allow the plant to self-seed.

The hybrid varieties become less vigorous with time, and self-sown seedlings may not come true to type. Sprinkle new seed in your foxglove bed each spring to ensure a steady show from the lovely flowers.

Tips

Foxglove is a must for the cottage garden or for people interested in heritage plants. It makes an excellent vertical accent along the back of a border. It also makes an interesting addition to a woodland garden. Staking may be required if it is in a windy location. If you remove the tallest spike, the side shoots will bloom on shorter stalks that may not need staking.

D. purpurea

D. purpurea (above & below)

Recommended

D. grandiflora (yellow foxglove) is a biennial or short-lived perennial. It is a clump-forming plant that grows 36" tall and spreads about 18". In summer it bears spikes of pale yellow flowers with brown markings in the throats.

D.* x *mertonensis (strawberry foxglove) is a true perennial but is short-lived, as is one of the plants in its parentage, *D. purpurea*. It forms a clump of foliage with flower-bearing stems 30–36" tall. The spring and early-summer flowers are light rose pink.

D. purpurea (purple foxglove) is a biennial that grows 24" wide and forms a basal rosette of foliage from which tall flowering spikes emerge,

The heart medication digitalis is made from extracts of foxglove. For over 200 years, D. purpurea *has been used for treating heart failure.*

growing 2–5' tall. The flowers bloom in early summer and come in a wide range of colors. The insides of the flowers are often spotted with contrasting colors. **Excelsior Group** (Excelsior Hybrids), available in many colors, bear dense spikes of flowers. They grow the same size as the species. **Foxy Group** (Foxy Hybrids), which also come in a range of colors, are considered dwarf by foxglove standards but easily reach 36" in height.

Problems & Pests

Anthracnose, fungal leaf spot, powdery mildew, root and stem rot, aphids, Japanese beetles and mealybugs are possible problems for foxglove.

D. purpurea (above & below)

Gaura

Gaura

Height: 2–5'   **Spread:** 24–36"   **Flower color:** white, pink   **Blooms:** late spring, summer, early fall   **Zones:** 5–8

GAURA, WITH ITS COOL AIRINESS OF BLOSSOM, MUST HAVE inspired the slogan a shop in Fripp Island, GA, put on a T-shirt long ago: 'Elegantly Shabby.' Many stems with buds along their length thread up from the base of this plant. The buds open sporadically, with the blossoms loosely clothing the plant instead of forming a mass display. From a distance, gaura looks as if it is engulfed by a swarm of small, white butterflies. This plant gives us a long performance instead of a quick run. You can find gaura with pink flowers as well, but it's not as showy or vigorous as the white-flowered selection.

Planting

Seeding: Start seed in spring or early summer when soil temperature is 65°–75° F.

Planting out: Spring

Spacing: 18–24"

Growing

Gaura prefers **full sun** but tolerates partial shade. The soil should be **fertile, moist** and **well drained**. Gaura is drought tolerant once it is established. Plants dislike sitting in wet soil over winter, so amend your soil to improve the drainage, if needed. Clumps rarely need dividing and resent having their roots disturbed. Most plants self-seed, and the new seedlings can be carefully transplanted, if desired.

Tips

Gaura is wonderful in mixed borders. Its airy habit softens the effect of brightly colored flowers. It bears only a few flowers at a time, but if the faded flower spikes are removed, it keeps flowering all summer. Plant gaura behind low, bushy plants like hardy geraniums, cornflowers or asters to display the delicate, floating flowers to best advantage.

Recommended

G. lindheimeri (white gaura, Lindheimer's beeblossom) forms a large, bushy clump 3–5' tall and 24–36" in spread. Spikes of small, white or pinkish flowers are borne on long, slender stems all summer. **'Corrie's Gold'** has a more compact habit, growing 24–36" tall. It has yellow-variegated foliage and its white flowers are tinged with pink. **'Siskiyou Pink'** has bright pink flowers. **'Whirling Butterflies'** is a compact, long-flowering cultivar that grows 24–36" tall. The white flowers are borne from late spring to early fall. This cultivar does not self-seed.

G. lindheimeri 'Corrie's Gold'

Problems & Pests

Rare problems with rust, fungal leaf spot, downy mildew and powdery mildew can occur.

G. lindheimeri 'Whirling Butterflies'

Golden Hakone Grass
Japanese Forest Grass
Hakonechloa

Height: 10–18"   **Spread:** 24–36"   **Flower color:** grown for its decorative, strap-like foliage; fall color   **Blooms:** grown for foliage   **Zones:** 5–9

THE ATLANTA BOTANICAL GARDEN HAS MANY DRIFTS OF GOLDEN Hakone grass growing in its Storza Woods. The grass is planted in combination with hellebore, hosta, ferns and more. The drifts are situated along the meandering paths with flowering shrubs behind them and mature hardwoods throughout. Not many grasses perform well in shade, but this one does. The denser the shade the more lime-green the foliage will turn, making a showier display. To intensify the lime-green coloration, underplant your golden Hakone grass with evergreen, black dwarf mondo grass. This combination contrasts colors and foliage textures and provides a wonderful year-round display.

This slow-growing grass is very well behaved and does not invade its neighbors.

Planting

Seeding: Not recommended

Planting out: Spring, when soil warms

Spacing: 24–36"

Growing

Golden Hakone grass grows well in **partial to light shade** in **moist, well-drained, moderately fertile, humus-rich** soil. The leaf color is enhanced in partial to light shade. Golden Hakone can tolerate full shade, its foliage turning lime green under such conditions. It also tolerates full sun as long as the soil remains moist. Divide in spring. Avoid locations with cold, drying winds.

Tips

Golden Hakone grass works well at the edge of a woodland garden but is also very effective in containers, beds, borders and rock gardens. It makes an excellent addition to larger gardens where it can be planted in drifts. The striking foliage cascades nicely over the edges of containers or low borders.

H. macra 'Aureola' (above & below)

Recommended

H. macra is a slow-spreading, mound-forming perennial that has bright green, arching, grass-like foliage that turns deep pink in fall, then bronze as winter sets in. **'Alboaurea'** has bright yellow foliage with thin, green, vertical stripes. **'Aureola'** also has bright yellow foliage with narrow, green streaks; the foliage turns pink in fall. Yellow-leafed cultivars may scorch in full sun and lose their yellow color in too much shade.

Problems & Pests

Golden Hakone grass rarely suffers any problems.

Goldenrod

Solidago

Height: 2–4' **Spread:** 18–30" **Flower color:** yellow **Blooms:** late-summer through fall **Zones:** 3–8

COMMON ALONG OUR ROADSIDES IN LATE SUMMER AND EARLY fall, the tall, self-seeding species of goldenrod should not scare you away from its desirable, smaller, more refined cultivars. Choosing the smaller cultivars means you won't have to stake your plants or tolerate rampant self-seeding. Goldenrod's dirty gold or ochre yellow blooms can be used to color echo your black-eyed Susan, coreopsis and the center cone of your purple coneflower. Although not found at larger nurseries, you can find this late-summer bloomer at an independent nursery, or order it online from a Georgia grower.

Planting

Seeding: Not recommended; desirable cultivars do not come true to type from seed.

Planting out: Spring or fall

Spacing: 18"

Growing

Goldenrod prefers **full sun** and tolerates partial shade. The soil should be of **poor to average fertility, light** and **well drained**. Too fertile a soil results in lush growth with few flowers and encourages invasive behavior.

Divide plants every three to five years in spring or fall to keep them from dying out, to control their growth and to keep them vigorous.

S. 'Crown of Rays'

Tips

Goldenrod is great for providing late-season color. It looks at home in a large border, cottage garden or wildflower garden. Don't plant goldenrod near less vigorous plants because it can quickly overwhelm them. Goldenrod is a great plant for xeriscaping.

Recommended

Solidago **hybrids** have been developed for an improved habit and better flowering than the common wild goldenrod. Plants form a clump of strong stems with narrow leaves. They grow about 2–4' tall and spread about 18–24". Plume-like clusters of yellow flowers are produced from mid-summer to fall. **'Crown of Rays'** holds its flower clusters in horizontal spikes. **'Golden Shower'** bears flowers in horizontal or drooping plumes.

x *Solidaster luteus* is a hybrid genus of a *Solidago* species and an *Aster* species. Growing 24–30" tall and wide, it bears daisy-like, pale yellow flowers with darker yellow centers.

Problems & Pests

Stem gall, leaf spot, rust and powdery mildew occur from time to time.

*Goldenrod has long been under suspicion as a source of hay fever allergens because goldenrod flowers at the same time as the less showy culprit—ragweed (*Ambrosia *species). People blamed the large, fuzzy, yellow flowers rather than the diminutive plants underfoot. Goldenrod has insect-borne pollen, not airborne pollen, and does not stimulate hay fever allergies.*

Green and Gold
Golden Star
Chrysogonum

Height: 8–10"   **Spread:** 18–24"   **Flower color:** bright yellow
Blooms: spring, then sporadically through summer   **Zones:** 5–9

GREEN AND GOLD IS A LOW-GROWING, SHADE-LOVING GROUND-cover with bright yellow, foliage-hugging flowers that can be seen from many feet away. It is a native plant whose foliage helps create a natural-looking garden, even though the showy yellow blossoms appear to be cultivated for their intensity of color. I have seen green and gold blooming on Christmas day at the base of a mature loblolly pine in a high-shade woodland. Green and gold is not guaranteed to bloom in your garden in winter, but it is nice to know there is an insouciant plant that didn't read the book about being a summer bloomer.

A native perennial groundcover, green and gold is found growing at the woodland's edge from southern Pennsylvania to Florida.

C. virginianum

Planting

Seeding: Start freshly ripened seeds in a cold frame in fall.

Planting out: Spring

Spacing: 18–24"

Growing

Green and gold prefers **partial to full shade** but tolerates full sun at the northern edge of our state; flowering is decreased in full shade. This plant adapts to most **moist, well-drained** soils and benefits from the addition of **organic matter** to the soil. Plants can be propagated by dividing in spring or fall. The daughter plants that grow from the nodes of the runners are easily transplanted.

Tips

This spreading perennial is often used as a flowering groundcover.

It can be used for a blast of bright color in woodland and native gardens and at the front of perennial and shrub borders.

Recommended

C. virginianum forms an attractive mat of toothed, coarse-textured foliage that spreads by runners that root at the nodes. Starry-shaped, bright yellow flowers bloom prolifically in early spring and in fall, with sporadic blooms throughout summer. A number of cultivars are available with dark green leaves, wider spreads, longer blooming periods or more vigorous growth habits.

Problems & Pests

Green and gold rarely suffers any problems.

Hardy Ageratum
Mistflower, Blue Mistflower
Eupatorium

Height: 24–36"   **Spread:** 24–36"   **Flower color:** light blue to lavender
Blooms: late summer to fall   **Zones:** 6–10

WITH ITS HABIT OF SPREADING BY RHIZOMES, HARDY AGERATUM can be a pass-along plant or a take-it-to-the-compost-pile plant. It is not too aggressive and is worth the small amount of effort needed to keep it in bounds. Now growing where I didn't think to plant it, hardy ageratum knew better than I did where it would look best. Blooming and peaking during late summer's most brutal assault of sun, heat and humidity, this charming flower effortlessly parades its cool blue blossoms in full clusters at the end of every stem, and there are lots of stems. Deadheading produces a slight second bloom.

Hardy ageratum attracts butterflies and provides a punch of color in the fall garden.

E. coelestinum

Planting

Seeding: Start seed in containers in a cold frame in late winter or early spring.

Planting out: Spring

Spacing: 18–24"

Growing

Hardy ageratum grows well in **full sun** or **partial shade** in **fertile, moist** soil. Wet or dry soils are tolerated. It is the most heat tolerant of the *Eupatorium* species. It can be divided in spring.

Hardy ageratum tends to be a bit lanky in growth, but it can be cut or sheared back several times to create bushier plants and more flowers. To allow flowering, stop cutting back by mid- to late July.

Tips

Hardy ageratum can be used in a bed or border, at the edge of a woodland garden or near a pond or other water feature. It is easy to grow and is a great choice for cool fall color.

Hardy ageratum is sometimes considered weedy, but you can prevent it from coursing through your garden by planting it in a contained area where the rhizomes are restricted from spreading.

Recommended

E. coelestinum (hardy ageratum) is a bushy, upright plant that spreads by shallow rhizomes. It has attractive, medium to dark green, triangular, wrinkled, toothed foliage and bears clusters of flossy, light blue to lavender flowers from late summer to fall. The cultivars are not as invasive as the species.

Problems & Pests

Hardy ageratum may have occasional problems with powdery mildew, fungal leaf spot, rust, aphids, whiteflies and leaf miners.

Hardy Begonia

Begonia

Height: 12–24" **Spread:** 12–18" **Flower color:** pink, white **Blooms:** late spring to frost **Zones:** 6–9

PERHAPS HARDY BEGONIAS SHOULD BE NAMED "HARDY AND fertile begonias." They are true perennials with colonizing attributes. Hardy begonias have leaves that are chartreuse on top with a heavy detailing of red veins on the back. It is the latter feature that makes this plant a stunning choice. Aside from the showy foliage, hardy begonias grace your shady garden with a soft pink blossom from spring to frost. If you have lots of space, this is a good selection, but if you only have enough area for 3–5 plants, it isn't the wisest choice due to its "fertile myrtle" tendencies.

Planting

Seeding: Start seed in the garden or in containers in early fall or after the last frost in spring.

Planting out: Spring

Spacing: 12–18"

Growing

Hardy begonias do well in **partial to full shade,** as long as the shade is not too deep. The soil should be **fertile, rich in organic matter, slightly acidic** and **well drained.** Allow the soil to dry out slightly between waterings. Hardy begonias may require extra water during excessively hot summers.

B. grandis (above & below)

Hardy begonias can be tricky to grow from seed. The tiny seeds need sunlight, warm temperatures and precise levels of moisture for good germination. Hardy begonias are easy to grow from the bulbils that form in the axils where the upper leaves meet the stem. Simply allow the bulbils to fall off the plant, or gather them up and scatter them around or share them with friends.

Tips

This southern heirloom perennial works well in shady beds and borders.

Recommended

B. grandis (*B. evansina, B. grandis subsp. evansiana*) forms a clump of branched stems with attractive, large, medium to olive green foliage with red veins and red leaf undersides. The open clusters of fragrant, pendant, pink flowers are held above the foliage and bloom from late spring to frost. The plant dies to the ground in winter. **'Alba'** bears pink-tinged white flowers.

Problems & Pests

Problems with stem rot and gray mold can occur from overwatering.

Hardy Geranium

Cranesbill

Geranium

Height: 6–20"   **Spread:** 12–24"   **Flower color:** white, pink, magenta
Blooms: spring, summer, fall   **Zones:** 3–8

DON'T CONFUSE THIS GERANIUM WITH THE COMMON BEDDING plant geraniums sold at garden centers every spring and summer, which are annuals in the genus *Pelargonium*. Hardy geranium is a sun-loving, low and mounding perennial with a more subtle showiness. The flowers rise several inches above the foliage on an abundance of thin stalks. The finely cut foliage gives the plant the illusion of being delicate, but this tough perennial establishes a solid root system, making it drought tolerant. For zone 8, it is best to give hardy geranium some afternoon shade.

Planting

Seeding: Start species from seed in early fall or spring; cultivars and hybrids may not come true to type.

Planting out: Spring or fall

Spacing: 12–24"

This plant is often called cranesbill because the distinctive seed capsule resembles a crane's long bill.

Growing

Hardy geranium grows well in **full sun, partial shade** and **light shade**. Some species tolerate heavier shade. It prefers soil that is **well drained** and of **average fertility**, but most conditions are tolerated except waterlogged soil. This plant dislikes extremely hot weather.

Divide in spring. Shear back spent blooms for a second set of flowers. If the foliage looks tatty in late summer, prune it back to rejuvenate it.

Tips

This long-flowering plant is great in a border, filling in the spaces between shrubs and larger plants and keeping the weeds down. It can be included in rock gardens and woodland gardens or mass planted as groundcover.

Recommended

G. macrorrhizum (bigroot geranium) forms a spreading mound of fragrant foliage. Crushing the foliage will emit a pleasant citrus scent. This plant grows 12–20" tall and spreads 16–24". It is quite drought

G. sanguineum var. *striatum*

tolerant. Flowers in variable shades of pink are borne in spring and early summer. **'Album'** bears white flowers with pink stamens.

G. sanguineum (bloody geranium) forms a dense, mounding clump. It grows 6–12" tall and spreads 12–24". Bright magenta flowers are borne from late spring to early summer and sporadically until fall. **'Album'** bears white flowers. **Var.** *striatum* (veined bloody geranium) is heat and drought tolerant. It has pale pink blooms with blood red veins.

Problems & Pests

Rare problems with leaf spot and rust can occur.

G. macrorrhizum

Hardy Hibiscus

Rose Mallow

Hibiscus

Height: 18"–10' **Spread:** 3–8' **Flower color:** white, red, pink
Blooms: mid-summer to frost **Zones:** 5–10

RELATED TO COTTON AND OKRA, HARDY HIBISCUS ARE A FEAST FOR the eyes and a literal feast for hummingbirds. These plants are fast growers and produce huge flowers, but don't think they need super amounts of fertilizer—it will result in more foliage than blooms. Choose one of the newer cultivars, such as 'Lord Baltimore,' for abundant, beautiful, sterile blooms and resistance to Japanese beetles. Planting in sand or clay is fine, but the single constant should be moisture. Site them well because they don't like to be moved. Combine hardy hibiscus with banana plants and canna lilies for a tropical trinity.

Planting

Seeding: Sow seeds indoors, or seed outdoors in spring; soil temperature 55°–64° F

Planting out: Spring

Spacing: 3–6'

Growing

Grow hardy hibiscus in **full sun**. The soil should be **humus rich, moist** and **well drained**; it must remain moist because the foliage can suffer from dessication in windy conditions. Hardy hibiscus are heavy feeders and benefit from a side dressing of fertilizer when they begin to leaf out. Divide in spring.

Prune by one-half in June for bushier, more compact growth. Deadhead to keep the plants tidy. If you cut your hibiscus back in fall, be sure to mark their locations because these plants are slow to emerge in spring.

H. moscheutos 'Blue River' (above), *H. moscheutos* 'Southern Belle' (below)

H. moscheutos 'Kopper King' (above),
H. moscheutos (below)

Tips

These plants add interest to the back of an informal border or in a pondside planting. The large flowers create a bold focal point in late-summer gardens.

Hummingbirds are attracted to these plants.

Recommended

H. coccineus (scarlet rose mallow, swamp hibiscus) is an narrow, open perennial with stout, erect stems and large, lobed, medium to dark green foliage. It grows 6–10' tall and 4–5' wide, and it bears deep blood red flowers from mid-summer to frost. (Zones 6–10)

H. moscheutos is a large, vigorous plant with strong stems. It grows 3–8' tall and spreads about 3'. The huge flowers bloom from mid-summer to frost and can be up to 12" across. **'Anne Arundel'** bears deep pink flowers. **'Disco Belle'** is a small plant, 18–24" tall with 9" blooms. It is often grown as an annual, and its flowers can be red, pink or white. **'Lady Baltimore'** bears pink flowers with a dark red eye. **'Lord Baltimore'** bears red flowers. (Zones 5–9)

H. mutabilis (Confederate rose, cotton rose) is a large, erect to spreading, well-branched, woody perennial that has very stout stems and large, lobed, toothed, softly hairy, medium green foliage. It grows 8–10' tall and 5–8' wide and bears funnel-shaped, fall flowers that open white to pink, then turn red as they age. **'Flore Plena'** bears large, double, pink flowers. (Zones 7–10)

Problems & Pests

Hardy hibiscus may develop problems with rust, fungal leaf spot, bacterial blight, *Verticillium* wilt, viruses and stem or root rot. A few possible insect pests are whiteflies, aphids, scale insects, mites, Japanese beetles and caterpillars.

Hardy hibiscus are one of the last plants to start growing in spring. If a fast freeze follows a wet fall, they may die out.

H. coccineus

Hosta
Plantain Lily
Hosta

Height: 2–36" **Spread:** 6"–6' **Flower color:** white, blue, purple; plant grown mainly for foliage **Blooms:** summer, early fall **Zones:** 3–8

HOSTAS COME IN A RANGE OF HEIGHTS AND SPREADS, AND THEIR diverse foliage colors of blue, green, chartreuse and ivory allow them to mix in every type of garden. Most hostas turn an intense shade of yellow during fall, giving them a second peak season after their summer peak of beautiful foliage and bloom. Plant hostas with hellebores and other evergreen plants so your garden won't look naked in winter. Slugs can be a problem, but shallow bowls of beer placed around your plants will attract slugs, drawing them to their death. Hopefully your hostas will be slug-free for many years afterward, as has happened in my garden. Decades ago, the genus name for hosta was *Funkia*.

Hosta leaves develop best if the plants are left undivided for many years.

H. hybrid

Planting

Seeding: Direct sow or start in a cold frame in spring; young plants can take three or more years to reach flowering size.

Planting out: Spring

Spacing: 1–4'

Growing

Hostas prefer **light to partial shade** but do grow in full shade. Morning sun is preferable to afternoon sun. The soil should ideally be **fertile, moist** and **well drained,** but most soils are tolerated. Hostas are fairly drought tolerant, especially if mulched to help retain moisture.

Division is not required but can be done every few years in early spring, when the new growth is about 1" tall, to propagate new plants.

Tips

Hostas make wonderful woodland plants and look very attractive when combined with ferns and other fine-textured plants and the evergreen, tropical-looking foliage of lenten rose. Hostas work well in mixed borders, particularly when used to hide the leggy lower stems and branches that some shrubs develop. The dense growth and thick, shade-providing leaves of hostas help suppress weeds, but deer and voles consider hostas a tasty snack.

Although hostas are commonly grown as foliage plants, they are becoming more appreciated for their spikes of lily-like flowers, some of which are fragrant and make lovely cut flowers. Some gardeners, however, find that the flower color clashes with the leaves. If you don't like the look of the flowers, feel free to remove them before they open—doing so will not harm the plants.

Recommended

Hostas have been subjected to a great deal of hybridizing, resulting in hundreds of cultivars, many with uncertain parentage. There are many wonderful hostas on the market. Check with your local garden center to see what's available.

H. **'Blue Angel'** grows 18–30" tall and 3–4' wide and produces heart-shaped, wavy, blue-green to gray-blue foliage. White flowers appear in mid-summer on 3' scapes.

H. fluctuans **'Variegated'** (*H.* 'Sagae') forms a dense clump of horizontally oriented, dark, dull, olive-green foliage with wide, creamy gold, wavy margins. It grows 36" tall and wide and bears violet-tinged white flowers on slightly arching scapes.

H. 'Francee'

H. fortunei (Fortune's hosta) is the parent of many hybrids and cultivars. It has broad, dark green foliage and bears lavender flowers in midsummer. It quickly forms a dense clump of foliage 12–24" tall and 24–36" wide. **'Albomarginata'** has variable cream or white margins on the leaves. **'Aureomarginata'** has yellow-margined leaves and tolerates sun better than many other cultivars.

H. **'Francee'** has puckered, dark green leaves with narrow, white margins. It grows 15–21" tall and 30–36" wide. In early summer it bears lavender flowers on 30" scapes.

H. **'Gold Standard'** has chartreuse to bright yellow leaves with narrow, irregular, dark green margins. This plant grows 24–30" tall and 24–36" wide. It bears lavender flowers on 42" scapes in mid-summer.

H. hybrid (above & below)

H. **'Honeybells'** has sweetly fragrant, light purple flowers that bloom in late summer on 36" scapes. It is a vigorous selection, growing 30" tall and 4' wide. The foliage is heart-shaped, pale green and shiny.

H. plantaginea (fragrant hosta) has glossy, bright green leaves with distinctive veins; it grows 18–30" tall, spreads to about 36" and bears large, white, fragrant flowers in late summer. **'Aphrodite'** has white double flowers.

H. **'Royal Standard'** is durable and low growing. It grows 4–8" tall and spreads up to 36". The dark green leaves are deeply veined, and the flowers are light purple.

H. sieboldiana (Siebold's hosta) forms a large, impressive clump of blue-green foliage. It grows about 36" tall and spreads up to 4'. The early-summer flowers are a light grayish purple that fades to white. **'Elegans'** (var. *elegans*) has deeply puckered, blue-gray foliage and light purple flowers. It was first introduced to gardens in 1905 and is still popular today. **'Frances Williams'** ('Yellow Edge') has puckered, blue-green leaves with yellow-green margins. **'Great Expectations'** has pale yellow or cream leaves with wide, irregular, blue-green margins.

H. sieboldii (seersucker hosta) grows 12–30" tall and spreads about 20–24". It has undulating, narrow, green leaves with white margins. In late summer and early fall, it bears light purple flowers with darker purple veins. **'Alba'** has light green leaves with undulating margins and white flowers. **'Kabitan'** has narrow, bright

H. 'Gold Standard' (above), *H. hybrid* (below)

yellow foliage with undulating green margins. This compact cultivar grows about 8" tall and spreads 12".

H. 'Sum & Substance' is a sun-tolerant, pest-resistant plant 24–36" tall and 5–6' wide with thick, smooth, pale yellow to chartreuse foliage. Pale lavender flowers bloom in mid-summer on 30–36" scapes.

H. venusta is a miniature variety that forms small clumps of tiny, medium to dark green, oval to heart-shaped foliage. This plant spreads slowly by rhizomes and grows 2–6" tall and 6–12" wide. It bears abundant pale violet flowers on 14–16" tall scapes.

H. 'Royal Standard'

Problems & Pests

Slugs, snails, leaf spot, crown rot and chewing insects such as black vine weevils are all possible problems for hostas. Varieties with thick leaves tend to be more slug resistant.

Once established, these hardy plants need little attention other than occasional watering and mulching with a rich organic layer.

H. hybrids

Iris

Iris

Height: 4"–5' **Spread:** 6–36" **Flower color:** many shades of pink, purple, blue, white, yellow **Blooms:** spring, summer, sometimes fall **Zones:** 3–8

LET IRISES BECOME THE WORKHORSES OF YOUR PERENNIAL GARDEN. Even if they never bloomed, I would still recommend them because of their stunning, tough, sword-like foliage. Some irises prefer shade and others demand sun, so the element of repetition for your garden design can be fulfilled. Along with demands for either sun or shade, some irises prefer to grow in moist to wet soil at a pond's edge while others prefer moist, well-drained soil. On a list of preferred perennials, irises should be in the top three along with daylilies and black-eyed Susans. To modify the Chinese proverb, "He who plants an iris, plants happiness."

Irises are depicted on the wall of an Egyptian temple from 1500 BC, making this plant one of the oldest cultivated ornamentals.

Planting

Seeding: Not recommended; germination is erratic and hybrids and cultivars may not come true to type.

Planting out: Late summer or early fall

Spacing: 2–36"

Growing

Bearded iris, Japanese iris, yellow flag and Japanese roof iris prefer **full sun** or **partial shade**. Crested iris grows best in **partial shade** or **light, dappled shade,** but it tolerates full sun in soil that remains moist. Irises perform best in **average to fertile, humus-rich, moist, well-drained** soil. Yellow flag can grow in water up to 4" deep.

Garden irises benefit from a layer of organic mulch that is topped up in spring and fall. The mulch helps prevent possible frost-heaving of the shallow rhizomes. Make sure you keep the mulch away from the crown of the plant.

After flowering is complete, divide irises to propagate new plants, to reduce crowding and to maintain flowering vigor. Deadhead to keep the plants tidy. Winter-damaged foliage can be cut to within 2" of the ground in spring.

When dividing bearded iris rhizomes, replant with the flat side of the foliage fan facing the garden. Dust the toe-shaped rhizome with a powder cleanser before planting to help prevent soft rot. Plant so the rhizome is slightly exposed and do not mulch for winter.

I. germanica hybrid

Tips

All irises are popular plants for beds, borders and foundation plantings. Small species and dwarf cultivars make attractive additions to rock gardens. Crested iris is magnificent for naturalizing in a woodland garden. Japanese roof iris grows well alongside streams or ponds. Yellow flag and Japanese iris love wet "feet" and thrive around ponds and water features.

I. germanica 'Before The Storm'

I. tectorum

Powdered iris root, called orris, smells like violets and is added to some perfumes and potpourris as a fixative.

I. germanica hybrid

Irises can cause severe internal irritation if ingested. Always wash your hands after handling them. Avoid planting irises where children play.

Recommended

I. cristata (dwarf crested iris) is a compact, native plant, 4–8" tall and 6–12" wide, that has bright green, strap-like foliage and pale purple-blue flowers in spring. Each lower petal, known as a fall, has a white patch with yellow to orange markings. This iris spreads rapidly through its creeping rhizomes, forming dense colonies. Many cultivars are available with a large variation in color and markings. (Zones 5–8)

I. ensata (*I. kaempferi*) (Japanese iris) is a water-loving species. It grows up to 36" tall and spreads about 18". White, blue, purple or pink flowers are borne from early to mid-summer. This species rarely needs dividing and is resistant to iris borers.

I. cristata

I. pseudacorus

I. ***germanica*** (bearded iris) has flowers in all colors. This iris has been used as the parent for many desirable cultivars and hybrids. Cultivars may vary in height from 6" to 4' and in width from 6–36". Flowering ranges from mid-spring to mid-summer, and some cultivars flower again in fall.

I. ***pseudacorus*** (yellow flag) is a vigorous perennial that grows 3–5' tall and 24" wide or wider, forming clumps of narrow, upright foliage. In late spring and early summer, it bears bright yellow flowers with brown or purple markings. Cultivars with variegated leaves or double flowers are available.

I. ***tectorum*** (Japanese roof iris) is a small iris that grows 10–16" tall and wide, and spreads somewhat quickly by rhizomes. Its attractive, sword-shaped, light green foliage is wider than that of most other irises. It bears large, flattened, light to dark purple flowers in early summer. 'Alba' ('Album') bears white flowers.

Problems & Pests

Iris borers can be lethal. They burrow their way down the leaf until they reach the root, where they eat until no root is left. The tunnels they make in the leaves are easy to spot, and if infected leaves are removed and destroyed, or the borers squished within them, the borers will never reach the roots. Leaf spot, slugs, snails and aphids may also cause some trouble.

Japanese Anemone
Windflower
Anemone

Height: 1–5'   **Spread:** 6–36"   **Flower color:** white, pink, red, blue
Blooms: spring, summer, fall   **Zones:** 3–9

WHEN PLANTED IN PARTIAL SHADE WHERE THE WOODLAND meets the more formal parts of the garden, Japanese anemones are cool, colorful harbingers of fall. The pink blossoms are a fresh surprise late in a season that isn't truly fall, but Indian summer. These plants are slow to establish. You might have to wait two to three years for appreciable growth, but once they are settled, you will be able to share these perennials with other parts of your garden. The foliage is low growing, but the flower stalks can grow 2–5' above the foliage. For taller stalks, some staking with fallen twiggy branches is helpful.

A. x hybrida

Planting

Seeding: Slow growing; some species take up to two years to germinate.

Planting out: Spring

Spacing: 4–18"

Growing

Most anemones grow well in **partial** or **light shade** in **humus-rich, moist, well-drained** soil. Provide protection from the hot midday sun. A bed or border beside an east-facing wall is an ideal location. Divide the plants in early spring or late fall, and grow them in containers for a year before replanting them in the ground in spring. In winter, Japanese anemones suffer in moist, wet or poorly drained soils. Deadhead only to keep a tidy look because removing spent flowers will not extend the bloom.

Tips

Anemones make beautiful additions to lightly shaded borders, woodland gardens and rock gardens. They look magnificent when planted en masse. To support Japanese anemones' tall stems, you can plant them behind shorter, shrubby roses.

Recommended

A. hupehensis var. *japonica* 'Bressingham Glow' is an erect, clump-forming plant 18–24" wide. It bears deep rose red to raspberry pink, semi-double flowers on 24–30" tall stems from mid-summer to fall. (Zones 5–8)

A. x *hybrida* (Japanese anemone) is an upright, suckering hybrid that grows 3–5' tall and 24–36" wide. It bears pink or white flowers from late summer to early fall. Many cultivars

Anemones look good when planted in front of red brick or wood siding, particularly natural or weathered, unpainted wood.

are available. **'Honorine Jobert'** is a heat-tolerant selection with pure white flowers. **'Whirlwind'** has white, semi-double flowers. (Zones 3–8)

A. tomentosa (grapeleaf anemone) is a fall-flowering species that produces white to light pink blooms on plants 24–36" tall and 24" wide. The foliage has white, woolly undersides. **'Robustis-sima'** has pink flowers that appear as much as three weeks earlier than the hybrid cultivars. The plants spread more if grown in shade. (Zones 3–8)

A. x hybrida

Problems & Pests

Rare but possible problems include leaf gall, downy mildew, smut, fungal leaf spot, powdery mildew, rust, foliar nematodes, caterpillars, slugs and flea beetles.

The name "anemone" (a-nem-o-nee) comes from the Greek anemos, 'wind,' referring to the windswept mountainside habitat of some species.

A. x hybrida

A. hupehensis var. japonica 'Bressingham Glow'

Japanese Painted Fern

Lady Fern

Athyrium

Height: 12–24" **Spread:** 24" **Flower color:** grown for foliage
Blooms: spores are produced in summer **Zones:** 4–8

PLANTING SILVER-FOLIAGED PLANTS IS ONE OF THE RULES
for designing a perennial garden. It is not an easy rule to follow
in the shade, but the tidy, elegant Japanese painted fern provides
the answer. Its foliage is intensely silver with deep-colored
burgundy veins running through it, and it stays silver
green for much of the year. This fern needs moist
soil—it is not a plant for dry shade or for
competing with large tree roots. Lady
fern spreads more easily than the
Japanese painted fern and is a
great choice if you want to create
a natural-looking fern glade.

A. nipponicum 'Pictum'

Planting

Seeding: Sow freshly ripened spores in containers in a cold frame or in the garden.

Planting out: Spring

Spacing: 18–24"

Growing

These ferns grow well in **full, partial** or **light shade** in **moderately fertile, humus-rich, acidic, moist soil.** Divide in spring when necessary. If Japanese painted fern is planted in full shade, the color may not develop. It is important to apply a layer of mulch in fall to maintain a better moisture level around the roots.

Tips

Lady fern and Japanese painted fern look very attractive in mixed beds and borders and when planted en masse. The interesting foliage stands out beside other ferns in moist woodland settings and shady gardens.

Recommended

A. filix-femina (lady fern) forms a dense clump of lacy, bright green fronds. It grows 12–24" tall and has a 24" spread. Cultivars are available, including dwarf cultivars and cultivars with variable foliage.

A. niponicum (Japanese painted fern) is a creeping, compact fern that

Lady fern is a striking plant that adds a wonderful flare to an otherwise shady, green landscape. It is native to most of North America.

A. nipponicum 'Apple Court' (above), *A. nipponicum* 'Silver Falls' (below)

bears long, medium green fronds with reddish purple midribs. Plants grow 12–24" tall and 24" wide but will continue to spread by their rhizomes. The cultivars are more readily available than the species and come in a variety of foliage colors. Plants grown from spores show more varied foliage coloration than those grown from divisions. '**Pictum**' (var. *pictum*) produces burgundy-flushed, dark green fronds with purplish red stalks and a metallic, gray sheen.

Problems & Pests
Problems are infrequent if not rare. However, rust is a possibility.

A. filix-femina

Japanese painted fern is very well-behaved, adding color and texture to shady spots without growing out of control.

Kalimeris
Japanese Aster
Kalimeris

Height: 18–24"   **Spread:** 18–24"   **Flower color:** white with a pale yellow center   **Blooms:** late spring to frost   **Zones:** 4–9

TINY, WHITE, ALMOST BABY'S-BREATH-TYPE FLOWERS CLOUD THE entirety of kalimeris, with its slip of small, pale-green foliage showing underneath. More upright in seasons with average to low rainfall, the blossoms tend to flop with too much water or too much fertilizer. Grabbing a handful of flowers and cutting them back 6–10" will rejuvenate a flopping plant. After two or three years of growth, you will begin to think of this groundcover plant as a non-stop bloomer. Planted in combination with flowering shrubs or other perennials, kalimeris can be considered a Cinderella of the plant world, working hard to make her companions look good. Foxgloves arising from a base of Japanese asters will be your calendar shot.

Planting

Seeding: Start seeds in containers in a cold frame in late fall or winter. Seeds need a cold treatment to germinate.

Planting out: During the cooler weather in spring or fall

Spacing: 18–24"

Growing

Kalimeris grows well in **full sun to partial shade** in **moderately fertile, moist, well-drained** soil, but it does well in most Georgia soils. It is quite weather and heat tolerant when established. This plant can be divided in spring or fall to rejuvenate it when it loses vigor, or to propagate it.

Tips

Use kalimeris in beds, borders, informal gardens and at the edge of a woodland. It looks great when planted in large swaths or when dotted in the landscape as an accent plant. Its fine texture is good for softening any plantings, so it makes a good filler between colorful, coarse-textured plants and a good companion to plants that are past their prime by mid-summer.

K. pinnatifida (above & below)

Recommended

K. pinnatifida is an upright, bushy perennial that spreads slowly to form large clumps. It has serrated, apple-green foliage and long-lasting, double, white flowers that have pale, buttery yellow centers and bloom from late spring to frost.

Problems & Pests

Kalimeris rarely suffers from pests or disease. It is more mildew resistant than many other asters.

Lily
Lilium

Height: 2–5'   **Spread:** 12"   **Flower color:** many shades of orange, yellow, peach, pink, purple, red, white in solids and bicolored   **Blooms:** early, mid- or late summer   **Zones:** 2–9

RESEARCHING THE GENUS *LILIUM* FOR A GARDEN CLUB presentation many years ago yielded a clear trinity of choices to plant in Georgia. My investigations included reading literature and talking to growers and gardeners with decades of experience. Every resource indicated the best lily to plant is also one of the prettiest, *L. candidum*, the Madonna lily. It is pure white with yellow stamens and a sublime fragrance. The second choice was a nice surprise—*L. speciosum* var. *rubrum*, the pink and white, hyper-fragrant lily found in many bridal bouquets. The last of the trinity, *L. tigrinum*, the tiger lily, has up to 40 orange flowers on each stem and likes sun or shade. Let this trinity be the start of your lily shopping list.

L. hybrid

Planting

Seeding: Sow ripe seed in a cold frame in early spring, or indoors under lights 65–70°F.

Planting out: Spring

Spacing: 12–24"

Growing

Lilies grow best in **full sun** but like to have their **roots shaded**. The soil should be **rich in organic matter, fertile, moist** and **well drained**. *L. candidum* needs neutral to alkaline soil. *L. speciosum* var. *rubrum* needs acidic soil and benefits from some shade from the hot midday sun.

Plant bulbs in fall immediately after purchasing or digging them up. Do not let the bulbs dry out. Most lilies are stem rooting, which means they produce roots on the stem above the bulb. These bulbs can be planted 6–8" deep. *L. candidum* is not a stem-rooting plant, and the bulbs must be planted shallowly, with the top of the bulb 1–2" beneath the soil surface. *L. candidum* bulbs also need to be planted earlier in fall than other lily selections.

Deadhead the flowers unless you want seeds, but allow the foliage to die back on its own. Divide the clump when the center begins to die out immediately after flowering, when clumps become crowded or when flowering diminishes.

L. hybrid (above & below)

Tips

Lilies are often grouped in beds and borders, and they can be naturalized in woodland gardens and near water features. They look great in the back of a bed or in the center of a flower display. Grow at least three of these tall but narrow plants together to create some volume.

Recommended

The many species, hybrids and cultivars available are grouped by type. Check with your local garden center to see what's available.

L. **Asiatic hybrids** are considered the most reliable lilies. They bear clusters of flowers in early or mid-summer and are available in a wide range of patterns and colors, including white, yellow and orange to pink, red and lavender. (Zones 4–8)

L. candidum (Madonna lily) has been cultivated for thousands of years. It produces a tuft of shiny, dark green, lance-shaped, basal foliage in fall that lives through the winter. In early to mid-summer, it produces clusters of up to 20 sweetly fragrant, outward-facing, white flowers that have yellow anthers and are yellow at the base of the petals. This species is very susceptible to gray mold. (Zones 6–9)

L. lancifolium (*L. tigrinum*, tiger lily) has narrow, lance-shaped foliage and dark purple stems. It bears large clusters of non-scented, nodding, orange to orange-red flowers with dark purple spots in late summer. It also produces black bulbils that form in the upper leaf axils. These bulbils can be planted to propagate more plants.

L. **Oriental hybrids** are relatively short lived and are considered a little fussy. They bear clusters of large, fragrant, mid- or late-summer flowers, usually in white, pink or red that are sometimes banded or spotted. (Zones 4–8)

L. speciosum **var.** *rubrum* (red Japanese show lily) is one of the last lilies to bloom. It has purple-brown stems and broad, lance-shaped foliage. In late summer it produces clusters of large, fragrant, deep carmine red to magenta flowers. The petals are darker colored down the center stripe of the petals and lighter toward the edges. *L. speciosum* is one of the ancestors of the Oriental Hybrids. (Zones 4–8)

L. lancifolium

Problems & Pests

Lilies are generally trouble free when planted in the right location. *Botrytis* (gray mold), viruses, aphids, slugs, red lily beetles, snails and wildlife such as deer, birds, voles, rabbits and groundhogs can all cause damage.

Lily bulbs should be planted in fall before the first frost, but if cold-treated bulbs are available, they can be planted in spring.

L. hybrid

Meadow Rue
Columbine Meadow Rue
Thalictrum

Height: 24–36"   **Spread:** 24–36"   **Flower color:** lilac purple, white
Blooms: early summer   **Zones:** 3–8

YOU WILL BE GLAD YOU CHOSE MEADOW RUE BECAUSE OF ITS
blue-green, charmingly lobed foliage, which is similar in shape to maidenhair
fern and columbine. Plants with foliage in other shades of green are accentu-
ated by meadow rue's blue hue. The foliage is also rabbit resistant. The flowers are borne on stalks rising above the foliage, but they don't last very long,
only about two weeks, even with deadheading. Be wary of generic books and
tags written about meadow rue that indicate full sun and regular garden soil
are acceptable—in Georgia, the plant will need some shade and regular
moisture.

Planting

Seeding: Direct sow in fall or start indoors in early spring; soil temperature 70° F

Planting out: Spring

Spacing: 12–24"

Growing

Meadow rue prefers **light or partial shade** but tolerates full sun with moist soil. The soil should be **humus rich, moist** and **well drained**. This plant rarely needs to be divided. If necessary for propagation, divide in spring as the foliage begins to develop. Meadow rue may take a while to re-establish once it has been divided or has had its roots disturbed.

T. aquilegifolium (above & below)

Tips

In the middle or at the back of a border, meadow rue makes a soft backdrop for bolder plants and flowers, and it is beautiful when naturalized in an open woodland or meadow garden.

This plant often does not emerge until quite late in spring. Mark the location where it is planted so that you do not inadvertently disturb the roots if you are cultivating its bed before it begins to grow.

Do not place individual plants too close together because their stems can become tangled. The taller the species, the more support it needs in an exposed location; otherwise, a good wind may topple it.

Meadow rue flowers are generally petal-less. The unique flowers consist of showy sepals and stamens.

Recommended

T. aquilegifolium forms an upright mound 24–36" tall with an equal spread. Small, plentiful lilac flowers appear in early summer on plants with blue-green foliage similar to that of columbine. 'Album' (var. *album*) bears white flowers and is slightly larger than the species.

Problems & Pests

Infrequent problems with powdery mildew, rust, smut and leaf spot can occur.

Mondo Grass
Lilyturf
Ophiopogon

Height: 2–12"   **Spread:** 4–12"   **Flower color:** white, sometimes lightly tinged purple   **Blooms:** summer   **Zones:** 7–10

SHADE'S QUINTESSENTIAL GROUNDCOVER, MONDO GRASS should be first on your planting list. Its dark green, grass-like foliage makes it a mat to whatever you are framing. A prophet without honor because of its almost ubiquitous use for troublesome areas, mondo grass should be appreciated for its elegance and used accordingly. Mass plantings of dwarf mondo grass under azaleas, camellias and hydrangeas, or woven throughout a shady perennial border, guarantee your garden will be beautiful all year. Mondo grass is adaptable to areas under large trees with raised tree roots and along streams where erosion is occurring. It is a spreading groundcover that will reduce the need for purchasing mulch.

Planting

Seeding: Sow fresh, ripe seed in containers in a cold frame in fall.

Planting out: Spring, summer, fall

Spacing: 4–12"

Growing

Mondo grass prefers to grow in **partial to full, dense shade** in **moist, moderately fertile, well-drained, humus-rich** soil. Apply some good compost or leaf mold around the plant in fall. This plant appreciates some winter protection of thick mulch in the northern tip of our state. Divide in spring just as new growth resumes.

Tips

Mondo grass is best used as a dense groundcover and for erosion control. It is also useful for edging beds and borders, and it does quite well in containers. The smaller cultivars are great in rock gardens and between stepping stones.

Recomended

O. japonicus is a clump-forming, evergreen perennial that spreads

O. japonicus cultivar

quickly by rhizomes and grows 8–12" tall and wide. It has narrow, arching, grass-like, dark green foliage. Short clusters of white flowers, possibly with purple tinges, nestle in the foliage in summer and are followed by persistent, shiny, black-blue berries. **'Compactus'** ('Nana') forms a dense mat of 2" tall, dark green foliage. **'Kyoto Dwarf'** grows 4" tall and wide. **'Silver Mist'** bears variegated green and white foliage.

Problems & Pests

Mondo grass may experience problems with slugs, snails, leaf spot and root rot.

O. japonicus

Muhly Grass

Mist Grass, Hairy Awn Muhly, Pink Muhlygrass, Purple Muhlygrass, Pink Hair Grass

Muhlenbergia

Height: 2–4' **Spread:** 24–36" **Flower color:** pink, purple, white
Blooms: mid-summer to fall **Zones:** 5–10

DISTINCTIVE AND DEMANDING OF NOTICE FOR ITS AIRY, SMOKE-like cloud of pink or purple blooms, muhly grass will make you fall in love even if you previously disliked all ornamental grasses. This native plant forms a large, round, cascading fountain of glossy, green foliage before coloring in blossom in late summer through fall. The blooms and seeds are attractive to birds and butterflies and are good for cut arrangements. Plant muhly grass at the front of the border to soften lines, or let it weave through the middle of your garden. Also, try combining this long-lived perennial grass with hydrangeas and dwarf conifers in a mixed border.

Planting

Seeding: Sow seed indoors or direct sow in spring.

Planting out: Spring or fall

Spacing: 24–36"

Growing

Muhly grass thrives in **full sun** but tolerates light shade. The soil should be **well drained, slightly acidic** and **moist,** but this plant is tolerant of just about any type of soil. Muhly grass prefers infrequent watering once it is established. However, the more water it is given, the larger it will become.

For thicker clumps, leave the ripened seedheads in place to allow self-seeding. Otherwise remove the seedheads before they ripen and fall. Muhly grass can be cut back in spring just as the new growth begins, but it can be equally stunning when the new growth emerges through the previous year's growth.

Tips

This wild-looking, medium-sized grass is suited to mixed beds and borders. It looks great with coarse-textured plants that bring attention to its delicate form. It's also useful for naturalizing areas of your garden that require little attention or care, and it works well as a groundcover in areas with poor soil. Muhly grass's fall color stands out while most other plants look spent.

Recommended

M. capillaris produces a dense, showy, knee-high clump of fine, wispy, grayish green to dark green grass. Purplish to pinkish flowerheads begin to emerge in late summer and last for up to two months. **'Regal Mist'** bears rosy pink flowers. **'White Cloud'** has white flowers.

Problems & Pests

No serious pest problems occur.

M. capillaris (above & below)

Muhly grass is a tough-as-nails grass that tolerates drought, floods, salt, heat and humidity. It is at home in a wild, native garden or in a formal border.

Northern Maidenhair Fern

Adiantum

Height: 12–24"   **Spread:** 12–24"   **Flower color:** grown for foliage
Blooms: spores produced in summer   **Zones:** 3–8

YOU'LL BE GLAD YOU DISCOVERED THIS DELICATE-LOOKING,
perennial fern. Northern maidenhair fern holds its nearly lime green foliage
on what appear to be little black wires running horizontal to the ground, and
it looks more like something a florist would use for filler in ornamental dish-
gardens. You can confidently copy this florist's idea in your shade garden.
Imagine a giant hosta arising from a bed of northern maidenhair fern and
underplanted with dark green, dwarf mondo grass. Wonderful! The delicate
foliage and wire-like stems will also provide movement in the garden. This
fern is a few weeks slower to send up its fiddleheads than other ferns, so don't
think it has died.

Some Adiantum
*species have been used
to cure bronchitis,
coughs and asthma.
They are also known
as good hair tonics
and restoratives.*

Planting

Seeding: Sow ripe spores outdoors in early fall.

Planting out: Spring

Spacing: 8"

Growing

Northern maidenhair fern grows best in **partial to full shade,** in **slightly acidic, fertile, moist, well-drained** soil.

Tips

Northern maidenhair fern works best at the edge of a woodland garden. It makes a good addition to a shaded border or shaded rock garden and does well in a streamside planting. When left to its own devices, maidenhair fern spreads to form colonies.

This fern is easy to propagate in fall. Just slice off a section of the thick root mass and replant it in a cool spot.

A. pedatum (above & below)

Recommended

*A. **pedatum*** is an upright, deciduous plant with dark brown to black stems. It bears branched, horizontally oriented, lance-shaped fronds. The lobed, fan-shaped, medium green foliage turns yellow-green to yellow in fall. A waxy coating on the leaflets rapidly sheds water and raindrops.

Problems & Pests

Northern maidenhair fern rarely suffers from any problems.

Pampas Grass
Cortaderia

Height: 7–10'   **Spread:** 5–6'   **Flower color:** tan, silvery white
Blooms: late summer   **Zones:** 7–10

WHEN MY OLDER SISTER WAS 13, I MANEUVERED HER IN FRONT of some mature pampas grass and pushed her in with all my might. With her hands and feet wriggling, and lots of screaming, she was rescued by friends while I enjoyed the show. Pampas grass foliage is sharp enough to draw blood, a good reason not to plant it near pathways or patios. If you aren't creating a wicked-child garden, use this large ornamental grass for the back of the border. It is stunning in drifts of five to seven plants in combination with large, evergreen shrubs like *Camellia sasanqua* or *Ligustrum*. When mature, pampas grass will require gloves and a chainsaw to prune.

Purchase pampas grass when the plumes are present so you can distinguish the showier female specimens from the males.

Planting

Seeding: Sow seed indoors or outdoors in spring.

Planting out: Spring

Spacing: 8"

Growing

Pampas grass prefers **full sun** in **fertile, well-drained** soil. It tolerates light shade and can adapt to many soil types. Fertilizer and supplemental watering is unnecessary once this grass is established. Divide in spring and cut back the foliage and stems in late winter or early spring.

C. selloana 'Pumila'

Tips

Pampas grass requires adequate space to reach its mature size. It makes an excellent specimen plant and is ideal for planting on dry slopes. It can be used at the back of borders and beds and is an effective windbreak.

Ensure that you do not plant pampas grass too close to walkways or patios because the edge of each blade is razor sharp. Wear gloves and long sleeves when working with this plant.

Recommended

C. selloana is the true pampas grass; other species that are often sold as pampas grass are much weedier. This species produces sharply edged, grayish green leaves and tall, fluffy, tan to silvery white flower plumes that may be tinged pink or purple. It grows 7–10' tall and 5–6' wide. Dwarf cultivars and cultivars with variegated foliage are available.

Problems & Pests

Pampas grass may have problems with *Helminthosporium* leaf spot. Ensure good air circulation.

Patrinia

Patrinia

Height: 1–6' **Spread:** 10–24" **Flower color:** yellow, white
Blooms: mid-summer, late summer, fall **Zones:** 5–8

IT WAS LOVE AT FIRST SIGHT WHEN I ENCOUNTERED PATRINIA one sunny day in late summer. It was backed by a mature 'Compacta' holly hedge (*Ilex glabra* 'Compacta') and was beside the peacock blue of *Salvia* 'Indigo Spires.' The clear yellow blooms rose to five feet in thick, airy clusters and had a nice fragrance. As the flowers faded, the chartreuse bracts became showy. Patrinia's first full year is commonly spent establishing itself without its showy blooms, but afterward it is long lived and free flowering. The blooms are good cut flowers. The foliage remains basal and turns reddish in fall.

Planting

Seeding: Sow fresh, ripe seed in containers in a cold frame in fall.

Planting out: Spring

Spacing: 18–24"

Growing

Patrinia prefers to grow in **full sun to partial shade** in **moderately fertile, humus-rich, moist, well-drained** soil. *P. triloba* does best in morning sun and afternoon shade. Patrinia tolerates heat, humidity, rain, wind and cold, and it is somewhat drought tolerant. This plant self-seeds unless deadheaded. Divide in spring.

P. scabiosifolia

Tips

Patrinia can be used in beds and borders and at the edge of a woodland. It is a good filler in bouquets and arrangements and when mixed with bolder plants in the garden. The smaller species can be used as groundcovers and in rock gardens.

Recommended

P. scabiosifolia (golden lace) is an upright perennial, 3–6' tall and 18–24" wide, that has large, ferny, coarsely toothed, medium green foliage that may turn yellow or red-tinged in fall. Over a long period from late summer to fall, it bears airy, flat-topped clusters of small, fragrant, bright yellow flowers on tall, branched stems. **'Nagoya'** is a dwarf specimen that reaches 36" tall.

P. triloba is a vigorous, clump-forming perennial that spreads by short stolons and grows 12–24" tall and 10–14" wide. It has red-tinged stems and deeply lobed, coarsely toothed, medium green foliage that turns yellow in fall. The airy clusters of fragrant, golden yellow flowers bloom from mid- to late summer.

P. villosa (white patrinia) is a fast-growing, clump-forming perennial that grows 24–36" tall and 18–24" wide. It has bright green, slightly hairy foliage and clusters of fragrant, white flowers from late summer to fall.

Problems & Pests

Snails and slugs may be a problem.

Patrinia species are the alternate hosts for daylily rust. Dig up, remove and destroy any plants that show signs of rust. Do not plant patrinia in close proximity to daylilies.

Peacock Moss
Blue Spikemoss, Rainbow Fern
Selaginella

Height: 1–4"   **Spread:** 18–24"; indefinite spread   **Flower color:** grown for foliage   **Blooms:** spores produced in summer   **Zones:** 6–11

WHENEVER THERE IS A STONE OR BRICK PATH IN A PARTIAL SHADE to full shade area, you should plant peacock moss at its edge. This moss softens the edges and will give the illusion that a year-old stone path is almost a decade old. A good spreader, this moss will fill in areas that you didn't know needed filling, yet is easy to keep within bounds. In summer, the ground-hugging, blue-green, fern-like foliage makes this groundcover visible from a distance. The foliage becomes more exotic in winter when it takes on a metallic blue sheen, like roast beef in a college cafeteria. A terrible color for roast beef, but an awesome color for plants!

Planting

Seeding: Sow ripe spores outdoors into warm soil in early fall.

Planting out: Spring, fall

Spacing: 18–24"

Growing

Peacock moss prefers **partial to light shade** in **moist, humus-rich, well-drained, slightly acidic** soil. It tolerates full shade as long as the shade is not too deep. Place this moss in a site out of the wind. Propagate it by transplanting rooted daughter plants.

Tips

Peacock moss works well as a trailing plant at the edge of a container. It makes a nice groundcover and can be used to edge a bed or border. It can also be used in a shady rock garden.

S. uncinata (above & below)

Recommended

S. uncinata is a semi-evergreen, mat-forming perennial that has trailing, branched stems that root at the nodes. It has tiny, bright blue-green to metallic blue foliage. The foliage may take on orange tinting when it receives more sun.

Peacock moss is a distant relative of the true ferns.

Problems and Pests

Peacock moss may experience stem rot and leaf spots.

Penstemon

Beard-Tongue

Penstemon

Height: 18"–5' **Spread:** 12–24" **Flower color:** white, pink, purple, red
Blooms: late spring, summer, fall **Zones:** 3–9

PENSTEMON SEEMS TO GO IN AND OUT OF FAVOR WITH GARDENERS
at the whim of how well it is stocked by garden centers. I'll see penstemon in
many perennial borders for a while, then none for years in gardens or nurseries. It is not a long-lived perennial, but it's definitely worth having because it
makes you look like you know a lot about gardening. Individual penstemon
flowers are shaped like bells and are attached to a tall stalk. The entire outline
gives the illusion of a cone shape from a distance.

*Penstemon's flowers
are highly attractive
to hummingbirds.*

Planting

Seeding: Start indoors in late summer or early spring; soil temperature 55°–64° F

Planting out: Spring or fall

Spacing: 12–24"

Growing

Penstemon prefers **full sun** but tolerates some shade. The soil should be of **average to rich fertility, sandy** and **well drained**. This plant is drought tolerant and rots in wet soil. Mulch in winter with chicken grit or pea gravel to protect the crowns from excessive moisture and cold. Good air circulation minimizes the occurrence of fungal diseases.

Pinch penstemon when it is 12" tall to encourage bushy growth. This plant tends to be short lived, often from four to five years. Divide every two to three years in spring. Cuttings of non-flowering stems can be taken in late spring to mid-summer. This plant will self seed, but the offspring of hybrids and cultivars may not resemble the parents.

P. digitalis 'Husker Red' (above & below)

P. hybrids (above & below)

Tips

Use large penstemons in mixed or herbaceous borders. These plants also look great in a cottage garden. The smaller species and varieties look great in a rock garden.

Twiggy branches pushed into the ground around a young penstemon plant will support it as it grows.

Recommended

P. barbatus (beardlip penstemon) is an upright, rounded perennial. It grows 18–36" tall and spreads 12–18". Red or pink flowers are borne from early summer to early fall. **'Elfin Pink'** is very reliable and has compact spikes of pink flowers. It grows up to 18" tall. (Zones 3–8)

P. digitalis (foxglove penstemon) is a very hardy, upright, semi-evergreen perennial. It grows 2–5' tall and spreads 18–24". It bears white flowers, often veined with purple, all summer. **'Husker Red'** combines white flowers with vibrant burgundy foliage that adds season-long interest. Chosen as the 1996 Perennial Plant of the Year by the American Perennial Plant Association, this cultivar was developed for hardiness as well as good looks. (Zones 4–8)

P. hybrids (garden penstemon, border penstemon) are upright, bushy plants that bloom in a wide range of colors. They grow 18–48" tall and 18–24" wide. From mid-summer to fall, **'Alice Hindley'** bears pinkish purple flowers with white throats. It grows 24–36" tall and spreads 12–18". **'Apple Blossom'** bears pink-flushed, white flowers from late spring to mid-summer. This rounded perennial grows 18–24" tall, with an equal spread. (Zones 6–9)

P. smallii (Small's penstemon) is an upright, shrubby perennial that usually grows 18–24" tall and wide but can grow larger in ideal conditions. The medium green, toothed foliage compliments the dark stems. It bears a bounty of rosy pink to lilac pink blooms for an extended period in mid- to late spring. The insides of the flowers are white with purple stripes. It is native to the northeast mountain area of Georgia. Allow the plant to go to seed, because it is somewhat short lived. (Zones 5–8)

Problems & Pests

Powdery mildew, rust and leaf spot can occur but are rarely serious.

Over 200 species of Penstemon *are native to varied habitats throughout North and South America, from mountains to open plains.*

P. barbatus cultivar (above), P. 'Alice Hindley' (below)

Perennial Sunflower

Helianthus

Height: 3–7' **Spread:** 3–4' **Flower color:** yellow with brown to purple centers **Blooms:** late summer and fall **Zones:** 4–9

ON GRAY OR RAINY DAYS, THE GOLDEN BLOOMS OF THESE sunflowers are a full blast of sunshine. They also bloom when not much else is in fresh bloom during late summer and early fall. Cut sunflowers back once or twice before July 4 to make them shorter, so they won't flop, and to increase the number of blooms. If powdery mildew is a problem on the lower foliage, pull out a few stems to increase airflow. *H. angustifolius* is a vigorous spreader but is easily kept in check. I wait until the stalks grow tall enough to pull up without having to bend over.

These plants are in the same genus as annual sunflowers, though the flowers are often not as large. Butterflies are attracted to these plants.

Planting

Seeding: Start in spring; seedlings may not come true to type.

Planting out: Spring

Spacing: 24–36"

Growing

Perennial sunflowers grow best in **full sun**. In general, soil should be of **average fertility, neutral to alkaline, moist** and **well drained**. The two species mentioned below prefer a constantly moist soil.

Plants should be cut back hard after flowering. They can also be cut back in early summer to produce shorter plants that flower later in the season. Divide every three or so years in spring or fall.

Tips

These impressive perennials deserve a spot at the back of a border or in the center of an island bed. Both of these species are water loving and can be planted near ponds or other water features. These tall plants can be used to provide a temporary summer screen.

Recommended

H. angustifolius (swamp sunflower, narrow-leaved sunflower) is a large, salt-tolerant, upright, clump-forming perennial with rough, hairy stems and rough, narrow, lance-shaped, medium green foliage. It bears lots of yellow flowers with brown to purple centers and grows 5–7' tall and 3–4' wide. (Zones 6–9)

H. angustifolius

H. x *multiflorus* (many-flowered sunflower) forms a large, upright clump. It grows 3–6' tall and spreads about 3'. Many daisy-like flowers with yellow petals and brown centers are borne in late summer and fall. **'Loddon Gold'** bears golden yellow, double flowers. **'Soleil d'Or'** bears double, yellow flowers. (Zones 4–8)

Problems & Pests

Problems with powdery mildew, downy mildew, fungal leaf spot and leaf-chewing insects such as caterpillars, beetles and weevils can occur.

H. x *multiflorus* 'Loddon Gold'

Phlox

Phlox

Height: 2"–5'   **Spread:** 12–36"   **Flower color:** white, red, purple-blue,
purple, pink   **Blooms:** spring, summer, fall   **Zones:** 3–8

IF THERE IS AN OLD-FASHIONED GARDEN PLANT UNITING ALL
of Georgia in early spring, it is the tiny-leafed, low-growing, drought-
tolerant evergreen, *P. subulata*. It thrives in poor or amended soil and flowers
in shades of pink, white or purple-blue. For later in the season, choose the
taller *P. paniculata*, which grows to 5' tall and is herbaceous. This plant looks
best in a drift of at least three plants, preferably more. Its foliage is prone to
mildew, so keep the stalks thinned to only four or five per plant. Phlox likes
an amended soil that is moist yet well drained. It demands full sun and
appreciates deadheading before it sets seed.

Planting
Seeding: Not
recommended
Planting out: Spring
Spacing: 12–36"

*Phlox is from the Greek word for
"flame," referring to the colorful
flowers of many species.*

Growing

P. paniculata, P. maculata and *P. subulata* prefer **full sun** but tolerate partial shade. *P. divaricata* and *P. stolonifera* prefer **partial to light shade** but adapt to full shade. *P. nivalis* grows well in **full sun to light shade**. All do well in **fertile, humus-rich, moist** soil that is very **well drained**. *P. subulata* grows in poor soil as long as the soil is well drained.

Divide in fall or spring. The low-growing phlox species often have stems that grow roots where they touch the ground. These plants are easily propagated by detaching and planting the rooted stems in spring or early fall. Do not cut back creeping phlox or moss phlox in fall—both species bloom early and will have already formed next season's flowers.

Tips

Low-growing species are useful in a rock garden or at the front of a border. Taller species may be used in the middle of a border, where they are particularly effective planted in groups.

To keep powdery mildew to a minimum, thin out phlox's stems to increase air movement; plant it in full sun when possible; eliminate or reduce overhead watering; and reduce fungal spores by removing infected leaves and stems in fall. High-quality, fungal-dominated, compost tea can also be used as a preventative.

Recommended

P. subulata (moss phlox, moss pinks) is very low growing, only 2–6" tall, with a spread of 20". Red-purple to

P. subulata (above & below)

violet purple, pink or white flowers are produced in early to mid-spring. Plants tolerate heat, poor soil and drought when planted in the proper conditions. **'Candy Stripe'** bears bicolored pink and white flowers.

P. paniculata 'Eva Cullum'

P. paniculata 'David' (above), *P. subulata* (below)

P. paniculata (garden phlox) blooms in summer and fall. It has many cultivars, which vary greatly in size, growing 20"–5' tall and spreading 24–36". Many colors are available, often with contrasting centers. **'David'** bears white flowers and is resistant to powdery mildew. **'Eva Cullum'** bears pink flowers with red centers.

P. divaricata (woodland phlox, blue phlox) is a low, bushy, mound-forming, semi-evergreen plant that spreads by sterile, creeping stems that root at the nodes. It grows 12–15" tall and spreads 12–20" wide. It has dark green foliage and bears flowers on erect stems in shades of lavender blue to pale violet and white for most of summer and early fall. (Zones 4–8)

P. maculata (early phlox, meadow phlox, wild sweet William) forms an upright clump of hairy stems, and narrow leaves that are sometimes spotted with red. It grows 24–36" tall and spreads 18–24". Pink, purple or white flowers are borne in conical clusters in the first half of summer. This species has good resistance to powdery mildew. **'Miss Lingard'** is an old-fashioned variety that bears white flowers all summer.

P. nivalis (trailing phlox) is a low, mat-forming, evergreen perennial with trailing stems that are upturned at the tips and root at the nodes. Individual plants grow 6–8" tall and about 12" wide and bear pink, purple or white flowers in summer. These plants do well in heat and humidity. (Zones 6–8)

P. stolonifera (creeping phlox) is a low, spreading plant that spreads by stolons. It grows 4–6" tall, spreads about 12" and bears flowers in shades of purple in spring. This species was named Perennial Plant of the Year in 1990.

P. divaricata hybrid

Problems & Pests

Occasional problems with powdery mildew, stem canker, rust, leaf spot, leaf miners and caterpillars are possible.

Phlox comes in many forms, from low-growing creepers to tall, clump-forming uprights. The many species can be found in diverse climates including dry, exposed mountainsides and moist, sheltered woodlands.

P. subulata 'Candy Stripe' (above), *P. paniculata* cultivar (below)

Pinks

Dianthus

Height: 2–24"   **Spread:** 8–24"   **Flower color:** pink, red, white, lilac purple, purple-red   **Blooms:** spring, summer   **Zones:** 3–9

EVERY SUNNY PERENNIAL GARDEN MUST HAVE THE SILVERY, evergreen foliage of 'Bath's Pink.' This bright spark will anchor your garden in winter when so many other perennials are dormant. The flowers are fragrant and long blooming, but I would forgo those pretty blooms for the capabilities of the silver foliage. *D. deltoides* is lower growing and dark green, forming a dense mat that adores full sun and looks good in combination with 'Bath's Pink.' Sweet William has broader, lighter green foliage than *D. deltoides* and has colorful blooms in a mix of white, pink and red, all on the same plant. All of the species and cultivars listed below require lime and excellent drainage.

Planting

Seeding: Not recommended; cultivars do not come true to type from seed.

Planting out: Spring

Spacing: 10–20"

Growing

Pinks prefer **full sun** in a **neutral to alkaline, well-drained** soil. The most important factor in the successful cultivation of pinks is drainage—they hate to stand in water. Mix organic matter and gravel into their area of the flowerbed to encourage good drainage.

Pinks may be difficult to propagate by division. It is often easier to take cuttings in summer once flowering has finished. Cuttings should be 1–3" long. Strip their lower leaves and keep the cuttings humid, but give them some ventilation so fungal problems do not set in.

Tips

Pinks make excellent plants for rock gardens and rock walls, and for edging flower borders and walkways. They can also be used in cutting gardens and even as groundcovers.

D. gratianopolitanus cultivar

The tiny, delicate petals of pinks can be used to decorate cakes. Remove the white part at the base of each petal before using the petals, or they will be bitter.

R. barbatus culitvars

Deadhead as the flowers fade to prolong blooming, but leave a few flowers in place to go to seed, especially for the sort-lived *D. barbatus.* Pinks self-seed quite easily. Seedlings may differ from the parent plants, often with new and interesting results.

Recommended

D. gratianopolitanus (cheddar pink) is long-lived and forms a very dense, spreading mat of silver gray, evergreen foliage that is 4–8" tall. It bears sweet-scented flowers in mid- to late spring, usually in shades of pink. **'Bath's Pink'** can reach 10" tall, has blue-green foliage and bears light to medium pink flowers in abundance. It easily tolerates our warm, humid conditions. **'Firewitch'** ('Feuerhexe') is an upright selection that bears clove-scented, rosy pink flowers.

D. barbatus (sweet William) is a biennial or short-lived perennial that reaches a height of 18–24" tall and spreads 8–12". Flattened clusters of often two-toned, white, pink, red or purple-red flowers bloom in late spring to early summer. Cultivars are available in a range of sizes and colors. **'Newport Pink'** has deep pink flowers and grows to 18" tall.

D. gratianopolitanus (above), *D. gratianopolitanus* 'Bath's Pink' (below)

D. ***deltoides*** (maiden pinks) grows 6–12" tall and 12–24" wide, forming a mat of dark green, evergreen foliage. The flowers bloom in late spring and into summer in shades of pink and red. **'Albus'** bears pure white blossoms. **'Red Maiden'** has red-purple flowers and looks great at the foot of a sunny mailbox. Use this popular species and its cultivars in rock gardens.

Problems & Pests

Providing good drainage and air circulation will keep most fungal problems away. Occasional problems with slugs, blister beetles, sow bugs and grasshoppers are possible.

Cheddar pink is a rare and protected species in Britain. It was discovered in the 18th century by British botanist Samuel Brewer, and it became as locally famous as Cheddar cheese.

D. barbatus cultivars (above), *D. deltoides* (below)

Pitcher Plants

Sarracenia

Height: 6–36"   **Spread:** 6–36"   **Flower color:** purple, red, pink, purplish red, yellow, yellow-green   **Blooms:** spring   **Zones:** 2–10

NOT MANY GARDENS HAVE A BOGGY AREA FOR GROWING PITCHER plants, but one can easily be created. Dig up a plot of ground and line it with a flexible pond liner that has some perforations. Mix topsoil with 25% to 50% peat moss for the best bogginess. Keeping the boggy soil acidic will allow pitcher plants to thrive and will also attract moss, which likes to grow in the same conditions. Several other perennials, such as *lobelia*, *iris* and *chelone*, also like growing in boggy conditions. My bog garden is in a rescued 1930's bathroom sink that we found on the side of the road. The drain is plugged with a small, plastic grocery bag to prevent excessive drainage. I also planted venus fly trap (*Dionaea muscipula*) in the old sink and let a few weeds grow to complete the illusion of a true bog garden.

S. purpurea

Planting

Seeding: Seeds need a short period of cold treatment to germinate. Sow treated seed into warm soil in the garden in spring.

Planting out: Spring

Spacing: 6–24"

Growing

Pitcher plants prefer locations with **full sun to partial shade**. The soil should be **humus rich**, consistently **moist to boggy** and **acidic**. Pitcher plants thrive in nutrient-depleted soils, so fertilizing isn't necessary and may actually kill the plant. These plants absorb the necessary nutrients from the insects they consume.

Division is required only if you want to propagate the plants. Carefully separate the crowns in mid-spring, avoiding damage to the roots, and replant the divisions immediately. Remove only dead foliage in fall—do not disturb the roots.

Tips

Pitcher plants are both beautiful and unusual, and they are excellent for locations that are kept consistently moist but not flooded, such as a bog garden. The insect-eating tubes that rise out of the damp ground are certain to be a conversation piece.

Do not dig these plants up from the wilderness. Buy them only from reputable nurseries.

S. leucophylla hybrid (above),
S. flava (below)

Recommended

S. flava (yellow pitcher plant) produces erect, pitcher-shaped foliage in yellowish green with crimson veining. It bears large, bright yellow, pendulous flowers that often rise above the pitchers. The species grows 24–36" tall and wide. (Zones 6–9)

S. **hybrids** are a group of many complex selections that are available in a wide array of forms, colors and sizes ranging from 9–12" tall and 12–18" wide. They are vigorous growers, painted with color beyond your wildest imagination. Ask your local garden center for their recommendations. (Zones 6–9)

S. leucophylla (*S. drummondii,* white trumpet, white-topped pitcher plant) bears slender, green pitchers 12–36" tall with purple-tinged, white tops. This plant spreads 12–18" wide and produces nodding, purple flowers in spring. (Zones 6–9)

S. minor (hooded pitcher plant) is a smaller, native plant that grows only 12" tall. It produces green and coppery red, pitcher-like foliage with domed lids and bears yellowish green flowers in late spring. (Zones 6–9)

S. purpurea (common pitcher plant, huntsman's cup) forms a clump of prostrate to erect, jug-shaped, purple-veined, green, purple or reddish pitchers that grow 6–12" tall and wide. Nodding flowers in shades of purple, red, pink or purplish red appear in spring. (Zones 2–9)

Problems & Pests

Scale insects, mealybugs and aphids can cause problems.

The tubes or pitchers are actually modified leaves. Hairs or spikes along the insides of the tubes allow insects to climb in but not out. Once an insect reaches the bottom of a tube, the plant digests it.

S. x 'Ladies-in-Waiting'

Plume Poppy

Macleaya

Height: 6–9'   **Spread:** 12–36"; clumps spread indefinitely   **Flower color:** cream; plants also grown for foliage   **Blooms:** summer   **Zones:** 3–10

EVERY TIME I SEE THIS PLANT IN A garden I wonder why I don't have it. Then I read about it again and remember why. It is a large perennial that spreads aggressively by rhizomes, and my small garden has "no room at the inn." The showy, deeply lobed, glaucous foliage contrasts extravagantly with almost any companion. Plume poppy prefers sun but will grow in partial shade. Growing it in partial shade is the best way to slow its spread while maintaining the glories of its foliage, blooms and seed pods, which is probably why I've always seen it in a partially shaded setting. The flowers and seedpods dry easily and look lovely in dried arrangements.

Planting

Seeding: Start seed in a cold frame in early or mid-spring.

Planting out: Spring

Spacing: 36"

Growing

Plume poppy prefers **full sun** but tolerates partial shade. The soil should be of **average fertility, humus rich** and **moist**. Plume poppy tolerates dry soils and is less invasive in poorer conditions.

Divide every two or three years to control the size of the clump. The mature size depends on conditions—in less fertile conditions, it reaches 4–5' in height; in optimal situations it grows to 9'.

Remove spent flowers if you want to avoid having too many self-sown seedlings popping up all over the garden. Pull up or cut back any overly exuberant growth as needed. Planting in a heavy-duty, bottomless pot sunk into the ground slows invasive spreading.

Tips

Plume poppy looks impressive as a specimen plant or at the back of the border. Give it lots of room, because it can quickly overwhelm less-vigorous plants. This plant is easy to care for and makes a nice summer screen. It is also a good choice for the centers of concrete-bordered medians and large island beds.

Recommended

M. cordata is a tall, narrow-growing, clump-forming plant with attractive, undulating, lobed leaves and plumes of creamy white flowers. Each clump spreads 12–36", but clumps of plants may spread indefinitely.

M. cordata

Problems & Pests

Slugs may attack young growth. Anthracnose can be a problem in warm, humid weather.

M. cordata 'Kelway's Coral Plume'

Purple Coneflower
Echinacea

Height: 18"–5' **Spread:** 12–24" **Flower color:** purple, pink,red, white
Blooms: mid-summer to fall **Zones:** 3–8

ONE OF GEORGIA'S TOP TEN PERENNIALS, PURPLE CONEFLOWER
should be planted immediately if you don't have it yet. Although it is beautiful in large drifts, it is an individual ballerina in my garden. Instead of drifts,
I let it seed as a single plant wherever it wants to. Strangely, this seems to be
where the soil is poorest, along compacted stone or gravel paths. Toward the
end of summer, the center of each flower takes on a strong, radiant, golden
cast. If the petals are ratty, remove them to show off the radiant, golden cone.
It will look like an entirely new flower.

E. purpurea

Planting

Seeding: Direct sow in spring.

Planting out: Spring

Spacing: 18"

Growing

Purple coneflower grows well in **full sun** or very **light shade**; in shade it may need staking. The soil should be of **average fertility, neutral to** **slightly alkaline** and **well drained**. This plant has thick taproots that help it resist drought, but it prefers to have regular water.

Echinacea was an important medicine for Native Americans, and today it is a popular immunity booster in herbal medicine.

Divide every four years or so in spring or fall. Deadhead early in the season to prolong flowering. Later in the season, you may wish to leave the flowerheads in place to self-seed, provide winter interest and attract birds. If you don't want to allow self-seeding, remove all the flowerheads as they fade. Pinch plants back or thin out the stems in early summer to encourage bushy growth that is less prone to mildew.

Tips

Use purple coneflower in meadow gardens and informal borders, either in groups or as single specimens. The dry flowerheads make an interesting feature in fall and winter gardens.

E. purpurea 'Magnus' (above), *E. purpurea* 'Magnus' and 'White Swan' (below)

Recommended

E. purpurea is an upright plant up to 5' tall and 24" wide with prickly hairs all over the leaves and stems. It bears purple flowers with orangy, cone-like centers. The cultivars generally grow to about half the height of the species. White-flowered plants tend to be shorter, less vigorous and shorter-lived than purple-flowered plants. **'Magnus'** flowers are up to 4 ½" wide. They are deep rose, and the petals are less droopy than those of the species. **'White Lustre'** bears white flowers with orange centers. **'White Swan'** is a compact plant, reaching 18–22" in height. It has white flowers.

Problems & Pests

Powdery mildew is the biggest problem. Also possible are leaf miners, bacterial spot and gray mold. Vine weevils may attack the roots.

E. purpurea 'White Lustre' (above & below)

Purple coneflower attracts wildlife; it provides pollen, nectar and seeds for various hungry visitors.

Purple Loosestrife
European Wand Loosestrife
Lythrum virgatum

Height: 2–4'   **Spread:** 18"   **Flower color:** pink, purple   **Blooms:** mid-summer to fall   **Zones:** 4–9

ATTRACTING BUTTERFLIES IS NOT AN ATTRIBUTE NORMALLY written into most accounts of purple loosestrife. However, butterflies do flock about the flowers, more flocking than I've ever seen at butterfly bush (*Buddleia davidii*). When in peak flower, which lasts from mid-summer to fall, this perennial is a focal point of color. It prefers moist, well-drained soil, yet it adapts easily to a dry, sunny slope. Purple loosestrife is long lived and needs little attention, but it will reward you for deadheading. Noted as being invasive in other states, the species is less invasive in Georgia, and the cultivars are less invasive than the species.

Planting

Seeding: Sow seed indoors or direct sow in spring.

Planting out: Spring or fall

Spacing: 18"

Growing

Purple loosestrife grows well in **full sun to partial shade** in **moist, fertile** soil. Deadhead the flower clusters to prevent self-seeding. Divide in spring or fall. Plants can also be propagated from basal cuttings taken in late spring to early summer.

Tips

Purple loosestrife works well as an accent in the middle or back of a border and makes an excellent specimen plant. It performs well in moist to boggy beds and borders. Do not plant purple loosestrife where it may escape into native wetlands.

Recommended

L. virgatum is an upright, clump-forming, branched perennial that grows 3–4' tall and 18" wide. It has lance-shaped, medium to bright green foliage and spiky clusters of flowers in shades of pink, purple and purple-red that bloom for a long period from early to late summer. **'Dropmore Purple'** has deep purple-pink flowers. **'Morden Pink'** grows 36" tall and bears clear pink to magenta flowers.

L. **'Rose Queen'** is a compact selection that grows 24" tall and bears bright pink flowers from purple buds.

L. virgatum 'Morden Pink'

Problems & Pests

Slugs, snails and Japanese beetles may attack purple loosestrife.

L. virgatum *is closely related to* L. salicaria, *which is a very invasive weed that has destroyed wetlands and has been banned from many states.* L. virgatum *is also banned in many states.*

L. virgatum

Ravenna Grass
Plume Grass, Hardy Pampas Grass
Saccharum

Height: 10–12' **Spread:** 3–6' **Flower color:** pink, purple **Blooms:** late summer to fall **Zones:** 6–10

SLOW TO GROW ITS FIRST YEAR, RAVENNA GRASS NEEDS A 10' diameter circle for comfort. Summer's glory and winter's focal point, the feathery pink flowers first turn to silver then mature into nice seedheads. Cut this plant back in late winter or early spring to within 4–6" of the ground. You can use shears when the plant is young, but power tools become necessary as each stem grows to be 1" thick. Occasionally this shallow-rooted plant dies out in the center due to shading, but it is easily lifted and chopped into healthy pieces for replanting.

S. ravennae

Planting

Seeding: Sow seed indoors, direct sow in spring or start seeds in containers in a cold frame in spring.

Planting out: Spring or fall

Spacing: 3–6'

Growing

Grow ravenna grass in **full sun** in **moderately fertile, well-drained** soil. Once established, this plant tolerates drought. Excessive fertility and overwatering can cause the stems to flop over. Provide protection from strong winds.

Cut back foliage and flowers in late winter to early spring to make room for new growth. Divide in spring or early summer to propagate more plants. Ravenna grass self-sows prolifically, so deadhead the flowers if you do not want any seedlings.

Tips

Ravenna grass is very effective as a specimen or accent plant. It can be used at the back of beds and borders as a textured backdrop for smaller, broadleaf plants, or as a seasonal screen or hedge. The large flower spikes are used in fresh and dried arrangements and are attractive in winter.

Recommended

S. ravennae is a large, erect, clump-forming, perennial grass. It has long, arching, strap-like, gray-green foliage with white stripes. The plume-like flowers are borne on tall, stiff stems that rise well above the foliage in late summer and early fall. The foliage turns orange to bronze in fall.

Problems & Pests

Ravenna grass is relatively pest free.

A large percentage of the world's sugar supply is derived from S. officinarum *(sugar cane), a close relative of ravenna grass.*

Red-Hot Poker
Common Torch Lily
Kniphofia

Height: 18"–6' **Spread:** 12–24" **Flower color:** red, orange, yellow, white
Blooms: summer, fall **Zones:** 5–9

RED-HOT POKER IS A PLANT OF SEDUCTION.
With rows of red-hot pokers in bloom, the
nurseries I've worked at sold out of this
plant before noon during spring's busiest
Saturdays. It is shocking that the entire
state isn't coated in or dusted with this
plant. Pay attention when told that red-
hot poker must have excellent drainage, which is especially true during
winter. Perhaps one reason we have
not seen more of this plant in the
past is its garish colors. Newer
cultivars are available that
aren't as garish, but they've
probably lost some vigor and
will absolutely need excellent
drainage—but they put on a
great show while they last.

Planting

Seeding: Not recommended; cultivars do not come true to type and seedlings may take three years to reach flowering size.

Planting out: Spring

Spacing: 24"

Growing

This plant grows best in **full sun.** The soil should be **fertile, humus rich, sandy, moist** and very **well drained.** Large clumps may be divided in late spring.

Red-hot poker is sensitive to cold. Do not cut back the foliage in fall in the colder areas of the state—it provides winter protection. Bundle up the leaves and tie them above the center bud to keep the crown protected over winter.

Tips

Red-hot poker makes a bold, vertical statement in the middle or back of a border. This plant looks best when planted in groups.

To encourage red-hot poker to continue flowering as long as possible, cut the spent flowers off right where the stem meets the plant.

Recommended

K. uvaria forms a large clump of long, narrow foliage. It grows 4' tall and spreads about half this much. In summer and often to first frost, bright red buds open to orange flowers that fade to yellow as they age. **'Bressingham Comet'** has flame red and yellow flowers and grows 18–24" tall and 12–18" wide.

K. uvaria cultivar (photos this page)

'Kingston Flame' bears burnt orange flowers on 4–5' tall plants.

K. **'Sunningdale Yellow'** grows 3–4' tall and 18–24" wide and bears bright yellow flowers. (Zones 7–9)

Problems & Pests

This plant rarely has problems but is susceptible to stem or crown rot. Thrips may cause flowers to drop off unopened.

Ribbon Grass
Gardener's Garters, Reed Canary Grass
Phalaris

Height: 2–4'   **Spread:** 36" to indefinite   **Flower color:** pale pink to white; plant grown for the foliage   **Blooms:** early summer   **Zones:** 4–9

WHY RECOMMEND A PLANT THAT CAN BE DIFFICULT TO KEEP IN bounds? For wet areas, dry sunny slopes and challenging areas that require erosion protection, the rhizomes of ribbon grass spread quickly to form a dense weave that holds the soil in place. For its invasive qualities, plant the species. If you want pretty foliage and slightly less aggressiveness, try one of the cultivars. The seedheads are displayed from June through to the end of October. Add ribbon grass to your pond, planted in a pot and placed 4–12" below the water's surface, to contrast nicely with the leaves of floating water lilies.

Planting ribbon grass in sunken containers allows you to place it in beds and borders without it taking over the garden.

Planting

Seeding: Not recommended.

Planting out: Spring or fall

Spacing: 36"

Growing

Ribbon grass grows well in **full sun or partial shade**. The soil should be of **average fertility** and **moist to wet**; this grass can grow in water up to 12" deep. It can be invasive and difficult to remove once established, although less so in dry locations, so consider restricting it to a large container to control its spread.

Divide ribbon grass as needed in spring or early summer. Cut the plant back to 4" tall when it turns brown in fall.

Tips

This vigorous grass is a great addition to a moist pond-side area or the margins of the pond. Ribbon grass can also be used as a groundcover or for erosion control on hard-to-maintain slopes.

Recommended

P. arundinacea is a clump-forming perennial grass that has dark green to blue-green foliage and spreads quickly by rhizomes. **'Feesey's Form'** has pink-tinged, light green foliage with wide, white stripes and pale pink flowers. **Var.** *picta* ('Picta') has long, narrow, arching, green leaves with white stripes. The pale pink to white flowers are held above the foliage in early summer.

P. arundinacea var. *picta*

Problems & Pests

Ribbon grass is subject to typical grass-family diseases including leaf spot, ergot, rust, smut and brown patch.

Rosemary

Rosmarinus

Height: 6"–6' **Spread:** 18"–5' **Flower color:** blue, pink **Blooms:** main blooming season in winter with some blooming in summer **Zones:** (6)8–10

INTERNATIONAL GARDEN DESIGNER RUSSELL PAGE SAID THAT rosemary is about as domesticated as a cat. Grow three of the same cultivar and you'll have three similar but different shapes. Try to prune rosemary how you would like, and you can hear her laugh—she'll continue to grow how she wants to. However, you must have rosemary—she's the coloratura of the winter perennial garden, evergreen and blooming, and she's a great companion to deciduous flowering shrubs in a mixed border. Use rosemary branches as a brush for marinades on the grill, or slip a branch into your postal correspondence, because rosemary is for remembrance. Breezy days waft rosemary's scent across your entire garden.

Rosemary's needle-like leaves are used to flavor a wide variety of culinary dishes. Cut woody spears of rosemary to use for spearing meat chunks on the barbecue.

Planting

Seeding: Start seeds in containers in a cold frame in spring.

Planting out: Spring

Spacing: 1–4'

Growing

Rosemary prefers **full sun** but tolerates partial shade. The soil should be of **poor to average fertility** and **well drained**. Removing the woody branches encourages fresh new growth. Rosemary can be propagated by semi-ripe stem cuttings in summer.

Tips

Grow rosemary in a shrub border where it's hardy, or plant it in a container as a specimen. Low-growing, spreading plants can be included in rock gardens, along the top of retaining walls or in hanging baskets. Container-grown plants rarely reach their mature size.

To overwinter a container-grown plant, keep it in very light or partial shade in summer, then transfer it to a sunny window indoors, away from sources of heat such as gas ranges, for winter. Keep it well watered, but not soaking wet.

Recommended

R. officinalis is a dense, bushy, evergreen shrub that grows 4–6' tall and 4–5' wide and has fragrant, narrow, dark green leaves. The blooms usually come in shades of blue, but pink-flowered cultivars are available. Cultivar growth habits vary from strongly upright to prostrate and spreading. Some cultivars can survive in zone 6 in a sheltered location

R. officinalis (above & below)

with winter protection. **'Prostratus'** has prostrate stems and grows 6–12" tall and 18–36" wide. **'Tuscan Blue'** is a fast-growing, upright plant that bears deep blue flowers.

Problems & Pests

Rosemary may experience root rot and leaf spots.

Russian Sage
Perovskia

Height: 3–4' **Spread:** 3–4' **Flower color:** blue, purple **Blooms:** mid- or late summer to fall **Zones:** 4–9

RUSSIAN SAGE IS A SILVER CLOUD OF CONTROLLED CHAOS. Enjoy how the many wand-like stems sway in the breeze. The foliage and four-sided stems are truly silver, providing contrast with nearby green companions, making everyone look better. The long bloom season begins in mid-summer and lasts almost four months. Full sun, lime and excellent drainage keep Russian sage thriving. Prepared soil is better than our Georgia red clay, and planting ¼" above the soil is best in the northern part of our state. Winter can be damaging, so wait to prune this herbaceous perennial until early spring when new growth is visible at its base.

Planting

Seeding: Not recommended; germination can be very erratic.

Planting out: Spring

Spacing: 36"

The airy habit of this plant creates a mist of silvery purple in the garden.

Growing

Russian sage prefers **full sun**. The soil should be **poor to moderately fertile** and **well drained**. Too much water and nitrogen causes the growth to flop, so take care when growing this plant next to heavy feeders. Russian sage is drought tolerant when established and does not need dividing.

In spring, when new growth appears low on the branches, or in fall, cut the plant back hard to about 6–12" to encourage vigorous, bushy growth.

P. atriplicifolia 'Longin'

Tips

The silvery foliage and blue flowers combine well with other plants in the back of a mixed border and soften the appearance of daylilies. Russian sage may also be used to create a soft screen in a natural garden or on a dry bank.

To enhance the plant's ability to survive winter in the coldest areas of the mountains, plant the crowns high in the soil or in a raised bed to keep winter moisture from collecting. A light mulch and a sheltered location also help.

Recommended

P. atriplicifolia is a loose, upright plant growing 3–4' tall and wide. It has silvery white, finely divided foliage. The small, lavender blue flowers are loosely held on silvery branched stems. **'Filigran'** has delicate foliage and an upright habit. **'Longin'** is narrow and erect and has more smoothly edged leaves than other cultivars.

The flowers make a nice addition to fresh and dried flower arrangements.

P. atriplicifolia

Salvia

Sage

Salvia

Height: 18"–6'   **Spread:** 1–6'   **Flower color:** purple, blue, pink, red, white,
yellow   **Blooms:** summer, fall   **Zones:** 5–11

MANY SPECIES OF SALVIA CLAIMING TO BE PERENNIALS ARE
tender perennials in Georgia. To improve their longevity, cease pruning them
in fall. Wait until all threat of frost has passed in spring, then prune. This is
good for the plants but bad for aesthetics if you've planted salvias near your
windows or in front of your home, because they can be somewhat ugly when
not cut back, kind of like naked sticks poking out of the ground. With so
many species and cultivars, I'll simply list my top three choices: *S.* 'Indigo
Spires,' *S. leucantha* and *S. greggi*. Most salvias are attractive to butterflies.

Planting

Seeding: Species can be started in early spring. Cultivars do not come true to type.

Planting out: Spring

Spacing: 1–6'

Growing

Salvias prefer **full sun** and tolerate light shade. The soil should be of **average fertility, humus rich** and **well drained**. These plants are drought tolerant once established.

Deadhead to prolong blooming. Cut plants back in spring to encourage new growth and to keep plants tidy. New shoots sprout from old, woody growth.

Division can be done in spring, but plants are slow to re-establish and resent having their roots disturbed.

S. involucrata 'Bethellii' (above), *S. guaranitica* (below)

Tips

Salvias are attractive plants for the back, middle or front of a border. They also look good when grouped and when planted in containers. The flowers are long lasting and make good cut flowers for arrangements.

Recommended

S. azurea (azure sage) is an openly branched, upright plant that grows 3–4' tall and 24–36" wide. It produces azure blue blooms in late summer and into fall. This salvia does not suffer in heat and humidity. (Zones 5–9)

S. elegans (pineapple sage) is an erect perennial that grows 3–5' tall and wide. It produces clusters of bright scarlet flowers from late fall to spring. Frost stops the plant from

blooming. The bright green leaves emit a mild pineapple aroma. The fresh leaves are used in cool drinks, teas and fruit salads. The flowers add flavor and color to desserts and salads. (Zones 8–11)

S. greggii (autumn sage) is an erect, vase-shaped, evergreen shrub or woody-based perennial that grows 18–30" tall and 12–20" wide. The summer to fall flowers are most often red, but they also come in shades of purple, red-purple, pink, yellow or white. This species needs dry conditions. It will die to the ground in a hard freeze but will reappear in spring. Cultivars are available. (Zones 7–9)

S. guaranitica (blue anise sage, Brazilian sage) is an upright, branched plant that grows 3–5' tall and wide. Rich, cobalt blue flowers bloom from early summer to fall. (Zones 7–11)

S. **'Indigo Spires'** is a big, bushy perennial that grows 3–5' tall and wide and has medium green foliage. It produces violet-blue flower spikes from mid-summer to frost. It is easily propagated from stem cuttings. (Zones 7–11)

S. involucrata (rosy-leaf sage, rosebud sage) is a fast-growing, open, shrubby perennial reaching a height of 5–6' and a spread of 3–5'. Dense, spiky clusters of purplish red flowers are produced from mid-summer to mid-fall. Each flower is surrounded by pink to purplish pink bracts that fall

S. involucrata 'Bethellii' (above)
S. leucantha (below)

S. guaranitica cultivar

away as the flower opens. **'Bethellii'** is a more compact plant that bears flowers in shorter, rounded clusters. (Zones 8–11)

S. leucantha (Mexican bush sage) is a shrubby perennial growing 3–4$^{1}/_{2}$' tall and 4–6' wide. White to pale lavender flowers with purple calyxes are produced freely from late summer to frost. This species needs to be cut to the base in winter to allow new spring growth. (Zones 7b–11)

Problems & Pests

Scale insects, whiteflies and root rot (in wet soils) are the most likely problems.

Read about your salvia before siting, particularly if it is not one of the species listed above. Some need drought conditions, yet others become like kudzu with plenty of moisture.

S. *elegans* (above)
S. *greggii* 'Furman's Red'

Sea Holly

Eryngium

Height: 1–6'   **Spread:** 12–24"   **Flower color:** purple, blue, white
Blooms: summer to fall   **Zones:** 3–8

ELLEN WILLMOTT SPREAD THE SEEDS OF SEA HOLLY IN GARDENS she thought were boring. Noticing this, gardeners began to call that seed "Miss Wilmott's Ghost." Sea holly is native to coastal areas and adapts to dry conditions. Full sun is best, and partial shade is acceptable, but it diminishes the intensity of the flower color. Sea holly prefers a gravel mulch in winter to protect it from rot. This plant attracts butterflies and makes a good dried flower, but don't expect blooms the first year from seed.

Planting

Seeding: Not recommended, though direct sowing in fall may produce spring seedlings.

Planting out: Spring

Spacing: 12–24"

Growing

Grow sea holly in **full sun** in **average to fertile** and **well drained** soil. Place this plant carefully because it has a deep taproot and doesn't like to be moved. Once it is established, sea holly is not a heavy feeder and is reasonably drought tolerant, but it suffers if left more than two weeks without water. Sea holly is very slow to re-establish after dividing. Root cuttings can be taken in late winter.

E. yuccifolium

The leaves of this plant are edged with small spines, making deadheading a pain—literally. Deadheading is not necessary unless you are very fussy about keeping plants neat.

Tips

Mix sea holly with other late-season bloomers in a border. It makes an interesting addition to naturalized gardens.

Recommended

E. amethystinum (amethyst sea holly) is a clump-forming perennial that grows 12–24" tall and wide and has silvery blue stems and spiny, jagged, medium green leaves. The steel blue flowers bloom from mid- to late summer.

E. planum (flat sea holly, blue sea holly) forms a wide clump of dark, toothed leaves with heart shaped bases. It grows 36" tall and 18" wide and has blue-tinged, silvery gray foliage and stems. The spherical, light blue flowers bloom from midsummer to fall.

E. yuccifolium (rattlesnake master) grows 3–6' tall and 24" wide, forming a rosette of long, narrow, spiny, blue-gray leaves. From mid-summer to fall it bears creamy green or pale blue flowers with gray-green bracts. (Zones 4–8)

Problems & Pests

Roots may rot if the plant is left in standing water for long periods of time. Slugs, snails and powdery mildew may be problems.

E. amethystinum

Sedum

Stonecrop

Sedum

Height: 2–24" **Spread:** 8–24" or more **Flower color:** yellow, yellow-green, white, red, pink, bronze; plant also grown for foliage **Blooms:** summer, fall
Zones: 3–10

IF YOUR FIRST EXPERIENCE WITH SEDUM WAS *S. ACRE*, A LOW-growing groundcover, you're probably still pulling it out of your garden, and you're probably still angry with yourself for having planted it in the first place. It's a runner that never pauses. Sedum is a large group of plants with literally hundreds of good choices, so it can be forgiven for the rogue child mentioned above. Some of the species are native. Sedum prefers good drainage, appreciates some afternoon shade and roots easily. It is drought tolerant and its leaves are succulent. Ants can be a problem during a prolonged drought, attacking the plants for moisture. A sedum that is over 10" tall looks best if pruned in half once during early summer.

Low-growing sedums make excellent groundcovers under trees. Their shallow roots survive well in the competition for space and moisture.

Planting

Seeding: Sow indoors in early spring. Purchased seed is often a mix of different species; you may not get what you expected, but you may be pleasantly surprised.

Planting out: Spring

Spacing: 18"

Growing

Sedum prefers **full sun** but tolerates partial shade. The soil should be of **average fertility** and very **well drained**. Divide in spring when needed. Prune back 'Autumn Joy' in May by one-half and insert pruned-off parts into soft soil, because the cuttings root quickly. Early-summer pruning of an upright species or hybrid produces a compact, bushy plant but can also delay flowering.

Tips

Low-growing sedums make wonderful groundcovers and work well in rock gardens or on rock walls. They also edge beds and borders beautifully. The taller types provide a lovely late-season display in a bed or border.

S. spathifolium

A recent change in taxonomy has seen many of the taller sedums split away from the genus *Sedum* to form their own genus, *Hylotelephium*. We include the taller sedums (*Hylotelephium*) here under the genus *Sedum* because many gardeners are unaware of the taxonomic change.

Recommended

S. acre (gold moss stonecrop) grows 2" high and spreads indefinitely. The small, yellow-green flowers are borne in summer. This plant may also be listed as Golden Carpet. (Zones 3–8)

S. **'Autumn Joy'** (*Hylotelephium* 'Autumn Joy') is a popular, upright hybrid. The flowers open pink or red

S. acre

and fade to deep bronze over a long period in late summer and fall. The plant forms a clump 24" tall with an equal spread.

S. kamtschatium forms a clump of glossy, dark green leaves and bears bright yellow flowers in late spring and early summer. It grows 4–8" tall and spreads 12–24". (Zones 3–9)

S. reflexum (*S. rupestre*; stone orpine) is a vigorous, mat-forming species that grows 4–10" tall and spreads 24" wide. It has needle-like, blue-green foliage and bears yellow flowers in early summer. (Zones 6–9)

S. sieboldii (*Hylotelephium sieboldii*) is a low-growing perennial that spreads by stout rhizomes and grows 4" tall and 8–18" wide. It has pink to reddish margined, blue-green to medium green foliage and bears clusters of pale pink flowers in fall. (Zones 3–9)

S. spurium 'Dragon's Blood' (above),
S. spectabile 'Brilliant' (below)

S. spathuifolium is a mat-forming species with pale blue-green leaves and yellow, early summer flowers. It grows 4–6" tall and spreads 24" wide. (Zones 6–9)

S. spectabile (*Hylotelephium spectabile;* showy stonecrop) is an upright species that blooms in late summer in white or various shades of pink. It forms a clump 16–24" tall and wide. **'Brilliant'** bears bright pink flowers, typically two weeks earlier than 'Autumn Joy.' **'Neon'** also has deep rosy pink flowers. (Zones 3–8)

S. spurium (two-row stonecrop) forms a mat about 4" tall and 24" wide. The mid-summer flowers are deep pink or white. Many of the cultivars have colorful foliage. **'Fulda-glut'** bears red or rose pink flowers above orange-red or maroon foliage. (Zones 3–8)

S. kamtschaticum

Problems & Pests
Slugs, snails and scale insects may cause trouble for these plants.

'Autumn Joy' brings color to the late-season garden, when few flowers are in bloom.

S. 'Autumn Joy'

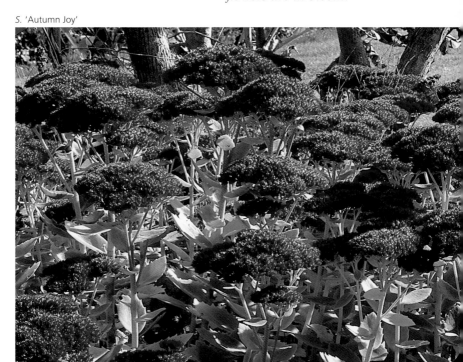

Shasta Daisy

Leucanthemum

Height: 1–4' **Spread:** 15–24" **Flower color:** white with yellow centers
Blooms: early summer to fall **Zones:** 4–9

YES, SHASTA DAISY WAS A *CHRYSANTHEMUM*, BUT IT IS NOW A *Leucanthemum*. Named for the whiteness of the snow on Mt. Shasta, this daisy looks great planted in your sunny perennial border next to the spiky flowers of foxglove, or arising from a base of coreopsis, whose yellow flowers echo the yellow centers of the shasta daisy flowers. Shasta daisy grows by my front door, backdropped by a red brick wall and color echoed with Gold Heart ivy (*Hedera helix* 'Gold Heart') climbing on the bricks. Its simple cheerfulness greets me from summer to almost frost. I became a "garden expert" the day I became unafraid to have the simplicity of a daisy in a prominent location. "Keep It Simple, Sweetie," is a good philosophy for garden design and for life.

Planting

Seeding: In spring, start seeds indoors or direct sow; soil temperature 70°–75° F

Planting out: Spring

Spacing: 24"

Growing

Shasta daisy grows well in **full sun** and **partial shade**. The soil should be **fertile, moist** and **well drained**. Pinch or trim this plant back in spring to encourage compact, bushy growth. Divide every year or two in spring to maintain plant vigor. Fall-planted Shasta daisy may not become established in time to survive winter.

Deadheading extends the bloom by several weeks.

Tips

Use this perennial in a border, where it can be grown as a single plant or massed in groups. The flowers can be cut for fresh arrangements.

Recommended

L. x *superbum* forms a large clump of dark green leaves and stems. It

L. x *superbum* (above & below)

bears white daisy flowers with yellow centers all summer, often until first frost. **'Becky'** is a vigorous, tough-as-nails plant that has strong, wind-resistant stems. It grows 36–40" tall and bears single white flowers with bright gold centers for an extended period lasting up to eight weeks. **'Thomas Killen'** ('Thomas E. Killin') is a thick-stemmed selection 30" tall and 18" wide, bearing flowers with a double row of white petals and raised golden centers. It is a great cut flower.

Problems & Pests

Occasional problems with aphids, leaf spot and leaf miners are possible.

Soapwort
Bouncing Bet
Saponaria

Height: 24–36" **Spread:** 18" **Flower color:** pink, white, red
Blooms: spring, summer, fall **Zones:** 3–8

A NATIVE EUROPEAN HERB, SOAPWORT HAS NATURALIZED WELL in the U.S. and can be found along moist streams or dry roads. Records from the 8th century BC show that soapwort was used as soap. Its leaves, when wet and crushed, emit a cleansing lather. Soapwort is a good plant for a rock garden. It is also a semi-evergreen groundcover that prefers neutral to alkaline soil but adapts to Georgia's acidic soil. Blooming from June to October, soapwort appreciates being cut back when flowering is finished, but this is not necessary. Soapwort is deer resistant due to its chemical make up. Numbing of the mouth occurs when this plant is chewed, and it is on many poisonous-plant lists.

Soapwort has been used for treating skin conditions and is probably effective because of the anti-inflammatory properties of its saponins.

Planting

Seeding: Start seeds indoors in early spring. Keep the planted seeds in a cool, dark place, about 60°–65° F, until they germinate, then move them into a lighted room.

Planting out: Spring

Spacing: 18–24"

Growing

Soapwort grows best in **full sun.** The soil should be of **average fertility, neutral to alkaline** and **well drained**. Poor soils are tolerated. Rich, fertile soil encourages lank, floppy growth.

Divide in spring at least every two to three years to maintain vigor and control spread. Cut rock soapwort back after flowering to keep it neat and compact. *S. officinalis* requires regular deadheading to keep it looking tidy after its initial bloom.

Tips

Use soapwort in borders, in rock gardens and on rock walls. Soapwort can sometimes overwhelm less vigorous plants and may self-seed in ideal conditions.

S. officinalis

Recommended

S. officinalis is an upright plant that grows 24–36" tall and spreads about 18". This plant is aggressive and can quickly spread by rhizomes. Pink, white or red flowers are borne from summer to fall. Cultivars are not as invasive as the species. **'Rosea Plena'** bears fragrant, rose pink, double flowers in early summer.

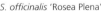

S. officinalis 'Rosea Plena'

Solomon's Seal

Polygonatum

Height: 18"–6'   **Spread:** 12–24"   **Flower color:** white with green tips
Blooms: spring, summer   **Zones:** 3–8

THE GRACEFUL, ARCHING STEMS OF SOLOMON'S SEAL DEMAND A
dark green foliage backdrop to showcase their architecture. Along the stems
are chartreuse-green leaves and white, pendent blooms dangling from the
base of each leaf node. Without a backdrop, the blooms are visually lost. If
you plant Solomon's seal in the dense shade of a hardwood forest, keeping it
away from the dry root zones, it will appear to be planted by providence.
After showing off its blooms in late spring and early summer, and its architecture all summer, Solomon's seal puts on its biggest show in fall with stunning, dirty French ochre fall color.

*The common name may
derive from the scars left on
the creeping rhizomes after the
flowering stems die off in fall.
They were thought to resemble
the six-pointed star associated
with King Solomon and
King David.*

Planting

Seeding: Sow seed in a cold frame in early spring.

Planting out: Spring or fall

Spacing: 12–24"

Growing

Solomon's seal prefers **partial to full shade**. The soil should be **fertile, humus rich, moist** and **well drained**. Propagate by division in spring once the rhizomes have begun to grow. Do not damage the young shoots. Division can also be done in fall. When division of the rhizomes is necessary, be sure that each division has at least one bud eye.

Tips

Solomon's seal seems to brighten up the dullest shade garden. It works well in mixed beds and borders but looks most at home in woodland settings or naturalized areas. It is suitable as a groundcover when mass planted.

The berries are highly **poisonous,** so do not plant Solomon's seal in areas that are easily accessible to children or pets.

Recommended

P. biflorum (*P.commutatum*; great Solomon's seal) grows 18"–6' tall and 24" wide and spreads by rhizomes. The tall, arching stems bear pendent, white flowers with green tips from late spring to mid-summer, followed by black berries.

P. odoratum (fragrant Solomon's seal) grows 24–36" tall and 12–24" wide. It has arching stems and

P. odoratum (above & below)

spreads slowly by rhizomes. Pendent, white flowers with green tips are borne along the stem in spring to early summer. Black, round berries follow the waxy flowers. **'Variegatum'** has variegated foliage. New stems are red. (Zones 4–8)

Problems and Pests

Slugs and sawfly larvae are possible problems.

Southern Shield Fern
Kunth's Maiden Fern, Southern Wood Fern
Thelypteris

Height: 12–36"   **Spread:** 2–4'   **Flower color:** plant grown for foliage
Blooms: spores produced in summer   **Zones:** 7–10

USING SOUTHERN SHIELD FERN HAS BEEN PART OF MY SECRET
arsenal of garden design tricks for years. This fern deserves to be outed. It
thrives in shade, but when planted in moist, well-drained soil, it can tolerate
the full sun of a Georgia summer. It makes a shocking addition to any sunny
perennial garden, where the unexpected, fine texture of this fern provides
good contrast with its neighbors. Be extravagant with your new trick. Plant
southern shield fern with dwarf Indian hawthorn, conifers, oakleaf hydrangea, abelia, rosemary, roses and more. A slow- to medium-spreading fern, it
is easily divided for other parts of the garden.

*The lovely, quick-spreading
southern shield fern is useful
for filling lightly shaded
locations.*

T. kunthii

Planting

Seeding: Sow freshly ripened spores in containers or in the garden.

Planting out: Spring

Spacing: 2–4'

Growing

Southern shield fern grows well in **light or partial shade**. The soil should be of **average fertility, slightly acidic, humus rich** and **moist**. Southern shield fern tolerates full sun when the soil is kept moist and grows adequately in hot, dry conditions, but it is most impressive in moist, shaded locations.

Divide the plants regularly in spring, or pull up extra plants to control the vigorous spread. Cut out crusty old foliage in spring before new growth begins.

Tips

This native fern makes an attractive addition to a shaded garden or to the edge of a woodland garden. It is best used where there is plenty of room for it to spread.

Recommended

*T. **kunthii*** (*T. normalis*) is a deciduous, perennial fern that spreads by rhizomes and spores. Where it is happy, it spreads quickly. It has gently arching, large, triangle-shaped, light green fronds and white stems. The fronds are not frost hardy.

Problems & Pests

This fern may have problems with scale insects and rust.

Spider Lily
Surprise Lily, Resurrection Lily, Naked Ladies
Lycoris

Height: 18–36"   **Spread:** 6–12"   **Flower color:** bright red, lavender-pink to rosy-pink   **Blooms:** mid- to late summer, fall   **Zones:** 5–10

IT IS TIME TO GET THIS PERENNIAL BULB, WHICH WAS COMMON to homesites circa 1960 and earlier, into new southern gardens. Spider lily's long, narrow foliage appears in spring and disappears by mid-summer. The plant is resurrected when a late summer storm provides water for the flowers, which appear from nowhere as if by magic. Arising on plain, leafless stalks (hence the common name "naked ladies"), the spider-like blooms are similar to those of *cleome*. Spider lily bulbs resent being moved, because it can prevent them from blooming for two to three years.

L. radiata

Planting

Seeding: Sow fresh, ripened seeds of *L. radiata* in containers or in the garden.

Planting out: Plant growing plants in spring; plant bulbs in fall

Spacing: 6–12"

Growing

Spider lily grows best in **full sun** or **partial shade** in **well-drained** soil of **average fertility**. Keep it moist while it is growing, and allow the soil to dry during dormancy. Spider lily tolerates drought once it is established. This plant can be divided after it goes dormant in summer. Plant the bulbs in fall, with the bulb neck at the soil surface. *L. squamigera* can be grown throughout the entire state in sun or shade. *L. radiata* appreciates a layer of mulch in zone 6.

Tips

Spider lily provides color when most of the garden has faded for the season. Use this plant in mixed beds and borders, in meadow and woodland gardens and for naturalizing.

Recommended

Spider lily is a long-lived, tough, colorful plant that can handle a range of environmental conditions from droughts to floods.

L. radiata (red spider lily, hurricane lily, red surprise lily) is a herbaceous perennial that arises from a true bulb. The bright red flowers are borne on long, naked flower stalks in early fall, seemingly out of nowhere, and they wither before the foliage appears. The long anthers (male sexual parts) give the flowers their spidery expression. The fleshy, strap-like basal foliage persists over winter and disappears by early summer. (Zones 6–10)

L. squamigera (below & right)

L. squamigera (Resurrection lily, magic lily) is similar to *L. radiata*. It is a bulbous perennial that produces gray-green, strap-shaped foliage in spring, which dies to the ground by early summer before the flowers emerge. In mid- to late summer it bears clusters of sterile, funnel-shaped, fragrant, pale lavender pink to rosy pink flowers. This species can only be propagated by division.

Problems & Pests

Spider lily rarely suffers any pest problems.

Spider lily makes a great cut flower, lasting for several days in an arrangement or bouquet.

Spiderwort

Tradescantia

Height: 6–24" **Spread:** 12–30" **Flower color:** purple, blue, pink, red, white
Blooms: early summer **Zones:** 3–11

WHEN SPIDERWORT FOLIAGE FIRST ARISES IN FEBRUARY, IT LOOKS
like a daylily, but by the end of March, its thick, fleshy stalks and wide, grass-like
leaves let you know this isn't a daylily. When I first planted spiderwort in my
garden, it thrived in full sun. The nearby trees have since matured, and now
my spiderwort thrives in full shade. I prefer the white-flowered plants, which I
have along a woodland path in my garden. Flowers with three sepals and three
petals, whose odd number attracts the eye, bloom heaviest at the beginning of
summer and later in fall. Shear the foliage back to 6–10" after the first bloom
for a second flush of pretty leaves and flowers. Combine spiderwort with hellebores so you won't miss them while they're dormant in winter.

T. x andersoniana 'Concord Grape'

Planting

Seeding: Not recommended

Planting out: Spring or fall

Spacing: 18–24"

Growing

Spiderwort grows equally well in **full sun** or **partial shade,** but it may appreciate some shade from the hot afternoon sun. The soil should be of **average fertility, humus rich** and **moist** but not soaked. If grown in overly rich soils with plentiful water, spiderwort can become weedy and fall open in the center.

To produce a fresh flush of foliage and possibly a second round of blooms late in the season, cut spiderwort back after flowering has ceased and the leaves have faded. Divide in spring or fall every four or so years.

Tips

Spiderwort is attractive in a lightly shaded wood-land or natural garden, but it also looks good in beds and borders. Once established, spiderwort grows almost anywhere. White-flowered varieties planted along a shady woodland path light up a garden.

One of the parent plants of these hybrids, T. virginiana, *is native to most of the eastern U.S.*

Recommended

T. pallida (purple heart) is a sprawling, quickly spreading groundcover that roots where the stem nodes touch the ground. It grows 6–12" tall and 12–18" wide and has attractive, smooth, purple foliage with bright purple-pink undersides. Pale pink to lavender flowers bloom in early summer. A hard frost will kill this plant to the ground, but it will regenerate from its roots. (Zones 7b–11)

T. x andersoniana

T*. x *andersoniana (Andersoniana Hybrids) forms a large clump of grassy foliage 16–24" tall and 20–30" wide. Clusters of purple, blue, pink, red or white flowers are produced on long stems in early summer. Many cultivars are available. (Zones 3–9)

Problems & Pests

Problems are rarely severe enough to warrant action. Aphids, spider mites, caterpillars, rot and leaf spot may afflict plants from time to time.

The name "spiderwort" apparently arose because the sticky sap of these plants can be drawn out from a broken stem in a cobweb-like strand.

T. pallida (below), *T.* x *andersoniana* 'I.C. Wegvelin' (above)

Stokes' Aster

Stokesia

Height: 12–24"   **Spread:** 12–18"   **Flower color:** purple, blue, white, pink, yellow   **Blooms:** mid-summer to early fall   **Zones:** 5–9

STOKES' ASTER IS A NATIVE WILDFLOWER THAT CAN BE FOUND growing in moist pinewoods or sunny meadows. When growing in your garden, it is most desirous of full to partial shade and excellent drainage. The blooms arise on somewhat lax stems, appearing to take a drunken delight in simply blooming. Sometimes I think Stokes' aster, by blooming with such intensity, is trying to blow itself up into a confetti of petals. My first Stokes' aster died because I didn't follow the command for good drainage. Stokes' aster is commonly found at nurseries with blue or white blooms. It is also worth your while to seek out the yellow-flowered 'Mary Gregory.'

Stokes' aster is named after English botanist and physician Dr. Jonathon Stokes (1755–1831).

Planting

Seeding: Start seeds indoors or out in fall; soil temperature 70°–75° F

Planting out: Spring

Spacing: 12"

Growing

Stokes' aster grows best in **full sun**. The soil should be **average to fertile, light, moist** and **well drained**. This plant dislikes waterlogged and poorly drained soils, particularly in winter when root rot can quickly develop. Those who garden in clay might consider planting this species in raised beds filled with amended soil. Provide a good winter mulch to protect the roots from freeze-and-thaw cycles. Divide in spring.

Deadheading extends the blooming period to up to 12 weeks.

Tips

Stokes' aster can be grouped in borders and adds some welcome blue to the garden late in the season when yellows, oranges and golds seem to dominate.

S. laevis (above & below)

Recommended

S. laevis forms a basal rosette of bright green, narrow, mostly evergreen foliage. The midvein of each leaf is a distinctive, pale green. The plant blooms from mid-summer to early fall. **'Blue Danube'** bears large, lavender to lavender blue flowers. **'Klaus Jelitto'** has dark green foliage and bears lavender to powder blue flowers that are larger than those of the species. **'Mary Gregory'** has creamy yellow flowers.

Problems & Pests

Leaf spot and caterpillars can cause problems. Avoid very wet and heavy soils to prevent root rot.

Thyme
Thymus

Height: 2–12"   **Spread:** 4–16"   **Flower color:** purple, pink, white; plant grown mainly for foliage   **Blooms:** late spring, summer   **Zones:** 4–8

SMOOTH OR FUZZY EVERGREEN LEAVES THAT ARE OFTEN variegated and range from green or blue to yellow or ivory keep thyme useful in sunny gardens. Thyme is great to use between stepping stones, in herb gardens, in container gardens or as a groundcover. Cut back yearly so the plants don't become leggy. With good drainage and amended soil, your thyme will grow for many years without much effort on your part. Amend the soil with rotted organic material, such as compost, and lime. Thyme, like most herbs, does not like acidic soils. Along with rosemary, it is a good evergreen anchor in perennial and herb gardens. Poaching a chicken with your garden thyme will make you think the chicken was raised eating this herb.

Planting

Seeding: Many popular hybrids, particularly those with variegated leaves, cannot be grown from seed. Common thyme and mother of thyme can be started from seed. Start indoors in early spring.

Planting out: Spring

Spacing: 16–20"

Growing

Thyme prefers **full sun**. The soil should be **neutral to alkaline** and of **poor to average fertility**. Very **good drainage** is essential. Work some leaf mold into the soil to improve structure and drainage. Divide thyme in spring.

It is easy to propagate thyme cultivars that cannot be started from seed. As the plant grows outward, the branches touch the ground and send out new roots. These rooted stems can be removed and grown in pots to be planted out the following spring. Unrooted stem cuttings can be taken in early spring, before flowering.

T. x *citriodorus* 'Argenteus'

Tips

Thyme works well in a sunny, dry location at the front of a border, between or beside paving stones, in a rock garden, on a rock wall or in a container. Creeping thyme makes a good lawn substitute for areas with reduced foot traffic. Thyme helps keep the herb garden evergreen.

T. praecox subsp. *arcticus* 'Lanuginosis'

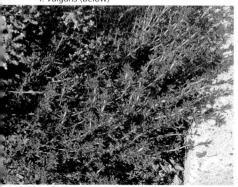

T. praecox subsp. *arcticus* (above)
T. vulgaris (below)

Once the plant has finished flowering, it is a good idea to shear it back by about half to encourage new growth and to prevent the plant from becoming too woody.

Recommended

T. x *citriodorus* (lemon-scented thyme) forms a mound 12" tall and 10" wide. The dark green foliage smells of lemon, and the flowers are pale pink. The cultivars are more ornamental. **'Argenteus'** has silver-edged leaves. **'Aureus'** has leaves variegated with golden yellow. **'Golden King'** has yellow-margined leaves.

T. praecox subsp. *arcticus* (*T. serpyllum*; mother of thyme, creeping thyme, wild thyme) is a popular, low-growing species. It usually grows about 5" tall and spreads 12" or more. The flowers are purple. There are many cultivars available. **'Albus'** (white creeping thyme) bears white flowers. **'Elfin'** forms tiny, dense mounds of foliage, but it rarely flowers. It grows up to 2–3" tall and spreads 4". **'Lanuginosis'** (woolly thyme) is a mat-forming plant up to 3" high and 8–10" in spread, with fuzzy, gray-green leaves. It bears

T. x *citriodorus* 'Golden King' (below)

pink or purplish flowers in summer. **'Minimus'** grows 2" high and 4" wide. **'Snowdrift'** has white flowers.

T. vulgaris (common thyme) forms a bushy mound of dark green leaves with purple, pink or white flowers. It usually grows about 12" tall and spreads about 16". **'Silver Posie'** is a good cultivar with pale pink flowers and silver-edged leaves.

Problems & Pests

Thyme rarely has problems unless it is subjected to poor drainage or over-head irrigation. Seedlings may suffer damping off, and older plants may get gray mold or root rot. Good circulation and adequate drainage are good ways to avoid these problems.

In the Middle Ages, it was believed that drinking a thyme infusion would enable one to see fairies.

T. praecox subsp. *arcticus* 'Purple Carpet' (above), *T. praecox* subsp. *arcticus* (below)

Toad-Lily

Japanese Toad Lily
Tricyrtis

Height: 24–36"   **Spread:** 12–24"   **Flower color:** white, blue, purple, maroon, bicolored, with or without spots   **Blooms:** late summer and fall   **Zones:** 4–9

PLANT THESE SHADE LOVERS NEAR THE EDGE OF YOUR WOODLAND walk, at the base of a low window or at your doorway. Toad-lily blooms are exotically shaped, similar to small orchids. Their flower color patterns are something that William Morris, a well-educated and philosophical textile designer, might have designed after taking the grand tour of Europe in 1884. The small flowers bloom in fall and run the length of the 36" long, arching, leafy stems. Most of the foliage I see on toad-lilies looks a bit rough, but who cares when the plants have such incredible blooms. The species and cultivars hybridize easily, producing original progeny.

Planting
Seeding: Sow ripe seeds indoors or in a cold frame in early spring.

Planting out: Spring, summer

Spacing: 12–24"

Toad-lilies are sometimes mistaken for orchids. They are actually part of the lily family, hence the common name; however, they do look very similar to exotic orchids.

Growing

Toad-lilies grow well in **partial, light** or **full shade**. The soil should be **fertile, humus rich, moist** and **well drained**. Toad-lilies appreciate a sheltered site, especially in mountain areas. Divide in early spring when they are dormant.

Toad-lily foliage may suffer tip burn if the plants are under stress or if they get too hot, but it won't harm the plants.

Tips

These diminutive plants are well suited to woodland gardens and shaded borders. If you have a shaded rock garden, patio or pond, toad-lilies make good additions to locations where you can approach them for a good look at their peculiar, spotted, almost orchid-like flowers. They can also be grown in containers when the perfect location just simply cannot be met.

Recommended

T. hirta forms a clump of arching stems bearing light green leaves. In

R. hirta 'Guilty Pleasure'

late summer and fall it bears star-shaped, white flowers with purple to maroon spots singly or in clusters at the stem tips. Many wonderful cultivars are available. **'Miyazaki'** produces white blooms with purple spots. **'Variegata'** bears similar flowers; however, the leaves are edged in creamy white.

Problems & Pests

Slugs and snails are the only problems toad-lilies experience.

T. hirta

Turtlehead

Chelone

Height: 2–4'   **Spread:** 18–30"   **Flower color:** white tinged with pink to dark pink   **Blooms:** late summer and fall   **Zones:** 3–8

BEACONS OF PINK IN SUMMER'S SHADY, MOIST AREAS, turtleheads begin blooming in mid-summer and continue for several weeks. They do their best in shade, so if you only have a sunny spot, it must be a boggy location. Turtleheads are native plants, and like most plants commonly found along streams, they are deer resistant. They are also attractive to butterflies and make good cut flowers. They spread by thickened, creeping roots. The blossoms do look like turtleheads, or if you can't imagine that, think of a snapdragon blossom. Prune back new growth in spring for bushier plants with more blooms.

When used as cut flowers, turtlehead blooms last 8–10 days.

Planting

Seeding: Indoors in January, outdoors in late spring; soil temperature 59°–68° F

Planting out: Spring

Spacing: 18"

Growing

Turtleheads grow best in **partial shade** or **full sun**. The soil should be **fertile, humus rich, moist** and **well drained**, but these plant tolerate clay soil and boggy conditions. Plants may become weak and floppy in too shaded a spot, so pinch tips in spring to encourage bushy growth.

C. lyonii (above & below)

Divide plants in spring or fall. They can be propagated from stem cuttings taken in early summer.

Tips

Turtleheads can be used in a pondside or streamside planting. They also do well in a bog garden or in a moist part of the garden where plants requiring better drainage won't grow. Along a moist, shady path, the pink blossoms are an exclamation point.

Recommended

C. glabra (*C. obliqua* 'Alba') is an upright plant that forms a dense mound of foliage and bears white flowers tinged with light pink.

C. lyonii (pink turtlehead) is an erect plant with square stems and dark pink flowers. (Zones 3–7)

Problems and Pests

Rare problems with powdery mildew, rust and fungal leaf spot can occur.

Verbena

Verbena

Height: 8"–6'   **Spread:** 12–36" or wider   **Flower color:** lavender blue, lilac, purple, pink, blue, white, red, magenta   **Blooms:** early summer to frost **Zones:** 6–10

"I THOUGHT YOU WERE MY FRIEND," BEGAN A PHONE conversation I had with the culprit who gave me *V. rigida*. I discovered I had the wild child of the genus. This species is pretty and spreading and loves sun and good drainage, similar to most verbenas. However, choose a named cultivar instead of the species—the cultivars have better manners. *V. bonariensis* has basal foliage, which is as rough as a kitten's tongue, and tall airy stems with multiple branches topped by purple flowers that attract hungry butterflies. It is good for self-seeding in interesting places. *V. canadensis* 'Homestead Purple' is a low-growing, evergreen groundcover that blooms from late spring to frost and looks great at the front of borders or in containers. You'll definitely want more than one type of verbena.

Planting

Seeding: Direct sow in late summer or fall or indoors in mid-winter.

Planting out: Spring or fall

Spacing: 12–36"

Growing

Verbena grows best in **full sun**. The soil should be of average **fertility, moisture holding** and very **well drained**. *V. bonariensis* and *V. rigida* tolerate drought when established. Cut or pinch *V. bonariensis* and *V. rigida* back by one-half in mid-summer to encourage bushy growth and a lot of fall blooms. Divide in spring or fall every three years or so.

Chill seeds for one week before sowing. Moisten the soil before sowing seeds. Do not cover the seeds with soil. Place the entire seed tray or pot in darkness, and water only if the soil becomes very dry. Once the seeds germinate, move them into the light.

Tips

Upright species may be used at the front, middle or back of beds and borders and to add height to containers. *V. bonariensis* and *V. rigida* are somewhat wispy plants when in flower and look best when mass planted. Use short verbenas on rock walls and in beds, borders, rock gardens, containers, hanging baskets and window boxes. They make good substitutes for ivy-leaved geranium where the sun is hot and where a roof overhang keeps the mildew-prone verbenas dry. Verbenas are excellent for filling in the spaces between other plants.

V. bonariensis

Recommended

V. bonariensis (tall verbena, Brazilian vervain, purpletop verbena, purpletop vervain) forms a low clump of foliage from which tall, stiff, flower-bearing stems emerge. The small, purple flowers are held in clusters at the tops of the long stems in early to late summer. The plant grows 3–6' tall but spreads only 12–24". Butterflies love tall verbena, and it self-seeds where it is happy. The seedlings are easy to keep under control. (Zones 6–9)

V. canadensis (clump verbena, rose vervain) is a low-growing, spreading plant native to south-central and southeastern North America. It grows 12–18" tall and spreads up to 36". It bears clusters of pink flowers

from mid-summer to fall. The following are excellent garden hybrids that have *V. canadensis* as one of the parents. **'Homestead Purple'** is a very popular and common cultivar. It bears dark purple flowers for an extended period and is mildew resistant. **'Taylortown Red'** bears a plethora of bright red flowers and is hardy to zone 6. (Zones 7–10)

V. rigida (rough verbena, vervain, tuberous vervain) is an erect to spreading perennial that arises from thickened tubers and has rough-textured, hairy, toothed, medium green foliage. It grows 18–24" tall and 12–36" wide and bears dense clusters of fragrant, bright purple to magenta flowers from early summer to frost. It tolerates heat and humidity and looks like a small version of

V. canadensis (above), *V. canadensis* 'Greystone Daphne' (below)

V. bonariensis. It also self-seeds and attracts butterflies. (Zones 7–10)

V. *tenuisecta* (moss verbena) can be low growing or somewhat upright. It grows 8–12" tall and spreads 36" or more. The stems usually sprawl along the ground. The flowers come in shades of lavender blue, lilac, purple, blue or white and bloom from early summer to frost. (Zones 7–10)

Problems & Pests

Aphids, whiteflies, slugs and snails may be troublesome. Good air circulation around this plant prevents fungal problems. Tall verbena is prone to powdery mildew in humid summers. Overall health and flowering are usually not affected, but severe outbreaks can really weaken a plant.

Verbena needs lots of sunlight to flower abundantly and stay free of fungal disease.

V. *bonariensis* (above)
V. *tenuisecta* (below)

Veronica
Speedwell, Spike Speedwell
Veronica

Height: 1–4' **Spread:** 18–24" **Flower color:** blue violet, blue, purple, red
Blooms: summer **Zones:** 3–8

CONE SHAPES IN A GARDEN ATTRACT THE EYE, AND VERONICA'S blooms are narrow, cone-shaped spikes. Grow this plant next to the flat-topped flower clusters of yarrow or the disc-shaped blooms of purple cone-flower to highlight Veronica's flower form. Prune off the old foliage when new growth has appeared at the plant base in early spring. Deadheading encourages a good second flush of flowers. Veronica appreciates an amended, enriched soil with good drainage and full sun. 'Sunny Border Blue' should be one of the first Veronicas, or perennials, you plant. It is one of the best spiky flowers among perennials.

Planting

Seeding: Not recommended; seedlings do not always come true to type. Seeds germinate quickly when started indoors in early spring.

Planting out: Spring

Spacing: 18"

Growing

Veronica prefers **full sun** but tolerates partial shade. The soil should be of **average fertility, moist** and **well drained**. Lack of sun and excessive moisture and nitrogen may be partly to blame for the sloppy habits of some plants. Frequent dividing ensures strong, vigorous growth and decreases the chances of flopping. Divide in fall or spring every two to three years.

When the spikes begin to fade, remove the entire spike where it sprouted from the plant to encourage rapid re-blooming. For a tidier plant, shear back to 6" in June.

Tips

Veronica is a beautiful, easy-to-grow plant for dotting through the garden as an accent or for edging. It is useful in a rock garden and works well en masse in a bed or border.

Recommended

V. spicata (spike speedwell) is a low, mounding plant with stems that flop over when they get too tall. It grows 12–24" tall, spreads 18" and bears spikes of blue to purple flowers in summer. Many cultivars of different colors and sizes are available, some up to 4' tall. **'Red Fox'**

V. spicata 'Red Fox'

has dark red-pink flowers. **'Sunny Border Blue'** grows 15–20" tall and has bright blue flowers.

Problems & Pests

Problems with scale insects are possible, as are fungal problems such as downy and powdery mildew, rust, leaf smut and root rot.

V. spicata 'Sunny Border Blue'

Virginia Bluebells
Virginia Cowslip
Mertensia

Height: 12–24" **Spread:** 10–18" **Flower color:** blue, purple-blue, pink
Blooms: mid- and late spring   Hardiness: zones 3–8

SOME PERENNIALS ARE PERSONAL DELIGHTS IN A GARDEN BECAUSE their subtle blooms are not shouting to be seen. Instead, they are our private dancers. Virginia bluebells are so subtle you'll probably forget you have them until their foliage arises in spring. The foliage appears first, followed by pink buds that open to blue flowers. After the blooms disappear, the foliage begins to yellow and is gone by mid-summer. The disappearing foliage is a normal attribute and not something to worry about. Plant evergreen hellebores nearby so the space isn't empty when Virginia bluebells disappear, and use a stone marked with 'Virginia Bluebells' in grease pencil (grease pencil writing is very weather proof) to help mark the spot.

Planting

Seeding: Start in a cold frame in fall.

Planting out: Spring or fall.

Spacing: 12–18"

Growing

Virginia bluebells grow best in **light to partial shade** with **shelter** from the hot afternoon sun. Soil should be of **average fertility, humus rich, moist** and **well drained**. Plants self-seed in good growing conditions. Virginia bluebells go dormant in mid-summer and can be divided at that time or in spring, just as new growth begins. They can be propagated by root cuttings in late fall to early winter.

Tips

Include Virginia bluebells in a shaded border or moist woodland garden. Make sure to plant them with plants that cover the bare spaces left when Virginia bluebells go dormant by mid-summer.

M. virginica (above & below)

Recommended

M. virginica (*M. pulmonarioides*) grows 12–24" tall and spreads 10–18", forming an upright clump with light green to blue-green leaves. It bears clusters of blue or purple-blue flowers that open from pink buds in late winter to early spring. **'Rosea'** produces rose-pink flowers.

Problems & Pests

Virginia bluebells have infrequent problems when grown in good conditions. Plants may experience slugs, snails, powdery mildew and rust.

Wild Ginger

Asarum

Height: 3–6" **Spread:** 12–24" or more **Flower color:** dark purple, burgundy, green; inconspicuous; plant grown for foliage **Blooms:** late spring to early summer **Zones:** 2–9

TAXONOMISTS ARE AT WORK AGAIN, THIS TIME WITH THE GENUS *Asarum*. The evergreen wild gingers are being split into a new genus, *Hexastylis*, while the deciduous wild gingers remain as *Asarum*. If you have a naturally wooded backyard, you probably have at least one of these wild gingers already growing. Good foliage growth in dense shade and deer resistance are their best attributes. Their flowers, sometimes called 'little brown jugs,' are hard to find because they are carried under the leaves and blend with leaf litter.

A. canadense

Planting

Seeding: Not recommended.

Planting out: Spring or fall

Spacing: 12"

Growing

Wild gingers need **full or partial shade** and **moist, humus rich** soil to grow and spread their best. All *Asarum* species prefer **acidic** soils, but *A. canadense* tolerates alkaline conditions. Wild gingers tolerate dry conditions for a while in good shade, but prolonged drought eventually causes the plants to wilt and die back.

Division is not necessary, except to propagate more plants. Cut the thick, fleshy rhizomes into sections with at least one pair of leaves growing from them. Be careful not to damage the tiny, thread-like roots that grow from the rhizome below the point where the leaves attach.

Wild ginger flowers have a unique shape, an unusual brown-maroon color and an unpleasant, slightly fetid odor that attracts their beetle pollinators.

A. shuttleworthii 'Callaway'

The heart-shaped leaves can be tucked into simple flower arrangements

A. canadense

Tips

Wild gingers make beautiful ground-covers for woodland sites. They can also be used in shady rock gardens and borders. Wild gingers are easy to remove from places where they aren't welcome.

Recommended

A. canadense (Canada wild ginger) is a low, spreading, deciduous perennial that grows 3–6" tall and 12" or more wide. It has slightly hairy, heart-shaped, light green leaves. (Zones 2–8)

A. shuttleworthii (Shuttleworth ginger) is a native, prostrate, evergreen, mat-forming perennial that grows 3–6" tall and 12" or more wide. It has heart-shaped, shiny, dark green foliage with silver marbling and unusual burgundy or green flowers.

'**Callaway**' is a robust selection with heavily silver-marbled foliage. (Zones 6–9)

A. splendens (Chinese ginger) forms a dense, spreading mass of evergreen, arrow-shaped, dark green, silver-mottled leaves and bears large, very dark purple flowers. It grows about 6" tall and spreads 24" or more. (Zones 5–9)

Problems & Pests

These plants rarely suffer attack by pests or diseases.

*A. shuttleworthii '**Callaway**' was discovered at Callaway Gardens in Pine Mountain, north of Columbus. Make sure you spend some time visiting the wonderful gardens we have in our state.*

Mixed *asarum* and *hosta* species (above)
A. splendens (below)

Yarrow

Achillea

Height: 7"–4'   **Spread:** 12–36"   **Flower color:** white, off-white, yellow, red, pink, purple   **Blooms:** early summer to fall   **Zones:** 3–9

PLANT YARROWS FOR THEIR FLAT-TOPPED FLOWER CLUSTERS, which provide great contrast with the disc and spike shapes of your other sun-loving perennnials. The flowers are also attractive to butterflies. Not lovers of rich soils, fertilizer or water, yarrows reward you for benign neglect. Most have fern-like foliage with hints of gray and a fragrance that is unattractive to deer. *A.* 'Coronation Gold' is one of the best and prettiest yarrows in the garden. It is a good cut flower and also dries beautifully. This is a great plant to have if you're on a budget, because after five years your clump can be divided into 20 to 30 new plants.

Planting

Seeding: Direct sow in spring; don't cover the seeds because they need light to germinate.

Planting out: Spring

Spacing: 12–24"

Growing

Grow yarrows in **full sun** in **average, well-drained** soil—avoid heavy clay. These plants tolerate drought and poor soil, and they abide, but do not thrive in, heavy, wet soil or very humid conditions. Excessively rich soil or too much nitrogen results in weak, floppy growth.

A. filipendulina and *A. millefolium* often need staking. Deadhead and divide every two or three years in spring to keep these cultivars vibrant, the flowerheads upright and the foliage from becoming a tangled mass. Once the flowerheads begin to fade, cut them back to the lateral buds. Basal foliage should be left in place over winter and tidied up in spring.

A. filipendulina 'Gold Plate'

Tips

Yarrows are informal plants and grow best in cottage gardens, wildflower gardens and mixed borders. They thrive in hot, dry locations where nothing else grows.

Yarrows make excellent groundcovers, despite being quite tall. They send up shoots and flowers from a low basal point and may be mowed periodically without excessive damage to the plant. Mower blades should be kept at least 4" high. Do not mow more often than once a month, or you will have short yarrows with no flowers!

A. millefolium 'Summer Pastels'

Yarrows can be used in fresh or dried arrangements. Cut flowerheads only after pollen is visible, or they die very quickly.

Recommended

A. **'Coronation Gold'** is an *A. filipendulina* hybrid that has clusters of bright golden yellow flowers 3–4" in diameter. Plants grow 24–36" tall and wide.

A. filipendulina (fern-leaf yarrow) has yellow flowers and grows up to 4' tall. It has been used to develop several hybrids and cultivars that come in various heights with flowers in shades of yellow. **'Gold Plate'** has flowerheads up to 6" across. **'Parker's Variety'** is an old variety bearing large, flat flower clusters.

A. millefolium (common yarrow) forms a mat of dark green foliage 12–24" tall. Its off-white, disk-shaped flowerheads appear from late June until September. Because it is quite aggressive, the species is almost

A. millefolium cultivar

The ancient Druids used yarrows to divine seasonal weather, and the ancient Chinese used the stems to foretell the future.

A. filipendulina 'Gold Plate'

never grown in favor of the many cultivars that have been developed. **'Cerise Queen'** has pinkish red flowers. **'Fire King'** has bright pink to cherry red flowers. **'Fireland'** bears red flowers with yellow centers; the flowers mature to coppery salmon and then soft gold. **'Summer Pastels'** has flowers of many colors, including white, yellow, pink and purple. This cultivar tolerates heat and drought very well and has fade-resistant flowers. **'Terra Cotta'** bears flowers that open orangy pink and mature to rusty orange.

A. **'Moonshine'** is another *A. filipendulina* hybrid that bears clusters of lemon yellow blooms 2–3" wide that are held above highly dissected, grayish green foliage. The plants grow 12–24" tall and wide.

Problems & Pests

Rare problems with powdery mildew and stem rot are possible.

A. millefolium 'Cerise Queen'

Yarrows have blood-coagulating properties that were recognized by the ancient Greeks. Achillea is named after the legendary Achilles because during the battle of Troy he is said to have treated his warriors' wounds with this herb.

A. millefolium

Height Legend: Low: < 12"-•-Medium: 12–24"-•-Tall: > 24"

SPECIES by Common Name	White	Pink	Red	Orange	Yellow/Tan	Blue	Purple	Foliage	Spring	Summer	Fall	Winter	Low	Medium	Tall
Artemesia								•		•	•		•	•	•
Aster		•				•	•			•	•		•	•	•
Astilbe	•	•					•		•	•				•	•
Autumn Fern			•					•		•				•	•
Barrenwort	•	•	•		•		•		•				•		
Beebalm														•	•
Black-eyed Susan				•	•					•	•			•	•
Blackberry Lily				•	•					•				•	•
Blanket Flower				•	•					•	•			•	•
Blazing Star	•	•				•	•			•	•				•
Bleeding Heart	•	•	•				•		•	•				•	•
Bloodroot	•								•			•	•		
Blue Lyme Grass					•			•		•					•
Blue Star	•					•			•					•	•
Boltonia	•	•					•			•	•				•
Butterfly Weed	•	•	•	•	•		•			•				•	•
Candytuft	•								•				•		
Canna Lily	•	•	•	•	•					•	•			•	•
Cardinal Flower	•		•			•	•			•	•				•
Carolina Lupine					•				•						•
Christmas Fern					•			•		•				•	
Christmas Rose	•	•			•		•		•			•		•	•
Chrysanthemum	•	•	•	•	•		•			•	•			•	•
Cinnamon Fern								•		•					•
Columbine	•	•	•		•	•	•		•	•			•	•	•
Coral Bells	•	•	•						•	•				•	•
Coreopsis		•		•	•					•				•	•
Crocosmia			•	•	•					•				•	•
Daffodil	•	•		•	•				•				•	•	
Daylily		•	•	•	•		•			•				•	•
Dwarf Plumbago						•				•	•		•		

| LIGHT | | | | SOIL CONDITIONS | | | | | | | | SPECIES by Common Name |
Sun	Part Shade	Light Shade	Shade	Moist	Well Drained	DT*	Fertile	Average	Poor	USDA Zones	Page Number	
•					•		•	•		3–8	74	Artemisia
•	•	•	•		•	•		•	•	3–10	78	Aster
	•	•			•	•		•		3–9	82	Astilbe
	•				•	•		•		5–9	86	Autumn Fern
	•	•			•			•		4–8	88	Barrenwort
•	•	•			•	•			•	3–9	90	Beebalm
•						•			•	3–9	94	Black-eyed Susan
•	•				•	•			•	5–9	96	Blackberry Lily
•						•	•	•	•	3–9	98	Blanket Flower
•					•	•			•	3–9	100	Blazing Star
		•			•	•		•	•	3–9	102	Bleeding Heart
	•	•	•		•	•		•		3–9	106	Bloodroot
•					•	•			•	4–10	108	Blue Lyme Grass
•	•	•			•	•			•	3–9	110	Blue Star
•					•	•			•	4–9	114	Boltonia
•					•	•	•	•		3–9	116	Butterfly Weed
•					•	•		•	•	3–9	118	Candytuft
•					•	•		•		8–11	120	Canna Lily
	•	•	•		•			•		3–9	124	Cardinal Flower
•	•	•				•	•	•		5–9	128	Carolina Lupine
	•	•	•		•			•	•	3–9	130	Christmas Fern
		•	•			•		•		4–9	132	Christmas Rose
•					•	•			•	4–9	136	Chrysanthemum
	•	•			•			•		3–9	138	Cinnamon Fern
	•	•			•	•		•		3–8	140	Columbine
	•	•			•	•		•	•	3–9	144	Coral Bells
•	•					•			•	3–9	148	Coreopsis
•					•	•			•	5–9	150	Crocosmia
•		•				•		•	•	3–8	152	Daffodil
•					•	•		•		2–9	154	Daylily
•					•	•	•	•	•	5-9	158	Dwarf Plumbago

*Drought Tolerant

Height Legend: Low: < 12"-•-Medium: 12–24"-•-Tall: > 24"

SPECIES by Common Name	White	Pink	Red	Orange	Yellow/Tan	Blue	Purple	Foliage	Spring	Summer	Fall	Winter	Low	Medium	Tall
Eulalia Grass		•	•		•			•		•	•				•
Evening Primrose	•	•			•					•	•		•	•	
False Indigo	•						•		•	•					•
False Sunflower				•	•					•	•				•
Feather Reed Grass		•	•		•		•			•	•				•
Foamflower	•	•							•	•			•		
Foxglove	•	•	•		•		•		•	•					•
Gaura	•	•							•	•	•				•
Golden Hakone Grass								•					•	•	
Goldenrod					•					•	•				•
Green and Gold					•				•				•		
Hardy Ageratum						•	•			•	•				
Hardy Begonia	•	•							•	•	•			•	
Hardy Geranium	•	•							•	•	•		•	•	
Hardy Hibiscus	•	•	•							•	•			•	•
Hosta	•					•	•	•		•	•		•	•	•
Iris	•	•			•	•	•		•	•			•	•	•
Japanese Anemone	•	•	•				•		•	•	•			•	•
Japanese Painted Fern *Lady Fern								•		•				•	
Kalimeris	•								•	•	•			•	
Lily	•	•	•	•	•		•			•					•
Meadow-rue	•						•			•					•
Mondo Grass	•						•			•			•		
Purple Muhly Grass	•	•					•			•	•				•
Nothern Maidenhair Fern								•		•				•	
Pampas Grass	•				•			•		•					•
Patrinia	•				•					•	•			•	•
Peacock Moss								•		•			•		
Penstemon	•	•	•				•		•	•	•			•	•
Perennial Sunflower					•					•	•				•

| LIGHT | | | | SOIL CONDITIONS | | | | | | | | SPECIES |
Sun	Part Shade	Light Shade	Shade	Moist	Well Drained	DT*	Fertile	Average	Poor	USDA Zones	Page Number	by Common Name
•				•	•		•			5–9	160	Eulalia Grass
•					•			•	•	3–10	164	Evening Primrose
•					•			•	•	3–9	166	False Indigo
•				•	•	•	•	•		2–9	168	False Sunflower
•				•	•		•			4–9	170	Feather Reed Grass
	•	•	•	•			•			3-8	172	Foamflower
	•	•		•			•			3–8	174	Foxglove
•				•	•	•	•			5–8	178	Gaura
	•	•		•	•			•		5–9	180	Golden Hakone Grass
•					•			•	•	3–8	182	Goldenrod
	•	•	•	•	•			•		5–9	184	Green and Gold
•	•			•			•			6–10	186	Hardy Ageratum
	•	•	•		•		•			6–9	188	Hardy Begonia
•	•	•			•	•		•		3–8	190	Hardy Geranium
•				•	•		•			5–10	192	Hardy Hibiscus
	•	•		•	•		•			3–8	196	Hosta
•	•	•		•	•		•	•		3–8	202	Iris
	•	•		•	•		•			3–9	206	Japanese Anemone
	•	•	•	•				•		4–8	210	Japanese Painted Fern *Lady Fern
•	•			•	•			•		4–9	214	Kalimeris
•				•	•		•			2–9	216	Lily
	•	•		•	•			•	•	3–8	220	Meadow-rue
	•	•	•	•	•			•	•	7–10	222	Mondo Grass
•				•	•	•		•		5–10	224	Muhly Grass
	•	•	•	•	•		•			3–8	226	Northern Maidenhair Fern
•					•		•			7–10	228	Pampas Grass
•	•			•	•		•	•		5–8	230	Patrinia
	•	•		•	•		•	•		6-11	232	Peacock Moss
•					•	•	•	•		3–9	234	Penstemon
•				•	•			•		4–9	238	Perennial Sunflower

*Drought Tolerant

Height Legend: Low: < 12"-•-Medium: 12–24"-•-Tall: > 24"

SPECIES by Common Name	White	Pink	Red	Orange	Yellow/Tan	Blue	Purple	Foliage	Spring	Summer	Fall	Winter	Low	Medium	Tall
Phlox	•	•	•				•		•	•	•		•	•	•
Pinks	•	•	•				•		•	•			•	•	
Pitcher Plant		•	•		•		•		•				•	•	•
Plume Poppy	•									•					•
Purple Coneflower	•	•	•				•			•	•			•	•
Purple Loosestrife		•					•			•	•				•
Ravenna Grass		•					•			•	•				•
Red-hot Poker	•		•	•	•					•	•			•	•
Ribbon Grass	•	•						•		•					•
Rosemary		•				•						•	•		•
Russian Sage						•	•			•	•				•
Salvia	•	•	•	•		•	•			•	•			•	•
Sea Holly	•					•	•			•	•				•
Sedum	•	•	•		•			•		•	•		•	•	
Shasta Daisy	•									•	•			•	•
Soapwort	•	•	•						•	•	•				•
Solomon's Seal	•								•	•				•	•
Southern Shield Fern								•		•				•	•
Spider Lily			•	•			•			•	•			•	•
Spiderwort	•	•	•			•	•			•			•	•	
Stoke's Aster	•	•			•	•	•			•	•			•	
Thyme	•	•	•				•	•	•	•			•		
Toad-Lily	•					•	•			•	•				•
Turtlehead	•	•								•	•				•
Verbena	•	•	•			•	•			•	•		•	•	•
Veronica			•			•	•			•				•	•
Virginia Bluebells		•				•	•		•			•		•	
Wild Ginger							•	•	•	•			•		
Yarrow	•	•	•		•		•			•	•		•	•	•

LIGHT				Moist	Well Drained	DT*	Fertile	Average	Poor	USDA Zones	Page Number	SPECIES by Common Name
Sun	Part Shade	Light Shade	Shade									
•	•	•		•	•		•			3–8	240	Phlox
•					•			•		3–9	244	Pinks
•	•			•				•		2–10	248	Pitcher Plant
•				•		•		•		3–10	252	Plume Poppy
•		•			•			•		3–8	254	Purple Coneflower
•	•			•			•			4–9	258	Purple Loosestrife
•					•	•		•		6–10	260	Ravenna Grass
•				•	•		•			5–9	262	Red-hot Poker
•	•			•				•		4–9	264	Ribbon Grass
•					•			•	•	8–10	266	Rosemary
•					•	•		•	•	4–9	268	Russian Sage
•					•			•		5–11	270	Salvia
•					•		•	•		3–8	274	Sea Holly
•					•	•		•		3–10	276	Sedum
•	•			•	•		•			4–9	280	Shasta Daisy
•					•			•		3–8	282	Soapwort
	•	•	•	•	•		•			3–8	284	Solomon's Seal
	•	•		•				•		7–10	286	Southern Shield Fern
•	•				•	•		•		5–10	288	Spider Lily
•	•			•				•		3–11	292	Spiderwort
•				•	•		•	•		5–9	296	Stoke's Aster
•					•		•	•	•	4–8	298	Thyme
	•	•	•	•	•		•			4–9	302	Toad-Lily
•	•			•	•		•			3–8	304	Turtlehead
•				•	•			•		6–10	306	Verbena
•				•	•			•		3–8	310	Veronica
	•	•		•	•			•		3–8	312	Virginia Bluebells
	•	•	•	•				•		2–9	314	Wild Ginger
•					•	•		•		3–9	318	Yarrow

*Drought Tolerant

Glossary of Terms

acid soil: soil with a pH lower than 7.0

alkaline soil: soil with a pH higher than 7.0

annual: a plant that germinates, flowers, sets seed and dies in one growing season

basal foliage: leaves that form from the crown

basal rosette: a ring or rings of leaves growing from the crown of a plant at or near ground level; flowering stems of such plants grow separately from the crown

biennial: a plant that germinates and produces stems, roots and leaves in the first growing season; it flowers, sets seed and dies in the second growing season

crown: the part of a plant at or just below soil level where the shoots join the roots

cultivar: a cultivated plant variety with one or more distinct differences from the species, such as flower color, leaf variegation or disease resistance

damping off: fungal disease causing seedlings to rot at soil level and topple over

deadhead: to remove spent flowers to maintain a neat appearance and encourage a longer blooming period

direct sow: to plant seeds straight into the garden, in the location you want the plants to grow

disbud: to remove some flower buds to improve the size or quality of those remaining

dormancy: a period of plant inactivity, usually during winter or unfavorable climatic conditions

double flower: a flower with an unusually large number of petals, often caused by mutation of the stamens into petals

genus: a category of biological classification between the species and family levels; the first word in a Latin name indicates the genus

harden off: to gradually acclimatize plants that have been growing in a protective environment to a more harsh environment, e.g., plants started indoors being moved outdoors

hardy: capable of surviving unfavorable conditions, such as cold weather

humus: decomposed or decomposing organic material in the soil

hybrid: a plant resulting from natural or human-induced crossbreeding between varieties, species, or genera; the hybrid expresses features of each parent plant

knot garden: a formal design, often used for herb gardens, in which low, clipped hedges are arranged in elaborate, knot-like patterns

neutral soil: soil with a pH of 7.0

invasive: able to spread aggressively from the planting site and out-compete other plants

node: the area on a stem from which a leaf or new shoot grows

pH: a measure of acidity or alkalinity (the lower the pH, the higher the acidity); the pH of soil influences availability of nutrients for plants

perennial: a plant that takes three or more years to complete its life cycle; a herbaceous perennial normally dies back to the ground over winter

rhizome: a food-storing stem that grows horizontally at or just below soil level, from which new shoots may emerge

rootball: the root mass and surrounding soil of a container-grown plant or a plant dug out of the ground

runner: a modified stem that grows on the soil surface; roots and new shoots are produced at nodes along its length

semi-double flower: a flower with petals that form two or three rings

side-dressing: applying fertilizer to the soil beside or around a plant during the growing season to stimulate growth

single flower: a flower with a single ring of typically four or five petals

species: the original species from which cultivars and varieties are derived; the fundamental unit of biological classification

subspecies (subsp.): a naturally occurring, regional form of a species, often isolated from other subspecies but still potentially interfertile with them

taproot: a root system consisting of one main root with smaller roots branching from it

tender: incapable of surviving the climatic conditions of a given region and requiring protection from frost or cold

true: the passing of desirable characteristics from the parent plant to seed-grown offspring; also called breeding true to type

tuber: the thick section of a rhizome bearing nodes and buds

variegation: foliage that has more than one color, often patched or striped or bearing differently colored leaf margins

variety (var.): a naturally occurring variant of a species; below the level of subspecies in biological classification

Index of Plant Names

Page numbers in **bold** indicate main flower headings.